P9-CFT-772

PRAISE FOR *THE GOOD ENOUGH CHILD*

"A really good book on turning the war between parents and children into a mutually nourishing relationship."
—Rabbi Harold Kushner, author of *When Bad Things Happen to Good People*

"Brad Sachs has written more than a good enough book; he has created a totally engaging 'must read' for any mother or father."
—Diane Ehrensaft, Ph.D., author of *Spoiling Childhood*

"No one writes about the miraculous complexity of family life better than Dr. Brad Sachs. The book is funny, conversational, insightful, wise. I'm a better parent because of it."
—Roberta Israeloff, author of *Kindling the Flame*

"Brad Sachs has told parents what they've been longing to hear: their children don't have to be perfect. This book should do much to defuse the unnecessary pressure on families today."
—Marguerite Kelly, syndicated columnist and co-author of *The Mother's Almanac*

"If the parents of my patients heeded the advice in Dr. Sachs's hopeful and helpful book, their children might not need me. I wish my own parents could have read it."
—Jeanne Safer, Ph.D., author of *Forgiving and Not Forgiving*

"A far better than 'good enough' book to help parents in raising their kids."
—Lawrence H. Diller, M.D., author of *Running on Ritalin*

"This wise book will greatly enhance the parenting efforts of children of all ages."
—Dr. Judith Mishne, Shirley M. Ehrenkranz School of Social Work, New York University, and author of *The Learning Curve*

"*The Good Enough Child* stands out amongst the glut of simplistic parenting guides as a wise, eloquent, and valuable book that will be infinitely helpful and reassuring to parents."
—Nancy Samalin, M.S., author of *Love and Anger: The Parental Dilemma*

"This empathetic and well-written, functional book is full of very good advice for all parents and is solidly based on the author's long experience in the psychological care of parents and children."
—Dr. H. Paul Gabriel, Clinical Professor of Psychiatry, New York University Medical School, and author of *Anticipating Adolescence*

"With wisdom, warmth, and wit, Brad Sachs puts the fun back into parenting, giving us the courage we need to abandon our quixotic quest, and the confidence to recognize that sometimes being human is better than being perfect."
—Armin A. Brott, author of *The Expectant Father* and *The New Father*

"In *The Good Enough Child*, parents are given sage advice for combatting a panoply of unrealistic pressures they are likely to encounter in raising children. This is a warm, personal, and engaging book."
—Charles E. Schaefer, Ph.D., author of *How to Help Children with Common Problems*

The
Good
Enough
Child

The
Good
Enough
Child

HOW TO HAVE AN
IMPERFECT FAMILY AND
BE PERFECTLY SATISFIED

Brad E. Sachs, Ph.D.

HARPER

NEW YORK ▪ LONDON ▪ TORONTO ▪ SYDNEY

HARPER

The names and identifying details of all patients have been changed to protect their privacy.

HarperCollins books may be purchased for educational, business, or sales promotional use. For information please write: Special Markets Department, HarperCollins Publishers Inc., 10 East 53rd Street, New York, NY 10022.

FIRST EDITION

Designed by Elliott Beard

Library of Congress Cataloging-in-Publication Data

Sachs, Brad.
    The good enough child: how to have an imperfect family and be perfectly satisfied / by Brad E. Sachs.
        p.   cm.
    Includes index.
    ISBN 0-380-81303-3
    1. Parenting.   2. Parent and child.   3. Perfectionism (Personality trait).   I. Title.

HQ755.85.s223 2001
649'.1—dc21
                                                    00-051828

07 08 09 10   RRD   10 9 8

This book is dedicated with love to

The blessed memory of my father-in-law, Alvin Meckler, z"l (1926–2000)

To the grandchildren whom he so adored . . .

Josh, who gets me to laugh

Matt, who gets me to play, and

Jessica, who gets me to the bus stop five minutes earlier than necessary each morning

And to his daughter, Karen,

On the twentieth anniversary of our remarkable marriage.

"In the breathing of the shadows
We forget 'most everything
But the tender weight of love we love to carry . . ."

Biff: What is it that you want from me?
Willy: Greatness!
Biff: No . . .

—Arthur Miller
Death of a Salesman

When it hurts,
We return to the banks of certain rivers . . .
—Czeslaw Milosz

CONTENTS

Acknowledgments

My deepest gratitude goes to . . .

My parents, Herb and Claire Sachs—working on this book wasn't quite as hard as the puppet that I had to do in first grade, but at times it came awfully close. I would not have completed either project as well without your care and support.

My mother-in-law, Selma Meckler, who has always treated me like a son, and who raised a wonderful daughter.

My brother and sister-in-law, Paul and Janet Sachs, and their children, Danny, Rachel, and Adam, for helping me to compensate for the many "deleterious strains" we all contend with—I'll be looking forward to your decision regarding this book's resonating quote.

My brother and sister-in-law, Lee and Deborah Sachs, and their son, Anatole—aren't you proud of me? More than three hundred pages of text and I didn't mention Key Lime once (oops).

My uncle, colleague, and fellow Baltimore sports fan, Ken Sachs, and his wife, Karen, eternal purveyor of Dance Rags.

My grandmother, Anne Sachs, the original Bearer of the Bottomless Pitcher.

My great-aunt Dasia Cherson—see how all of those literary birthday gifts paid off?

My loving and devoted friends: Tom Burns, Greykell Dutton, David Gilberg, Norman Gross, Roberta Israeloff, Rick LaRocca, Eric Metzman, Andre Papantonio, Steve (mio fratello) Rosch, Scott Rosenthal, Kathy Santiago, Rob Schrier, Veronika Slaby, Scott Strahlman, and Ellen Talles.

Katie Smith, who has so good-naturedly anchored our family over the years that she has *become* family.

My patients, who have taught me so much and have so coura-geously invited me into their lives.

All of the schools, parent groups, agencies, and institutions that have invited me to lead workshops and share my evolving thoughts and perspectives over the years.

Rabbi Gary Fink and Congregation Oseh Shalom, a *shul* that has provided my family and me with a warm and sustaining spiri-tual community.

All of our friends and neighbors in the village of Long Reach, and throughout Columbia, who have been so generous and sup-portive during this challenging year.

Phyllis Stern, whose instruction in child and family therapy has nurtured and guided me for more than fifteen years, and whose consultations were the enzyme that catalyzed the birth of this book (see page 317).

My agent, Sarah Jane Freymann, whose faith in this project was a constant source of strength and motivation.

Beth Rashbaum, for once again helping me to discover the "book within the book."

Clare Hutton, of Avon Books, for her editorial acumen.

Ann Thoroman, for sticking her neck out and taking a chance.

George Martiyan, at Long Reach Parcel Plus.

Radio Stations WRNR 103.1 FM, WETA 90.9 FM, and WAMU 88.5 FM for their musical backdrops.

The Howard County Public Library System.

Bet Yeladim Preschool, for giving all three of our children such a good start.

And of course to Karen Meckler, M.D., the only person brave, steadfast, and loving enough to have read every word of every draft (and, believe me, there were plenty).

The
Good
Enough
Child

The Impossible Dream

By your stumbling, the world is perfected.

Sri Aurobindo

Here's how it is. As you await the birth of your first child, you are positive that you will be able to raise that child better than you were raised, and you look forward to proving yourself in this wonderful new endeavor. You have thought a lot about your own childhood. You know that you are made up of a constellation of joys and sorrows, big and little, which have affected how you live and how you love, who you've been and who you've become.

You know what your parents should have done differently, and you vow that you will repair their mistakes and see to it that your own son or daughter feels secure, nurtured, and protected in a way you couldn't even imagine when you were young.

And you go about this process of becoming a parent with a fervor, a passion that blossoms from the heart of your desire to heal yourself. You imagine your child's face and his future, creating and absorbing every detail. You read books and manuals on parenting and anticipate every encounter, how you will respond to even the tiniest of his gestures with gratitude and tenderness and warmth, how you will be tuned in to every shift in temperament, attentive to every developmental task.

You talk with your partner and you talk with your friends and you talk with your family, and you can't stop thinking about it, the prospect of parenthood is so compelling, so exciting. You find yourself speaking to your future child, singing to your child, dreaming of your child. You are reaching inward and upward with a zeal unlike anything you have experienced before, and you are ready, so ready, for this birth, for your own rebirth, when you will reclaim your own life through the creation of *new* life. You have never felt this way before—so open, so hopeful, so heartened.

And you're not just waiting for any child, of course, but for the Perfect Child, the child who will complete the life that you have begun, the child who will fill in your gaps, minister to your soul, amplify your attributes, and cancel out your flaws, the one who will make you so proud and so thrilled that at the very thought of her, your heart seems to be stamping in its stall, unable to contain itself.

The handmaiden to this Perfect Child will of course be the Perfect Family, with you and your partner blissfully playing your destined roles as Perfect Parents. And you will feel as if you need nothing else, and that the universe has granted you your most wildly imagined wish.

But at some point, maybe right away, as soon as your baby emerges red, squalling, and unruly from the womb, or maybe further down the road, during a colicky infancy, or a fractious toddlerhood, or the first days of school, or perhaps not until adolescence, your dream of perfection is going to shatter, and for reasons that you will not understand, and in ways that cannot be prevented no matter how hard you try, the shards of that dream will lie around you, mean, hard-edged, and treacherous. You will then feel a disappointment and a rage and an anguish unlike anything else you have experienced in your life.

At that moment you are going to flail about in a frenzy of blame, which you will direct at any of a number of convenient targets: yourself, your child, your partner, your parents, your pediatrician, the evil teacher at school. The list may grow to include everyone who has ever been important to you or your child.

But whenever it happens, and whoever you blame, you will have to come to terms with the fact that you are not raising the Perfect Child after all. Perhaps she was born with something missing, deformed, or malfunctioning, or perhaps she was simply one of those children who cry the entire first year. Or she was a sweet, sleepy newborn, but has grown into a moody, oppositional, foul-tempered 1-year-old. Or now that she's entered preschool, she won't play merrily with her classmates but kicks and bites them instead. Or she's become one of those obnoxious brats who mouths off to her teachers at the expensive private school you're working two jobs to afford and then comes home and hammers her little brothers any chance she gets. Or now that she's in high school, whatever free time remains from diligently piercing body parts and dyeing her hair a strange new color every week is devoted to conscientiously reminding you of how much she despises you.

And not only is your *child* imperfect, but so are you. You don't feel inspired and exhilarated by the experience of having created new life, you feel exhausted and demoralized. You are not the kind, tolerant, patient parent you fantasized you'd be, particularly when your child is in pain and really needs you, but an irritable and disappointed one. You lose your temper, and you think black thoughts, and you say terrible things you instantly regret but don't know how to take back.

The pernicious synergy of sleep deprivation and anxiety about money and trips to the pharmacy to fill prescriptions that don't seem to work and school conferences with guidance counselors who barely seem to know who your daughter is and teachers who seem even less experienced than you has put you at the end of your rope. You don't want to hear anything else about your daughter's "developmental stage." You just want her to change *now*—to look or sound "right," to sleep through the night, to get sick less often, to eat what's in front of her, to have more friends, to do better in French, or to just be more *likable*.

And, to make things worse, somebody else out there, someone in your very own neighborhood or family or school or network of friends, actually seems to have the Perfect Child that you long for, the child who would have been just right for you. This child loves to draw just like you love to draw, even though your own child won't even look at a crayon no matter how many boxes you leave lying about. This child can't wait to get outside and play just like you can't wait to get outside, while your own child could apparently stay in the house for days at a time without even looking out the window, and consistently throws a tantrum at the sight of his jacket. This child ends up running the youth group at church even though her parents haven't set foot in a house of worship for twenty years, while your own child, offspring of two devout, observant churchgoers, sleeps through Sunday school on the infrequent mornings that you're actually able to get her to show up there.

And of course, not only is there this Perfect Child out there whom you have to contend with, amazingly enough there appears to be a Perfect Parent, too, the one who you were supposed to be, the one who, unlike you, seems so happy and good-natured, so loving and creative, all of the time, the one who seems to have been transformed by parenthood rather than sacrificed to it, the one who makes her kids' Halloween costumes out of "scraps lying around the house," just like the parents' magazines recommend, or the one who writes and sings funny songs and plays them on the guitar while his bright little boy sits admiringly by, cheerful, obedient, and appreciative, or the one who enthusiastically coaches the softball team that his daughter is the captain and transcendent star of—or the one who just doesn't seem to see her son as a direct reflection of herself, who doesn't really take it personally that he's nasty with peers or lousy at spelling or clumsy at sports.

These parents don't seem ambivalent, these parents don't seem overwhelmed and perplexed so much of the time, these parents don't seem to argue with their spouses over and over again about how much television should be allowed or why their daughter sneaks out at night or what they should do when they take their son to the playground for some fresh air and exercise and he just stands at the bottom of the slide wailing because the other kids won't get off it.

And when these parents do have a problem, they smile, and they always seem to quickly find a solution and the solution is always so simple—and the solution always *works*. Their child was hyperactive but they took him to an allergist and discovered he had Food Allergies, and now everything is Fine. Their child wasn't sleeping at night but they read a book that teaches you a Surefire

Technique, and, by golly, now they can barely get him out of the bed in the morning, he Sleeps So Well. Their child was cranky and aggressive, but the pediatrician said he'd grow out of it by the time he was 4, and, promptly on the dot of his fourth birthday, he became As Gentle As A Lamb. Their child was failing all of his subjects, but they arranged for a Psychological Evaluation, immediately and precisely determined his Learning Style, got him a wonderful tutor, and he now has Straight A's and Scholarship Offers from several Ivy League Schools. Or so it appears on the surface.

Somehow, nothing is so clear-cut in your family. Problems emerge that never quite get solved, or they look like they're solved but then seem to reemerge, or the "solutions" wind up creating bigger problems than the problem they were addressing, or the problems are so quickly replaced by new ones that you feel like you are always playing the Whack-a-Mole game at the arcade, hammering down one plastic rodent with your cushioned club only to find three others simultaneously popping up, taunting you with their leering smiles.

Perhaps the funny little head twitch finally stops for a few months, but then, mysteriously, it starts up again. Or your daughter finally makes a friend who doesn't smoke, and stops smoking for a time herself—but then the friend moves, and your daughter is lonely and whiny again, and back to sneaking cigarettes in the park. Or your son stops sobbing and clinging to your leg as you leave him at day care to go to work, but now he's unable to go to bed at night without more than an hour of repetitive stories and clutching. Or your daughter, who you complained never read enough when she was in elementary school, now reads so much that her teachers complain about her inattention in class, her classmates tease her for being a "geek," and you can't get her involved in a conversation that lasts more than ten seconds.

Some nights you just lie in bed, tired but unable to sleep, sad and bewildered, trying desperately to knit up the unraveling sleeve of family life, and you wonder what you did wrong, how this happened to you, and, worst of all, what this says about you as a parent and a person.

Of course you know what it says. It says that you are worthless and undeserving, that you should never have been a parent, that you are harming your children every day that they have to live with you and observe your behavior, and that they would be better off in your friend's home, or your neighbor's home, or a foster home, or practially *any* home but yours. If they had to live in a forest raised by wolves they'd probably turn out better than they would with you hovering anxiously and incompetently about, losing your temper, engaging in loud shouting matches with your spouse. . . .

Sound familiar? If so, then you have come to the right place and you are reading the right book, because in reading what I have written you will not be falsely seduced into believing that children can be molded to conform to our expectations and specifications like Pinocchios carved by hopeful and adoring Geppettos out of the blond lumber of our dreams if we just love them, work hard, and follow the directions in the child-rearing manual.

What you *will* get out of this book is relief from a crippling burden—the belief that a healthy family is made up of perfect parents raising perfect children and that somewhere out there is the secret to joining this select group. Once you give up this desire for perfection, you will find a new joy, confidence, and spontaneity in your family life. These are the qualities that have been lost in the obsessive approach to child-rearing that is the defining characteristic of contemporary parenting.

While parents have always wanted the best for their children and always tried to shape them into the individuals that they wanted them to be, there are a number of reasons why the expectations that parents have for their families have recently become so greatly, and unrealistically, amplified.

For instance, when couples have fewer children, and have children later in life, this means that the stakes are raised for each child that they do have, and each has to fulfill a greater share of parental dreams. The number of mothers at the end of their childbearing years who have only one child rose from 9 percent to 16 percent in the past ten years, and the percentage is still climbing quickly. When we have only one or two children to raise and we are already approaching midlife, we pump all of our hopes and ideals into each of their tiny souls and insist that they swell and embody them.

Also, many parents have invested tremendous amounts of time, money, and energy into arriving at parenthood. People who couldn't have conceived a child even half a generation ago because of either genetic flaws or long delays in starting a family may now find themselves investing several years and thousands of dollars to overcome these problems. Couples who still can't conceive may then start the adoption process, which can take another year or two, and more money. When that much time and expense is involved, it is only natural to expect a high return on one's "expenditure."

Children who are the gratification of so many long-delayed hopes and dreams bring to mind a passage in Sigmund Freud's writings which refers to "His Majesty the Baby." But when Freud wrote that phrase, he was talking about the natural solipsism of the infant, not the child-centeredness verging on child worship I see in so many parents today. *No* child can support the weight of so many wishes.

Nor can any parent achieve the level of mastery required to minister to His or Her Majesty. Our culture has sanctified and idealized parenthood, making us all believe that we should shine like the radiant, eternally patient caregivers that the mass media create and tempt us with. Take a closer look at the advertisements that convey such improbable messages about parenthood and you will realize the extent to which we have been seduced.

In one magazine advertisement for a baby monitor, a photograph on the top half of the page shows a transmitter next to a gorgeous baby, asleep in his crib, while a photograph on the bottom half of the page shows a content, industrious mother, reassured by the soft buzz of the receiver. What's noteworthy, however, is what the mother is doing.

Most new parents, when their baby has finally fallen asleep, are either frantically returning the phone calls that couldn't be taken during the past several hours, trying in vain to stay on top of assorted piles of laundry, cleaning up a living room that may look like the target of Allied bombing from World War II, or collapsing, trancelike, on the couch, their brains squidgy from fatigue and overresponsibility.

What is this mother busy with? Wearing a fresh-looking smock, she is gaily refinishing a piece of furniture. I don't know about you, but refinishing furniture was way, way down at the bottom of my list of priorities during the vertiginous years of early parenthood.

But the juxtaposition of these images is a compelling one just the same. This is what parenthood should, and will, be like: pleasant, quiet, lovely, and convenient. How much more we despair, then, when the reality of family life as we come to live it is so different.

Another factor accounting for such widespread parental anxiety is that parents at the turn of the millennium are far better informed than any other group of parents ever were about the needs of their children, but the increased education and knowledgeability exact a steep price: we have become hyperaware of all the things that could go wrong if we don't do everything exactly right.

Sometimes, these concerns are real, and terrifyingly valid. For example, when we were adolescents, if the beliefs, advice, warnings, and exhortations of our parents did not deter us from embarking on a sexual relationship, we might have ended up having a life-altering experience, like an accidental pregnancy or gonorrhea, but not a life-*threatening* experience. In the age of AIDS, sexual experimentation by teenagers is not just a matter of right and wrong, but potentially a matter of life and death.

On the other hand, sometimes these concerns are less sound. Because we have so narrowed the range of what "normal" childhood is like, we inevitably find any deviation from this artificial and unlikely norm something to worry about. If our child isn't focusing well in first grade, we are encouraged to consider an evaluation for attention deficit disorder, rather than deal with him as a lively 6-year-old who isn't crazy about school and has energy to burn. If our child is more content playing by herself than with her peers, we conclude that she has low self-esteem, and set to work creating multiple opportunities for her to interact with other children, rather than valuing her individuality and honoring her choice to exercise it in the quiet fantasy play she so obviously enjoys.

In our overly psychologized and medicalized era, we are enticed into assuming that all childhood rough edges can and should be smoothed out. The companion and misguided belief is that if we read, watch, and listen to enough experts, purchase the right toys, equipment, and educational aids, and administer the right psychoactive drugs, we will be equipped to perform the psychological equivalent of cosmetic surgery on our offspring, resulting in the creation of the model child.

The drugging of American children has reached epidemic proportions. While advances in psychopharmacology have helped many to be relieved of unnecessary psychic suffering, they have also led us to conclude that we can *all* be "better" people—happier, calmer, more focused and attentive—if we brew and imbibe the appropriate neurochemical cocktails. Why shouldn't the same expectations apply to our children? So child after child is paraded into the doctor's office with a request for one of the magic potions that will eradicate "problem behaviors," without giving significant thought to the origin of these behaviors and whether they are truly problematic.

In fact, recent studies document that children as young as *1 year old* are being treated with psychiatric drugs that have never been tested on or approved for children under 6 years of age, that the use of antidepressants with children *between the ages of 2 and 4* has doubled and the use of stimulants with that same age group has tripled, and that each year American children are prescribed *five to ten times* as much Ritalin as the entire rest of the world combined. Could all of these children truly have neurological defects? What does this data say about our patience and tolerance for the children whom we claim to care so much about?

Yet at the same time that we so simplistically reduce our children to products of their biochemical circuitry, we also fret about them as products of the traumas we fear we ourselves may be inflicting on them. Dare simply to raise your voice, smack their hands, express annoyance, withdraw in anger, or criticize them—interactions that occur in most homes, between the vast majority of parents and children, surely hundreds of times a year—and, we are solemnly informed, they may be emotionally blunted and scarred for life.

Recently, I learned that a 10-year-old girl who was in therapy with me had been told by her mother that she had been "sexually abused" by her father, even though her father "refused to admit that this had happened." What was the nature of his abuse, I asked the mother, who explained that when her daughter, Natalie, was a toddler, she had seen Natalie reach out to touch her father's penis when he was getting dressed after a shower, and he hadn't "instantly" removed Natalie's hand. Sexual abuse, of course, constitutes a tremendous violation and betrayal. How terrifying it is for us to be parents in an age when there is such confusion about its very definition.

Another concern for most parents is the widening gap between the haves and the have-nots in our society, the sense, fed by an unpredictable economy, that there is no middle ground, and that if we don't give our children every possible opportunity and inclination to "make it," they will end up flipping burgers at the local fast-food joint or folding shirts at some mall, doomed to lead destitute, impoverished lives.

We push our children hard and fast, buying them tutors and putting them through elaborate test-prep courses so they'll score well on their college boards, all because we are so fearful for their futures. No wonder we tend to overreact when they show no particular skill or talent that might set them apart from the crowd of contenders and push them to the front of the line.

Not only must *all* our children be above average, as in Garrison Keillor's Lake Wobegon, but the converse is that any who are simply average are actually judged to be failures—subpar, underachieving slackers who have to be defended or apologized for when we are not goading and pushing them beyond their natural capacities. In the words of the father confronting a teacher in a cartoon: "Where do you come off, calling my son 'grade-level'?"

It is typical to want to see each child as unique, an individual with a one-of-a-kind matrix of gifts and attributes, but we've gone from seeing our children as unique to insisting that they be exceptional, stars in their (or our) chosen field of accomplishment. It's not enough that our child should have some innate talent, a natural inclination toward skating or the violin or mathematics—no, each child must be a *prodigy*. Too often the special instruction that we arrange for and the avid encouragement we give to jump-start these putative prodigies rob them of any opportunity to learn about themselves and the world through unstructured play.

When was the last time your child went outside just to kick a ball around or play hide-and-seek with the neighbors? Free time to daydream, play-act, or hang out with a friend in the tree house has just about disappeared from the lives of our children because anything as casual as that doesn't fit into the veritable religion we have made of child-rearing. There are too many rites and rituals to perform as we worship at the shrine of the Perfect Parent, hoping desperately that if we—and our children—perform them all properly, our prayers for perfection will be answered.

Unlike the religion of child-rearing, however, most religions have as their basis the acknowledgment that while we can work toward perfection, be it perfect peace, perfect holiness, or perfect godliness, perfection will always elude us. It is in bravely coming to terms with and learning to forgive ourselves for our imperfections, and others for theirs, that we become most enlightened and move closer, ever closer, to our God, to each other, and, perhaps most important, to ourselves.

This book is about forgiving, even embracing, imperfection, for I believe the search for the ideal is the enemy of the achievable and the realizable. Once we let go of the image of the perfect family and accept ourselves and each other for who we are, we will become the best and most loving parents a child could ask for. To do so requires that we say good-bye to a tantalizing dream, but it enables us to greet a delicious reality, the reality of family love, with its wonderfully complicated texture, its bright and its shadowy moments, its healing and redemptive power.

Of course, everyone pays lip service to the idea that we need to accept our children and ourselves, that children feel loved and do best when they're appreciated for who they are, not for what they do, and that acceptance involves distinguishing between what you want *for* your child and what you want *from* your child. We hear this, but unfortunately nobody tells us exactly how to do it in such a way that accepting your child doesn't mean simply giving up on him.

This book will not only encourage you to be more accepting, but will demonstrate, through vignettes and case histories, how to do that while still playing a positive, proactive role in the life of your child.

As a final note, I do want to add that I am writing from deep within the trenches of my own life, which features a twenty-year marriage, three children, a large and complex extended family, and a busy psychotherapy practice with children and adults.

Everything that I write about or recommend has been road-tested along the bumpy, winding pathways of either my personal life or my clinical work, or both. Thus, I hope that you will hear in these pages a voice that is grounded not in dreams and fantasies, but in the hard, daily realities faced by anyone who is raising children and trying to infuse a family with the sense of intimate connection that gives life dignity and meaning.

ONE

The Reluctant Embrace

Perfect love means to love the one through whom one became unhappy.

Søren Kierkegaard

Three Jewish women get together for lunch. As they are being seated at the restaurant, one takes a deep breath and gives a long, slow "Oy." The second takes a deep breath as well and lets out a long, slow "Oy." The third takes a deep breath and says impatiently, "Ladies, I thought we agreed that when we got together, we weren't going to talk about our children."

No one can make us feel as delighted and joyous as our children do, but no one can make us feel as disappointed and upset, either. All of us enter parenthood with wishes, hopes, and expectations for our children. Amazingly, there are children who in fact make their parents' dreams come true.

Appearing at the exact moment that their mother and father wanted or needed a certain type of child, with a uniquely appealing cluster of qualities consisting of the right gender, appearance, temperament, values, and interests, they confirm all expectations, fulfill all hopes, and become ideal partners in the unfolding script of family life. There is a fortuitous fit between who they are and who their parents desire, and both experience a meshing of goals and motives that is indescribably wondrous. Even when the inevitable parenting mistakes are made, the child is able to manage without difficulties or disintegration. Everybody marvels at this completely mutual and effortless gratification, and parent and child emerge with a sense of confidence and competence that is the irrevocable result of such magical reciprocity. These are, of course, the rare exceptions.

More typically, parents are, at some point along the developmental spectrum, shocked by the discrepancy between their ideal child and the unremarkable or disappointing child offered up by reality. She may come to appear unattractive or unappealing, reminding us of people we despise or parts of ourselves that we abhor. Far from being adored, she actually winds up being resented, and the guilt and worry that result cause everyone tremendous suffering, creating a climate of reproach and resentment, estrangement and misunderstanding. She withdraws hurtfully or lashes out angrily, feeling engulfed by our presence and asphyxiated by our demands, leaving us feeling rejected, both unheeded and unneeded. When this debilitating process is set into motion, the family key shifts from major to minor, love turns to war, and what may have been envisioned as a lifelong honeymoon is transformed into an unending nightmare.

EIGHT SELF-DEFEATING REACTIONS TO OUR CHILDREN'S PROBLEMS

When our interactions with our child culminate in feelings of personal failure rather than parental pride, we typically react in one or more of eight self-defeating ways, each of which has its short-term benefits and long-term risks. And each of these eight responses, which may seem on the surface to have been called into being because of a situation that has arisen with our child, can also tell us something about our own unresolved issues. But to hear that message about ourselves requires courage, honesty, and sometimes the kind of help that a psychotherapist can offer. Our self-defeating strategies look like this.

1) We Use Denial to Avoid Dealing with Our Feelings of Failure

The *benefit* of this approach is that immediate feelings of fear, grief, and anger are staved off for a time. The *risks* are twofold: the possibilities for closeness and exchange are greatly narrowed when a child is not seen for who she is, and the child's actual needs cannot be met and adapted to when denial clouds the parental lens.

Stephen, for example, chose not to face some of the possible explanations for his 14-year-old daughter Hannah's newly unpredictable behavior. Although she now consistently broke her curfew and came home past midnight on weekends, spent most of her free time at home in her room with the door locked, had twice been caught leaving school grounds during school hours, was suddenly getting C's and D's and even an occasional E after years of A's and B's, and frequently received phone calls in the middle of the night, somehow her behavior didn't arouse any persistent suspicions that something serious might be going on.

"What consequences have there been for her coming home past curfew or missing school?" I asked during our first session, one that had come about only after the guidance counselor at Hannah's school had repeatedly suggested to her father that she receive a psychological evaluation.

"Well, I ground her whenever she misses a curfew, which is tough to do because she'll try to sneak out anyway. And the school handled her cutting classes by giving her Saturday school."

"How do you understand Hannah's behavior and the fact that it's such a departure from what she used to be like?"

"I think she's coming of age, and that she's rebelling against authority. I did it. Some of the other kids in her class do it. I suspect that's what *she's* doing," was Stephen's reply.

"Do you think that she might be experimenting with drugs or alcohol?"

"I guess it's possible. The other day I was out back and noticed a bag under the porch. And when I looked inside, I saw that it was filled with empty beer bottles."

"How did you handle it?"

"I asked Hannah if she knew anything about it, and she said that she didn't."

"And you believed her?"

"Yes. She's always been honest. Even when she was a little girl, she could always be counted on to tell the truth."

"Any other evidence that she might be using drugs or alcohol?"

"Well, something did happen last summer, now that you men-tion it. Her mom and I are divorced. Her mom lives in another state with her new husband, so Hannah spends vacations and summers there. And when Hannah was coming home last August, her mom called to tell me that she had found a bag of marijuana in a pair of jeans one day while doing the wash."

"Did she ask Hannah about it?"

"Yeah, and she said she was just holding it for a friend."

"Do you believe that?"

"I did at the time. I had friends like that when I was growing up, buddies who would ask me to do them a favor."

"Have you gotten to know her friends very well?"

"Not really. When they're over, they don't do much more than say hi, and then head upstairs to Hannah's room. And when they're out, they're out. I don't really spend any time with them. Some of them seem a little strange, but they're basically nice kids, from what I can tell."

"What about when she comes home late, past curfew. Have you observed any behavior that suggests that she might be under the influence of drugs or alcohol at that time?"

"She certainly tries to avoid me, I know that. . . . I've tried to talk with her, but she says she's tired and she just wants to get to bed and that we can talk in the morning."

"And what about her grades? Why do you think they've fallen so dramatically?"

"She says her classes are much tougher this year and that a cou-ple of teachers really have it in for her."

"Have you ever asked Hannah straight out whether she's tried drugs or alcohol?"

"No. I mean, I think about asking her, because I know it's out there, but I think she'd just get angry and accuse me of not trust-ing her to make good choices. Plus, she could lie, so I'm not sure what the point would be."

"The point might be to see how she responds, because that could give you some clues about whether it's becoming a problem for her or not."

"What do you mean?"

"Well, if you bring the subject up and she reacts very angrily or defensively, even while saying she's not using anything, it would suggest that perhaps she's struggling with this more than you're aware of."

"But I still wouldn't know for sure."

"That's true. . . . That's why some parents in this kind of situation, being confronted with all kinds of worrisome changes in their child, decide it's worth doing a drug test or two, just so they have something more to go on than what their child says. After all, you already know about the beer bottles and the bag of pot in her pants pocket. Do you think that would be a good idea in this case?"

"I'm not sure. I think she'd really be offended if I suggest she take a drug test."

"That might tell you that she's concerned about the results of the test."

"I don't know. Like I said before, I think she'll just get angry and accuse me of not trusting her."

"From the sound of things, she's not giving you much reason to trust her right now."

"Well, I *do* trust her, though. I think she's basically a good kid."

"I don't doubt that. But she may be becoming involved with drugs or alcohol to the extent that it's interfering with her 'goodness' and getting in the way of her development as a young woman."

"I don't know about that. She can still be very sweet and kind a lot of the time. It's not like all she's doing is causing trouble."

From my first few minutes with Stephen, it was clear that he was working overtime to avoid acknowledging the depth of Hannah's problems and the likelihood that she was at least using, if not abusing, drugs and alcohol.

Often, when I see this level of denial in operation, I eventually discover that the roots of that denial can be found within the parent's own experience. Perhaps he used drugs or alcohol recreationally when he was an adolescent and came through it feeling unscathed, so he's having difficulty acknowledging that his own daughter is truly at risk, even though at some level he must know that she is. Perhaps he did or does abuse drugs or alcohol himself, and considering the possibility of his child's involvement would force him to live, or relive, his own feelings of shame and depression. Perhaps his family taught him to rely on denial to deal with life's difficulties. Perhaps someone dear to him suffers or suffered through chemical dependency, and the reminder of this is too painful for him to bear, so he blinds himself to what is uncomfortable to see.

Whatever the reasons, whenever a parent is battling as hard as Stephen was against the discomfort that would result from acknowledging his child's difficulties, he cannot be the support she needs as she faces the many temptations that arise during adolescence.

2) We Become Hyperactive Parents

The *benefit* of this approach is that, unlike denial, there is an actual recognition of disappointment and an effort to resolve it. The *risk* is that to cover up our feelings of anger and disillusionment, we overreact to the point of alienating the child who senses, rightly, that the parent's demands are excessive.

Andy contacted me because he was "devastated" by his son Craig's low scores on a standardized test that Craig's school administers to fourth-graders each year.

"This kid should be ahead of everybody. He's got every advantage: a smart mother, a smart father, a high IQ. How could he possibly be scoring in the thirtieth percentile on these tests?" Andy railed.

In our first session, as his son sat grim-faced, listening to what was in store for him, Andy outlined his plans for remedying this problem in a taut, businesslike way. Craig would be the recipient of a "full psychological evaluation," tutoring twice a week at a local learning center, weekly psychotherapy sessions "to get at the root of the problem," a psychiatric consultation "so that we can get him started on Ritalin," a monetary reward system for good grades, and participation in the homework club after school on the afternoons that he wasn't going to be tutored. "And he can forget about swim team for now. He can swim in the summer, but it's time to get cracking on his schoolwork now. Another couple of years, he'll be in middle school, and then he'll *really* have to work."

I could see Craig slowly shriveling in his chair as each component of his father's plan was articulated.

"How are Craig's grades at school?" I asked.

"They're okay, but they really could be better," his mother, Fay, said. "He's been getting mostly B's and C's, with an A here and there. But that wasn't a big deal until we saw those test scores and realized how little he must really be absorbing at school. There's got to be a problem."

"I'm impressed with the conscientiousness with which you're approaching this situation," I began, "and all of your ideas sound like good ones. But I'm wondering if it might be better to pick one or two to start with, see what results we get, and then, if you still have some concerns, we can always roll out one or two others."

"I'm concerned that time's a-wasting," was Andy's immediate response. "We've got to get on top of this, before he starts falling behind."

"Maybe so," I said, "but I'm concerned about implementing all of these interventions at the same time, particularly before we even have the results of any psychoeducational testing."

"That's the way I do things," Andy said. "I go full tilt, all the way."

"But if you do all of these things and see results, you won't know which ones did the trick. And if you *don't* see results, there won't be much left to try."

"Then we'll try him in a different school," Craig said.

Feeling stuck, I decided to take a different tack. "How does he like being on the swim team?"

"He loves it," Fay said. "He's not the best swimmer on the team by any means, but he likes the kids on the team and enjoys being in the relays at meets."

"Since we know that regular exercise is not just good for the body but also helps to keep the mind sharp, would you consider letting him stay on the team, at least for the remainder of the school year?"

"Well, I'd consider it," Andy said, "but it appears that it would interfere with the tutoring program that we contacted. They only have slots available on Tuesdays and Thursdays, and that's when he has swim practice. My feeling is that his schoolwork is more important, and, like I said, he can always do summer swim team."

"Could you ask the coach if he might be able to practice just *once* a week for a couple of months, so that he remains a part of the team and gets a good workout, and then see if you can arrange the tutoring once a week?"

"The tutoring place says that they like to start with their students twice a week," Andy said brusquely.

"What about the homework club at school? What days is that available?"

"That's every day except Fridays," Fay said.

"So maybe he could stay on the swim team and do the homework club on Mondays and Wednesdays," I offered.

"I still think he ought to do both the tutoring and the homework club," Andy insisted. "I doubt that the homework club does much more than give kids a chance to get their work done and have some questions answered. That's no substitute for actual tutoring."

My belief was that Andy's hypervigilant approach to his son's low scores was going to do nothing more than suffocate and alienate Craig, thus creating more of a problem than the one that currently existed. Looking into the possibility of a learning problem certainly made sense, and providing him with some additional academic support was surely a good idea. But depriving him of a chance to be with his friends on the swim team and making it appear as if his entire self-worth rotated on the axis of his academic performance was, to my mind, a recipe for disaster.

To be of some help in cases like this, I have to try to understand why the parent is so disturbed by his child's underachievement. Perhaps he wishes he himself had done better in school and regrets not having had any support from his parents to facilitate it. Or perhaps he did extremely well in school and needs the validation he would get if his son followed closely in his high-performance footsteps. Perhaps Craig reminds him of an academically underachieving brother who's never been able to hold a job in adult life and still comes to him for loans that he never pays back.

The hyperactive parent has to ask himself whether he is trying to redress something that went awry in his own life rather than dealing with the needs of his child. Only then can he respond to the child's problem in a sensitive and effective way.

3) We Blame Ourselves

The *benefit* of this approach is that there is an illusory sense of control that feels comforting: we know why our child is disappointing—it's our fault. The *risk* is that in blaming ourselves, we become paralyzed by the ensuing self-criticism and guilt. I once saw a bumper sticker that put it this way: "When it comes to guilt trips, parents are frequent fliers."

Jenny, for example, contacted me because her 6-year-old daughter, Siobhan, was still wetting the bed at night.

"We just can't seem to break her of this habit. The pediatrician told us she'd grow out of it, but she started telling us this when Siobhan was three, and now it's three years later, and there's no evidence she's growing out of it at all. I'm embarrassed to have her sleep over at friends' houses, and her classmates are starting to have slumber parties now. How can I send her when she's going to be wet in the morning?"

"What have you tried so far?" I asked.

"Well, we haven't really known what to do, other than to beg her to try to be more careful each night. We tried an elimination diet once or twice, to see if it was the result of an allergy, and we usually try to limit her fluids at night. But nothing we do or say seems to make much of a difference."

"Some parents that I work with have tried one of the medications that sometimes help kids with this problem. I'm not recommending this yet, but was wondering if you've thought about it."

"I really don't want to medicate my child. And our pediatrician is pretty conservative about this also. She said that plenty of kids are still wetting the bed at Siobhan's age, and that she doesn't recommend trying medication until she's seven or eight."

"What have you read about bed-wetting?"

"I can't tell you how many nights I've pulled stuff off the Internet, trying to find an answer. I know that just about every kid grows out of it eventually, but some don't until they're well into their teens, and I feel that would be just awful for her, to still be waking up in wet sheets as a teenager."

"What else?"

"Well, I know that emotional factors affect bed-wetting too."

"Is Siobhan stressed in any way?"

She paused, and then blurted out, "Her dad and I separated for six months when she was three. We got into counseling and got back together, and things are much better now, but I still wonder if that's why she's having trouble controlling her bladder."

"Was she wetting the bed before the two of you separated?"

"Oh, yes."

"And was there ever a time after she was toilet-trained when she stayed dry at night?"

"When she was first toilet-trained, at two and a half, she was sometimes dry at night. And since then, every six or eight months, there'll usually be a period of time when she's dry for some days in a row."

"So how is it that you can conclude she's wetting the bed because you and her dad separated, when she was wetting both before you split up and after you got back together?"

"I don't know," Jenny replied tearfully. "I just can't help thinking that we caused this somehow by letting her hear our fights."

"How is she doing at school and with her friends?"

"Very well. She started kindergarten this year and has really flourished. She loves drawing and practicing her letters and numbers. And she's made lots of new friends and loves getting together with them on the weekends."

"Is she sleeping and eating normally?"

"Yes."

"Behavior problems at home or in school?"

"No."

"Any nightmares?"

"No."

"Headaches, or stomachaches, or other physical complaints?"

"No, she's healthy as a horse. She's only missed a couple of days of school the whole year."

"This doesn't sound like the description of a girl who is feeling very stressed."

"But then why is she still wetting the bed?"

"Most research suggests that it's usually nothing more than a slight immaturity in the nervous system. That's why kids tend to grow out of it naturally, without any intervention—because their nervous system begins to mature and even itself out."

"So what are we supposed to do?"

"Well, it seems to me you can either speak with your pediatrician and see if she'll reconsider her decision about medication, or you can just assume that Siobhan will grow out of it, and in the meantime teach her how to change and wash her sheets, give her a sleeping bag for sleepovers and some advice on how to be discreet if she wakes up wet at a friend's house, and hang in there until she's past this."

"I can't just let it go. I can't just sit back and let this happen to her."

"Actually, you can. In this case that's a legitimate option. I can understand how frustrating it must be, for you and your husband as well as for her. But it's not a threat to her health or yours, it's not endangering her, and aside from the natural feelings of embarrassment—and there will always be *something* that a child gets embarrassed by—there's not much potential for long-term damage here. The fact that she's doing so well in all the other areas of her life should be very reassuring to you. Why not just wait for this to take care of itself, which at some point it will."

"I don't know," Jenny insisted, "I can't help thinking there's something I should be doing. I just wish we hadn't put her through that separation. I just wish we could turn back the clock."

For me to be of some help for this family, I would have to help disentangle Jenny from the belief that she and her husband were the sole cause of Siobhan's bed-wetting. Perhaps Jenny has a history of taking responsibility for other people's problems and is doing the same thing now. Perhaps there are still some issues left over from her separation from her husband that have not been dealt with, and focusing on her daughter's bed-wetting allows her to keep them from getting buried. Perhaps self-blame ("If only my husband and I could have gotten our act together before we had to go through splitting up") is simply a more comfortable, familiar experience for her than is acceptance ("This is a problem that for now has no ideal solution").

Whatever the explanation, Siobhan's temporary neurological lag will become a greater and greater source of frustration and anxiety until Jenny can forgive herself for her own imperfections.

4) We Blame Others

The *benefit* of this approach is that neither we nor our child are the sole recipient of unjustifiable blame. The *risk* is that in consistently blaming others for whatever problems exist, we dodge the legitimate responsibility that we and our child have to address a troublesome issue in an honest and creative way.

Marty had been called into the school more than once during his son's fifth-grade year to confer with the teacher, because Noah was bullying and tormenting other kids. "I know that Noah can be difficult, but this teacher of his just doesn't like boys, I can tell," was Marty's initial explanation of the problem. "That woman's got it in for him, and the moment any kid comes crying to her that something happened, she's going to turn around and point the finger at Noah."

"Has he displayed this kind of behavior in other years as well?" I asked.

"Yeah, I guess so. I mean, he's a big kid, and always has been, and I think that's made it hard for him. More has always been expected of him by teachers because he's big, and it's easy to single him out as the bully. The other kids know that they can get away with it, that he'll be the one who winds up getting into trouble, not them."

"I think you're making an interesting point about some of the disadvantages of being a big kid," I commented. "How have you tried to help him understand some of the liabilities that go with his good size?"

"Well, I've told him he's going to have to be more on his toes, that because of his size and strength he's got to be more careful with smaller kids, make sure not to hurt them when they're messing around. But the teachers, they just don't get it. This has happened every year—from when he was in preschool, even. It's always, 'Your son's out of control, your son's too aggressive, your son's got to learn better self-control.' I think it's very unfair."

"Have there been teachers who seem to have understood him better than others over the years?"

"I guess so. I mean, some years have started off pretty good, and his second-grade teacher really liked him. He had a good year that year. But he somehow winds up getting this reputation as the class bully, and then everything starts to unravel from there. From then on, it's all pinned on him."

"What do you think was different in second grade?"

"Like I said, I think the teacher really liked him."

"But how did she treat him?"

"She treated him like she liked him! She gave him a chance. She didn't blame him the second somebody came crying off the playground. But she wasn't afraid to be firm with him when he *was* at fault."

"So there were times, even *that* year, when he was a little too rough?"

"Well, yeah. Like I said, Noah's no angel, and I don't expect him to be. I just don't believe he's as bad as everyone says he is. Last year things had gotten so bad that I asked for him to be switched out of his class and transferred to another one."

"What happened?"

"The principal wasn't crazy about it, but she agreed to it—although I have to say that things weren't a whole lot better, I think that's probably because it was too late in the year by then. I shouldn't have waited until things got as bad as they did before I asked for the change."

"Does he play on any athletic teams?"

"Yeah, pretty much every season he's playing a sport."

"And how does he handle games and practices?"

"It all depends on whether the coach likes him or not. Like in basketball this past year, that coach seemed to have it in for him. He didn't get much playing time, and he would get frustrated because of this and mess around in practice. One evening the coach called me to let me know he was having trouble with Noah's behavior at practice, but I told him that Noah would probably take practices more seriously if he knew he was going to be playing in more games."

While it is likely that some of Noah's teachers and coaches tended to base their reactions to him on his reputation, Marty was not acknowledging that there were probably good reasons why Noah had *earned* that reputation, and that, either way, it appeared that Noah needed to develop some less aggressive ways of expressing himself.

Perhaps Marty felt victimized because he, too, had been a big kid who had been discriminated against because of his physical presence, and he has a hard time insisting on better behavior from Noah, because he empathizes with his plight. Perhaps Marty still models or sanctions aggressive behavior, and calling Noah to task for similar behavior would mean that he would have to reevaluate his own.

Either way, Noah will be unlikely to shape up and improve his social relationships as long as his father prefers to see the difficulties his son is having as someone else's responsibility.

5) We Blame the Child

The *benefit* of this approach is that we spare ourselves (and others) any burden of guilt or responsibility. The *risk* is that we drain our child of any self-worth by rejecting him for being who he is and for not being who he isn't.

Evan was a high school sophomore who was very good with his hands, able to disassemble and reassemble anything from alarm clocks to car engines. Although he had been tested and was not found to have either a learning disability or an attention deficit, school was a tremendous chore for him, and he rarely got grades above C. He spent most of his free time drawing diagrams for devices that he had dreamed up and hanging around a local body shop every day after school, helping the owner for free.

His parents, Michael and Kay, brought him to my office with a specific goal in mind: getting him to work harder in school.

"We want to know why he's not doing his class work and why he's not doing his homework, and what we can do to get him more motivated," Michael began.

I turned to Evan. "How would you answer those questions?"

"I'm just not interested in school. I wish they would understand that."

"Are you planning on graduating?"

"Sure."

"Have you thought of what you might want to do once you're done with high school."

"Lots of things. I love working on cars, and the guy who runs the body shop I work at says he'd be happy to hire me for a real job and give me some additional training if I keep helping him out part-time through high school."

"What kind of plan is that, working at a body shop?" Michael interjected. "I didn't raise my son to be a grease monkey."

Evan looked hurt. "Dad, I like doing it. I'm *good* at it. The guys at the shop say I do a great job."

"Have any of you looked into one of the school system's technical programs?" I inquired.

"He's not going to go to some vo-tech program. He's got to have options in his life, and options come with a regular diploma."

"Most technical programs these days aren't the dumping grounds for poor students that they were when we were growing up," I tried to explain. "Technical know-how is quite a marketable commodity these days, and getting good training in that can lead to a good living. Plus, it's still a high school diploma that he'd be earning."

"He's not changing schools just so he can spend more time getting his hands dirty. Even if he becomes a mechanic, he's got to know how to read and write and add and subtract."

"But I know how to do those things, Dad," Evan complained.

"I'm just not that interested in which countries fought in World War II or how to figure out sines and cosines."

"I think he ought to work harder, that's what I think," Michael insisted. "He needs to have more stick-to-it-iveness."

"How long have you been working at the body shop," I asked Evan.

"Almost two years now."

"Does that sound like decent stick-to-it-iveness?" I asked his dad.

"Sure, but that's because he enjoys doing it. You can't go through life only doing things that you enjoy."

"But it's not a bad idea to seek out what you love doing. It makes life go a lot more smoothly."

"His life isn't going to be very smooth if he spends it working on cars."

"That might be where he is now, but his intense interest in how things work might lead him into other areas, too."

"I'll believe that when I see it. For now, I wish he'd quit farting around and try to get a grade above a C for a change."

"At least I'm *getting* C's and passing," Evan said, sounding angrier than he had before. "It's not like I'm failing or dropping out, you know." It was difficult for me not to hear this as a warning: "Back off and appreciate who I am and what I do, or I'll *really* give you something to be angry about."

Instead of recognizing and nurturing Evan's obvious gifts, his father was relentlessly blaming him for being a square peg that didn't fit into a round hole. Perhaps Michael wasn't allowed to pursue what he loved to do when he was younger and feels that being a good father means that he needs to convey this same message to his son. Perhaps Michael *did* pursue what he loved, and it turned out to not be as satisfying or financially rewarding as he had hoped it might be, so he's worried that his son will experience the same disappointment. Or perhaps it's simply a social embarrassment to him to have a "grease monkey" for a son. My task in this family was to help Michael understand that his intolerance of his son's career goals was setting the stage for greater conflict and more significant problems around the corner.

6) We Distance Ourselves from the Child

The benefit of this approach is that we dull our feelings of disappointment in our child that seem too painful to bear and protect him from bearing the direct brunt of our anger and frustration. The risk is that our child feels given up on, making it difficult for him to acquire the self-esteem that is the necessary base for healthy growth and maturation.

PJ was a 10-year-old who was referred to me by his pediatrician because he was lethargic and overweight. He displayed little interest in any kind of physical activity, and the pediatrician was concerned about his weight gain and high blood pressure. Efforts to modify his diet had mostly been unsuccessful.

When I asked what kind of exercise PJ got, his mother, Indira, said, "Almost none. That's one of the problems. He's become a real couch potato. He'd be content just sitting in front of the TV or playing video games all day, rain or shine. He'd eat all day, too, if we let him. He just doesn't seem to care about his weight."

When I asked the parents what their exercise habits were, Indira admitted somewhat sheepishly that she was pretty out of shape herself and "could stand to lose a good twenty-five pounds. I think I need to exercise as much as PJ does, if not more."

PJ's dad, Raj, however, looked fit as a fiddle and emphasized that this was indeed the case. "I play in a men's soccer league twice a week, and I play racquetball on the weekends, too. And there's a pool right near my office, so I try to get a swim in during lunch breaks as well. My doctor says he can't believe my blood pressure is as low as it is."

"In what ways have you tried to help PJ to develop such good physical fitness for himself?" I asked.

Raj's face darkened. "I've tried a lot of things. When he was five, I signed him up for the kids' soccer league, but he didn't like it at all. Then when he was six, and baseball season rolled around, I not only signed him up, but I volunteered to be the assistant coach, thinking that might help get him involved. But it didn't. He seemed to like having me around, but mostly so he could complain about practice being too boring."

"What else have you tried to do to help him be in better shape?"

"I signed him up for a couple of other sports, too, but it was always the same result: He just didn't seem to care. Basketball was a disaster—he wouldn't even participate in the practices. I'm tired of extending myself and having him reject all my efforts."

"Have you invited him to the pool with you in the evenings or the weekends?"

"He says he doesn't like the water."

"Maybe the two of you could take a short jog in the evenings."

"I often don't get home until past seven o'clock. And by the time he gets his homework done and practices his flute, it's already late and getting dark out."

"Have you thought of getting a set of weights and putting together a workout for him that he could do on his own?"

"I know he wouldn't follow through, so why bother? He just avoids anything that has to do with physical activity."

Raj had many rapid excuses for not trying other ways to get PJ off the couch and into motion, suggesting to me that he had basically written his son off. If PJ wasn't going to exercise in any of the ways that Raj enjoyed, which mainly involved team sports, there was simply no point in trying anything else. Meanwhile, PJ was growing heavier with each passing month.

For things to change, I would have to learn more about why Raj was so hurt by PJ's lack of interest in team sports. Perhaps Raj was angry at his son for being out of shape because he has shameful memories from his own childhood, either about himself or about another family member. Perhaps he was sitting back in the hopes that his wife, who also could stand to be in better shape, would take charge and get herself and PJ moving. Perhaps he was feeling rejected by his son because PJ doesn't like doing the things that Raj likes to do. I knew that something was causing him to manage his feelings by pulling away from his son rather than responding more flexibly and creatively to find a new and different way of sharing healthy activities. In the several months this family spent in therapy, much of my focus was on Raj's problems rather than PJ's.

7) We Become Overanxious

The *benefit* of this approach is that no one person appears to be blamed or rejected for creating the problem. The *risk* is that we tend to create a bigger problem than existed in the first place by becoming so emotionally reactive to the situation.

All parents are frequently beset by pangs of worry about their children and have moments in which they shiver in the chill of catastrophic thinking. The key, however, is thinking the problem through and determining the degree to which anxiety is or is not justified.

Kim's 3-week-old son, Victor, for example, wasn't nursing very easily, and he didn't weigh a whole lot more than he had at birth. It might have been due to his sleepiness, his clumsiness, or an awkward fit between the size of his mouth and the shape of her nipple. The pediatrician wasn't concerned about his leisurely growth, but Kim was very worried and began trying to increase the frequency of his feedings to every two hours in an effort to "put some meat on his bones."

The more she tried to nurse him, however, the more difficulty he seemed to have. He had begun turning his head away and arching his back as soon as she unbuttoned her blouse and brought him close to her breast. Meanwhile, this intense regime was wreaking havoc with her own stability as she became increasingly exhausted and irate. In a panic over his slow grasp of the mechanics of nursing, she was responding in a way that only made the situation worse.

"I'm terrified that his development is being stunted by his refusal to nurse. I read that brain growth is incredibly rapid during the first few weeks of life, and here he is, not even gaining any weight. How can his brain grow right if his body's not getting enough nutrients?"

"But you said he was gaining weight, just more slowly than you'd like, and that your pediatrician wasn't worried about his development."

"She's not worried about him now, but if he continues to avoid nursing as much as he's doing, she's going to have to worry about him."

"Have you spoken to any other new mothers about their experiences with nursing?"

"Yes, and they all seem to be doing better at it than I am."

"You talk about it like it's a performance," I commented.

"Well, it is, kind of. I mean, what kind of mother am I that my son doesn't want my milk? Isn't that the basis for our bonding right now? What else is there? We can't have a conversation, we can't play a game."

"It's as if you see yourself as failing as a mother because he's not gaining weight as quickly as you think he should."

"I *am* failing," Kim shouted, tears streaming down her cheeks. "Look at him, he doesn't even want me," she sobbed, as Victor expertly avoided her efforts to place her nipple in his mouth.

Our task at this stage was not so much to get Victor to nurse more vigorously but to understand why Kim was choosing to respond to this situation in a way that was clearly backfiring for both of them. Perhaps Kim's parents or husband were promoting her anxiety by constantly commenting on Victor's small stature. Perhaps she felt guilty about something that happened before or during her pregnancy and subconsciously assumes that Victor is "punishing" her by refusing her breast. Perhaps she never learned that it was okay for her to "just say no" to an offer of nurturance, and it's hard for her to give Victor the room to do what *she* never could do.

Kim needed to sort out the origins of her anxious response to Victor's offhanded nursing. Only then could she create a better fit between his need for nourishment and her need to nourish.

8) We Become Overprotective

The *benefit* of this approach is that we recognize the existence of a problem without casting blame for it on the child, ourselves, or anyone else. The *risk* is that our concerns about our child become magnified to such a degree that we deprive him of developing his own ability to meet challenges.

Elaine contacted me because of her daughter's shyness around other children. Dawn was a timid 4-year-old who came into my office warily, shuffling along while tightly clutching her mother's handbag with both of her little fists. As soon as her mother sat down, she instantly crawled onto her lap and buried her face, making it impossible for us to have any eye contact with each other.

"Dawn just can't handle interactions with anyone," Elaine began. "I tried her in a preschool program on two different occasions, once this year, and once last year, and in both cases she did nothing but sit on the floor and bawl. When we go to the park she'll play quite happily until another kid shows up, and then she dashes over to me and won't leave my lap until the other kid leaves, which of course sometimes doesn't happen. If someone says hi to her, like in a store, she turns her head away and pouts.

"She was invited to the birthday party of a little girl up the street, but she spent the whole party doing what she's doing now, just sitting on my lap—she didn't play any games, didn't want any punch, didn't eat any cake, wouldn't even take the goodie bag that she was given, so I had to take it home for her. She has another invitation for another child on our block, and I don't think I'm even going to bother taking her. It's bound to be a repeat performance."

"Did the preschool teachers help her to manage your separating from her?"

"They tried, but it didn't work. I even told her I'd wait right outside, wouldn't even drive home, but she just wouldn't stop crying."

"Did you ever actually leave the room, just to see what would happen?"

"This last time, the teacher told me to just leave and wait right outside the door, and I did, but I could hear her crying and crying, and I just couldn't take it. I went in after a few minutes, and that was that."

"When she was at the birthday party, how did you help her get acclimated?"

"I let her stay with me at first, and I said I'd go over and sit with her on the floor when all the girls started playing a game, but she wouldn't let me do that. She wanted me to stay right where I was, out of the action."

"And what would have happened if you had said you were going to sit there for the game anyway, and she was free to join you or stay behind?"

"I don't know. I didn't think about trying that."

"What other public places do you take her to?"

"Not many, really, because she seems so unhappy. I don't even bother going to the pool because she goes nuts with all the noise and hates having water splashed on her. These days, I'd have to say, we mostly stay home because everything is so hard for her, and because I get tired of being clung to and having to fight her to be even a little bit more outgoing."

While Dawn was clearly a shy, uneasy child, it was also clear that Elaine was so intent on protecting her daughter (and herself) from discomfort that she wasn't giving Dawn adequate, workable opportunities to learn to cope with and overcome some of her timidity. In situations like this, I have to learn more about what impact the child's shyness has on the parent, and why she chooses to cushion her daughter so thoroughly that the child never has the chance to grow out of her shyness.

Perhaps Elaine was or is shy herself, and had been pushed to overcome it before she was ready to do so. Perhaps her brother or sister was shy growing up, and she saw this work to their disadvantage over time. Perhaps she values friendliness and sociability above all else, despises a child who doesn't display these qualities, feels guilty about this, and then tries to overcompensate for her guilt by not pushing her daughter at all.

By analyzing the origins of her overprotectiveness, she will be better able to find a safe and successful way to build up Dawn's social skills.

It is easy to see how responding in any of the ways discussed above will only exacerbate the very problems and imperfections that first troubled us. It is also easy to see, at least when the story concerns someone else, that parents bring their own unresolved issues to their interactions with their children, unconsciously looking to the child for surcease from old injuries, many of which date back to childhood and may have long since been forgotten.

But oh, how those demons raise their ugly heads when we replay our childhood tapes through our children!

Our ability to relate in a more positive, effective way when our children don't meet our expectations depends on our decision to recast the image of our child as "good enough," to honor who he is and relinquish who he isn't, and in doing so to heal the wound to our self-image that he has unintentionally inflicted on us.

To begin getting in the right frame of mind to do this, reflect on the following questions, and, if you think it would be helpful, write down your answers and keep them with you as a reference as you journey through the subsequent chapters of this book.

_____ EXERCISE ONE _____

1. In what ways were you a disappointment to your parents?
2. At what point in your development did this disappointment occur?
3. How did your parents handle their disappointment in you? In what ways did it reveal itself, directly or indirectly? (You can use as a guide or stimulus the eight typical ways of responding that were discussed above.)
4. How did you respond to their disappointment in you?
5. How has their disappointment affected your overall approach to life?
6. How has their disappointment affected your own parenting?
7. What emotions are linked to your being disappointing?
8. What emotions are linked to your being disappointed?

Let's look at how one parent, Elaine, the mother of the overly shy 4-year-old Dawn, answered these questions. Her response took the form of an essay rather than a question-and-answer format; through her essay she began to glean some insights into her own parenting.

I disappointed my parents several times, but one that comes to mind is when I didn't go to the prom during my senior year in high school. I think they saw that as a real coming-of-age ritual, and when I chose not to go with any of the guys who asked me, they were quite upset. My mother kept asking, even up until the night before the prom, if I might agree to go with the son of a friend of hers, but I just didn't feel ready for it. My father was coming into my bedroom almost every night, it seems, telling me how important it was to go to the prom, how it's a night that I would always remember, and I should just go.

But what I remember was how I was letting them down. And I felt so bad about it, I knew they wanted me to do this, and I knew most of my friends were going, but I was just too shy and too uncomfortable, the thought of dressing up fancy, and being picked up by a boy in a tux, and going out to dinner and then to a party— well, it was just too much. I was always a little behind the curve socially, and I simply could not get myself to go along with this.

And I still remember the Sunday after the prom, hearing my mom on the phone with the mother of a friend of mine who *had* gone, and how angry she looked as she was getting all the details, sort of repeating them out loud so I'd hear them—"And so everybody went out to breakfast? And they didn't get home until a couple of hours ago? And they rented a limousine?" I felt so small . . .

And so now that I'm a mom, I've tried to do things differently. I try not to push Dawn to do things that she's not ready to do. I don't want to put her in the position that my parents put me in, feeling bad for something that there's no real reason to feel bad about, because there's no worse feeling than disappointing your parents when there's nothing you can do about it.

In her writing, Elaine was able to pinpoint, with some precision, the experience of disappointing her parents and how they responded to their disappointment. She was also able to note how that experience has colored her own parenting, making her overly cautious about placing (what she believes are) unrealistic expectations on Dawn's shoulders.

However, her desire to be a different parent than her own parents were, a desire that all parents share, was also leading her to become overprotective of Dawn, to inadvertently convey to her daughter the belief that she was not able to grow beyond herself and develop some new skills and capacities.

As we discussed the ways in which this approach was backfiring, and resulting in Dawn feeling just as insecure as she used to feel, Elaine was able to begin resisting the temptation to overcompensate for her parents having pushed her, and to consider providing Dawn with *achievable* opportunities to grow.

——————————— TWO ———————————

Uncovering

The real voyage of discovery consists not in seeking new landscapes, but in having new eyes.

Marcel Proust

In my work with families, I have come to believe that every child actually has three births. There is the first birth, the birth of the fantasy child whose identity we begin to construct in our minds during our own childhood. This is the dream child who will flawlessly meet all of our expectations for perfection and remedy all the defects of the unavoidably flawed parent-child relationship we ourselves had to endure.

Then there is the second birth, the birth of the imperfect, flesh-and-blood child who enters life on his own terms, with his own will and heart and destiny, the child who will inevitably enrage and disappoint us somewhere along the way because he can never meet the expectations that we have for him.

And finally, if we are courageous enough to go through these labor pains, there will be a third birth, the birth of the good enough child, the child we can see with new and unencumbered eyes, who does not exist simply to please and gratify us, who can be appreciated simply for being himself no matter how far he diverges from the ideal.

How can a child successfully meet expectations that began blossoming years before she was born, or even conceived? How do we, as a family, make the bewildering journey from the first birth to the third? In my work helping hundreds of parents and children to navigate these choppy waters, I have found that there are five stages along the way, which are the core of this book:

1. *Uncovering* the origin of your expectations for your child, in which are rooted the qualities that you attribute and ascribe to your child
2. *Acknowledging* the ways in which you help to create the very behaviors or attitudes that so disappoint you
3. *Understanding* how your child goes about solving his problems and fulfilling his needs
4. *Forgiving* your child for not having fulfilled your expectations, releasing him from the unwritten contract that requires him to meet your needs rather than his own
5. *Changing* how you respond to your child, as if you have both been reborn

Once these stages have been worked through, you will feel a tremendous sense of relief, and a newfound conviction in your own competence. When you start to see both yourself and your child as good enough, you will also enjoy the relationship between you as never before. Unburdened of excessive anger and anxiety, guilt and fear, you will be amazed at the tender, joyous feelings that emerge.

As one parent said to me at the end of treatment, "I don't know whether she's changed, or whether I see her differently, but it finally feels like we're in love."

We'll continue by working on the first stage and taking a look at the origin of the expectations that we bring to parenthood.

I remember one day seeing two families back-to-back who had completely different reactions to the same data. It was June, the end of the school year, which is always a highly charged time in my practice.

My two o'clock patients, the Lewises, came into the room with their 15-year-old son, Brandon, triumphantly leading the way. He handed me his report card, his eyes ablaze with pride. "All B's and

C's!" he announced happily. This was a tremendous accomplishment after having earned D's and E's almost exclusively on his first three report cards that year. I spent the session congratulating the family on their hard work and making sure they understood how the changes that they had all been making over the past six months had made this payoff possible.

My three o'clock patients, the McKinneys, came into the room looking glum and irritable. "We're really not making the kind of progress in here that we had hoped to," began Mr. McKinney, as he took his son Derek's report card from his shirt pocket and thrust it toward me. "Look at this. More than two months of therapy now and not a single A. Nothing but a couple of B's, and the rest C's. I don't know that it makes much sense for us to continue in here if this is what the result is going to be," was his curt commentary, as Derek stared down at the floor, mortified, and Mrs. McKinney directed a stony glare my way.

Despite the unmistakable current of anger circulating throughout the room, I couldn't help having a private moment of amusement at the discrepancy between the reactions of the two families. The report cards were almost identical, but the Lewises were delighted, while the McKinneys were disappointed. Why?

The reason is that there was a significant difference between the two sets of parental *expectations*. Let's take a closer look at these two families to see how their expectations got established and how these expectations changed, or didn't change, over time.

The Lewises had struggled successfully in the past half-year to alter some of the patterns that had both contributed to and resulted from Brandon's low grades. Not particularly interested in academic matters, Brandon had still done reasonably well in primary and middle school, usually getting B's even though he was clearly more committed to making good friends than he was to making good grades. He began ninth grade by investing himself even more heavily in his social life than usual, at the expense of his academic life. With the increasing workload that high school classes offered, it was not surprising that his grades suffered.

He ended that first year of high school with C's and D's, which his parents attributed to his inexperience, hoping that things would straighten out on their own the next year. However, his first-quarter marks in tenth grade were even worse, and by the end of the second quarter, two very angry and desperate parents and a surly and demoralized young man made their way to my office for help.

Brandon's parents had responded to his falling grades by becoming punitive and overinvolved, calling his teachers every couple of days to see if he was up to date on homework, grounding him for weeks at a time when he failed tests or didn't turn in his assignments. They were constantly lecturing and hectoring him until their home had become an unpleasant battleground for all of them. The activities that were most important to him—rehearsing with the rock band that he had put together, going to concerts with his friends, playing his beloved electric guitar, or just sitting in his room listening to a stack of CDs or his favorite radio station—were the very ones that his parents started putting restrictions on.

As is often the case during adolescence, a time when most young men and women are striving for greater autonomy at any cost, this approach was backfiring: the more his parents pushed for productivity, the less productive Brandon seemed to become.

When I made some time for us to talk without his parents present during our first session, Brandon reported with surprising candor and self-awareness that he believed his parents cared more about his grades than he did, and that he was reluctant to show any improvement in school for fear of convincing them that their draconian measures were succeeding, which would result in their remaining in place.

"If they think that grounding me and calling my teachers and keeping me in my room to do homework two hours a night is going to improve my grades, they've got another think coming," he warned. "I'll get whatever grades I decide to get, and there's not a thing they can do about it."

I asked Brandon what he hoped to do with his life over the next several years. "Oh, I want to graduate, if that's what you're wondering," he said, "but I just don't think I want to go to college. My drummer's older brother is going to one of those institutes that teaches studio production and sound engineering, and I might enjoy that, because I'd really like to get into music and produce and record stuff. But I haven't told my parents that, because I know they'd go ballistic if they knew what I was thinking of doing."

When I talked to Brandon's parents without Brandon present, I of course heard a different version of things. "We've just been too lenient over the years, and it's catching up with him now," his father said. "Tenth grade is time to buckle down, and it's our job to help him do it. Otherwise, it'll be too late, and he won't have the grades to go to college."

"He really doesn't deserve to be out at concerts or playing around with that band of his if he can't even turn in his homework," Brandon's mother added. "He needs to get more serious, and it's got to happen now."

I learned more about the basis for his parents' concerns when I asked them about their own educational histories. Elliott, Brandon's father, said that he'd never been much of a student. He wound up graduating high school by the skin of his teeth and bumping around from one underpaying, unsatisfying job to another for almost a decade. Finally, he got involved selling insurance—"found my calling," in his words—and became very successful at it.

Mercedes, Brandon's mother, had been an excellent student her whole life and was in the midst of completing a second master's degree, in counseling, to go along with one in special education. An elementary school teacher who was planning on becoming a guidance counselor, she admitted with a chuckle that she had difficulty even *imagining* what it would be like to fail a test or neglect a paper, being unable to recall having ever done either.

So between Elliott's belief that his own lack of focus in school had resulted in ten years of feeling lost and financially unstable, and Mercedes's pride in her enduring conscientiousness, it was no mystery why Brandon's low grades were eliciting such a strong negative reaction from both of them.

I tried to address this with each parent separately. With his dad, I pointed out that the difficulties he had had as a young adult were not solely due to his low grades in high school, but to his not having found something he loved to do. If he had been fortunate enough to begin selling insurance right after high school, he probably would have taken to it just fine. It's just that nobody, himself included, had considered this as a possible career for him.

His parents had always aimed "higher"—they envisioned Brandon as a lawyer, a goal that had no appeal whatsoever to him—while he had responded to their aspirations by refusing to aim anywhere at all. He'd "get by," he kept telling them, and so he did, until the "getting by" became so discouraging that he got serious about finding something to do with his life.

With Brandon's mom, I pointed out that while opportunities for success in certain careers are closely linked with school performance, that is not true for every career, her husband's being a case in point. I also planted a seed by reminding her that good teachers are good not because of the grades they got in their college or graduate courses but because of the patience, caring, and compassion that they show their students, a statement to which she vigorously assented.

I then scheduled a session with Brandon and his parents together and encouraged him to talk to them more directly about some of the hopes he held for his future. At first, as he had predicted, they were dismayed. "I don't mind you getting into music as a career, but I think you've got to get a college degree before you make any decisions about this," Elliott said after a long pause. "Are you sure these schools will qualify you to do what you want to do?" Mercedes asked.

I encouraged Brandon to take his parents' concerns seriously, and he and I spent some time in a follow-up session cranking out a list of questions and calling three of the training institutes he'd heard about in the area. He learned that they all required high school diplomas or GEDs. Two of them had linkups with community colleges in the area that allowed for the pursuit of both a certificate and an associate's degree, and they all provided scholarships for promising students with good high school grade point averages.

Armed with this information, and with my encouragement, Brandon sat down with his parents one evening after dinner and went over what he had learned, and some of his thoughts and ideas. The three of them reported back to me in the following session that it was the first positive discussion they'd had together in months.

As Brandon began to realize that doing better in school might benefit *him* as much as, if not more than, his parents, by enabling him to get accepted into one of these institutes and qualify for a scholarship, he reclaimed control over his academic life and began investing more energy in it.

And as his parents began to realize that his future did not depend entirely on high grades, or even necessarily on a bachelor's degree, they were able to relax their expectations and loosen their stranglehold on their musically inclined son. I didn't advise them to let go of the reins completely, of course—we worked out a contract in which Brandon's right to go to a concert would be contingent on his having turned in all homework and passed all tests in the week preceding—but the other activities that were so important to him, his guitar practice, his band rehearsals, his "music listening time," were all left up to him to schedule and balance with his other responsibilities.

With the pressure off, and with Brandon finally seeing some reason to commit himself to his studies, his grades rose nicely— not as high as his parents might have liked, but high enough to afford him the flexibility to pursue some of the avenues that interested him. His final report card, in his and his family's eyes, was "good enough."

Now let's examine the McKinney family to see what can happen when expectations are *not* successfully adjusted to meet the nature of the child. Derek was a studious high school junior who had consistently gotten the most out of his abilities over the years.

While most of his friends breezed through their classes, Derek usually had to struggle, particularly when it came to anything involving reading and writing. However, his good global intelligence and his solid work habits had generally carried the day and enabled him to succeed, even in the gifted and talented classes that he took in middle school and the higher-level honors courses he had begun taking during freshman and sophomore years in high school.

In his junior year, though, it seemed that he had finally hit a wall. Despite sometimes spending more than four hours a night at homework, he simply could not get the A's and high B's he was used to getting. No matter how much effort he expended, his grades remained at the low B and C level in the very sophisticated physics, calculus, honors English, and European history classes his earlier success had propelled him into.

His parents could not understand what had happened to their sterling son. And their confusion was magnified by the fact that Derek's two older sisters had both been fine students throughout high school and were now enjoying further success in their college and postgraduate years. One was currently handling a demanding premed curriculum with ease, while the other had recently received a fellowship that allowed her to begin a doctoral program in linguistics.

Trying to trace the history of Derek's current problems, I learned that when his second "low" report card came in, at the end of January, his parents had arranged for him to start being tutored. Unfortunately, that seemed to do nothing more than increase his workload, along with the tension he was feeling. In fact, that tension was what had brought them into my office. When they came for their initial session with me in April, they reported that they had called me on the advice of their pediatrician, who was concerned about the chronic stomach pain that Derek was suffering from, pain for which the gastroenterologist they had consulted could find no apparent cause. The mention of Derek's grades was made only in passing.

In our second session, after hearing Derek tell me about his frustration with reading and writing, how long it took for him to read a page of text and remember what he had read, and how this had always felt like a problem to him, I suggested a psychoeducational evaluation. His parents eagerly followed through on this with a colleague of mine, and the tests revealed that Derek was wrestling with a learning disability that had probably been interfering with his achievement for years, without anyone's ever being aware of it.

The McKinneys didn't interpret the results in quite the way that I had hoped, however. "If he's got a learning disability, then he's going to have to work even harder to overcome it, it seems to me," mused Jack, Derek's father. "Do you think this is why his SATs weren't very high?" wondered Helaine, Derek's mother.

I pointed out that Derek deserved a lot of credit for having done as well as he had over the years while struggling with a heretofore unidentified handicap, and that the key now was not working harder, but working *smarter*, which would mean acquiring some learning strategies to help him compensate for the disability.

However, a few weeks later, when the last report card of the year rolled in looking pretty much like the previous three, it was clear, based on his parents' reaction, that they felt they had more work to do. Derek had had a few sessions with a reading specialist who was teaching him test-preparation techniques, but there hadn't been enough time for him to make any visible progress yet.

Meanwhile, his parents expected him to continue to operate at the level that they had become accustomed to, one that compared well with his sisters and reflected well on them. Clearly, this attitude was taking its toll on their son both mentally and physically, and making a difficult situation worse. My guess was that if they didn't begin to see Derek as "good enough" soon, unremarkable grades and minor stomachaches would be the *least* of their problems.

Every parent walks a tightrope when it comes to expectations. We know that having expectations of our children that are too high is a sure way to annihilate their self-worth and ensure that they will walk around feeling that they have let us, and themselves, down. On the other hand, having expectations that are too low is a sure way to dilute their self-respect and makes it difficult for them to believe in themselves and their capacity to overcome roadblocks, handle setbacks, and attain their goals. So what is a parent to do?

The solution, of course—easier said than done—is to establish expectations that are *realistic*, that honor who our children are and what they are and are not capable of, expectations that are high enough that our children can internalize our confidence and belief in them and feel challenged to achieve and excel, but not so high that they are constantly experiencing failure and defeat.

How do we arrive at realistic expectations? One way is to take a look at the origins of our expectations for our children. Knowing more about how we formed our expectations is the first step toward making adjustments and creating a sense of "good-enoughness."

When our child is first handed to us, through birth or adoption, we are being asked to make an extraordinary commitment: we are agreeing to take care of a total stranger for our entire lives. From this point on, not a single day will pass in which we are not subject to feeling *some* sense of parental responsibility, no matter how old we or our children are. As a television comedienne once commented, "Every mother watches her middle-aged children for signs of improvement."

Now just as nature abhors a vacuum, we humans abhor anything that is unrecognizable, so we instantly set about making this "stranger" someone we can feel more familiar with. We attribute to this for-now-unknown entity an identity that enables us to connect with him right away, and to feel better about investing and sacrificing so much of ourselves in his care.

Often, the attributions that we make are pleasant ones. "She's got her mother's gorgeous eyes," we observe. "Look at her swat at that mobile—she's so *coordinated*," we marvel. Or, "He's such a flirt, just like his dad."

Sometimes the attributions we make are more negative. "He's always breathing heavy. Do you think he inherited my asthma?" "He's never satisfied, no matter what I do for him." "She's certainly got her grandfather's temper, I can tell you that."

But no matter if the attributions are positive or negative, we create them so that our child becomes someone we can identify with, good or bad. Once we can identify with our child, we have in place the basis for establishing an emotional bond. The bond may turn out to be a gratifying one or a disappointing one, but *there has to be some kind of bond there* or we will not be able to summon and justify the enormous energy required to raise our children.

And it is here, right in the middle of the constellation of qualities that we choose to attribute to our children, that we must look to find the origin of our expectations for them. The way in which we read complex meanings into even the subtlest, tiniest characteristics that our child displays speaks volumes about our visible and invisible wishes, motives, and fears, all of which conspire to define what we demand of him.

Understanding the way in which parental *attributions* connect with parental *expectations* is crucial to the raising of a "good enough child," so let's take some time to look at how these connections evolved for two different parents.

Lisa, a single parent, came to me upset about the chronic fighting that she and her 11-year-old daughter, Samantha, had been engaging in for the past year. Things had been getting worse and worse throughout fifth grade, but had finally come to a head when Samantha had stormed off the field in the middle of a losing soccer game and refused to go back in, despite her coach's and teammates' efforts to convince her to do so.

Lisa told me, "I think it's just so disrespectful to leave your team in the middle of a game and not have the decency to hang in there, even if there's no way you're going to win. I'm just fed up with her attitude, this business that if things aren't going her way, then she doesn't have to participate anymore. She's walked out of practice twice already this season, and now she does it during a *game!* She should apologize to her coach and she should apologize to her teammates, and frankly, now that I think about it, she should apologize to me, too. I'm the one who signed her up, who pays the fees, who washes her uniform, who practices with her, who gets her to all of her games and cheers her on from the sidelines. It's an insult to me as well."

"That's just the problem." Samantha wasted no time jumping in. "You weren't *cheering* me from the sidelines, you were yelling at me to 'Get in the game! Get in the game!' Do you know how sick I am of hearing you yelling at me the whole time? How do you think it makes me feel?"

"I'm trying to get you *focused*, Samantha," Lisa retorted. "I know how good a player you can be, and when I see you drifting out there on the field, I yell to try to wake you up and get you back in there. I'm only trying to help."

"Well, it doesn't feel like help, Mom," Samantha snarled. "It's

embarrassing, and I'm sick of it, and I don't even want to play soccer anymore. I've been playing in that stupid league for six years
now, and I'm done!"

"Honey, when you're at your best, you're the best player on
your team, and one of the best in the whole league. You can't quit
something that you're so good at! The coach says she sees players
like you come through the ranks only once every couple of years.
Do you know what kind of future you can have? Do you know
that if you keep at it you could possibly qualify for the Olympic
development team next year? Do you know what an honor that
would be? How can you stop now?"

Samantha seemed to be more interested in sorting through the
crayons on my end table than she was in listening to her mother,
so I stepped in and redirected the conversation.

"What are some of the other things you spend your time doing
besides playing soccer?" I asked, almost falling into the trap of
asking her what else she "liked" doing, when she had already made
it clear that she didn't "like" playing soccer, at least not in the way
that she was being expected to.

She held up a crayon. "I love to draw," she said quietly. "I like to
design clothes, and I like to draw people, and I'm learning how to
make stained glass in art at school."

"What do you think of your daughter's interest in art?" I asked
Lisa.

"I think it's really neat," she said quickly, but a bit cautiously.
"Her art teacher, Mr. Ortega, took me aside the other day when I
was picking her up and told me how impressed he was with
Samantha's creativity."

"Then how come you never want to see what I draw?" asked
Samantha, her anger starting to rise again. "How come I couldn't
take Mr. Ortega's pottery class?"

"Honey," Lisa began patiently, "I think we went through this
already. Mr. Ortega's class was on Wednesday afternoons after
school. If you took his class, you'd be missing one of your soccer
practices, and the coach said that if you miss a practice, you can't
play in the game. I thought we made a choice here. We had to
pick something, and you agreed to pick soccer."

"I picked soccer because I knew you'd be angry if I didn't. I *hate* having to practice two days a week and plan my entire weekend around games. I don't want to do it anymore, don't you understand?!"

After having led thousands of therapy sessions over the years, if there's one thing I recognize when I see it, it's a dead end. I cut this discussion short and suggested that Lisa rejoin me without Samantha for our next session so that I could learn more about her and the history of her relationship with her daughter.

During that session I discovered that Lisa, too, was a talented athlete, one who had always loved sports, and who had begun to display her ability even before she started school. By the time she was a senior in high school she had been elected captain of both the lacrosse and the ice hockey teams, and she won a scholarship to a top-ranking college based on her athletic achievements and leadership.

After graduating, she had pursued a career marketing sportswear for women, and continued to derive enormous satisfaction from sports, playing in recreational soccer, hockey, and softball leagues throughout the year.

Lisa had generally sounded very up, almost perky, during our first session and during the first part of this second one, but when I asked her what pregnancy and early motherhood had been like, gloom seemed to descend upon her. Her hands stopped their constant movement and fell, folded, into her lap, her voice slowed, and she broke eye contact with me.

"It wasn't a very happy time, I hate to say," she responded. "When I was expecting, I wasn't all that comfortable physically, and my blood pressure skyrocketed, so I had to be on bed rest for the last three months, and I couldn't exercise, couldn't get out much, and it was just very depressing.

"And things didn't seem to get much better after Samantha was born, either. She was a decent baby, nursed well and slept well, but I took six months of maternity leave from work, which I think was a mistake, because I lost touch with everybody and just felt lonely and out of sorts most of the time. I tried to join a mother's group in the neighborhood, but I just didn't fit in. Everybody was busy comparing napping schedules and feeding schedules and all I wanted to do was get back to work, or get back to the gym, or do something besides hang around with infants all day."

"What was your relationship with Samantha like during that time?" I asked.

"Well, like I said, I found motherhood pretty boring at first, so although we spent all of our time together, I couldn't quite get into it."

"Did it ever change?"

"Yeah, I can remember the day it changed," Lisa said, and suddenly she came back to life again, her eyes lighting up and her hands flying up into the air again. "I was lying on my bed with her, she was no more than six months old, it was getting to be spring, and I just kind of rolled this fuzzy little ball over to her, for no particular reason, and, honest to god, she swatted it right back at me. And I stared at her, and she stared back at me, and her eyes were sparkling! So I rolled it back to her, and she did the same thing again! And all of a sudden I realized how coordinated she was. Here was a six-month-old already playing a version of catch! And from that point on, it was like something had lifted, and I felt like a real mother, with a daughter who was truly mine. I started dreaming about her getting into sports just like I got into sports, and how much we could share, and it was like I was saved."

It was easy for me to imagine that these sweet, exhilarating dreams were exactly what Lisa needed to get through the dreary, endless days of early parenthood, when nothing feels quite right, when everything seems out of kilter, when life stretches ahead as nothing more than an unending series of feedings, diaperings, doctor's visits, laundry baskets, and interrupted naps.

Lisa had attributed the quality of athleticism to her infant daughter in an effort to bond with her. In this case, it turned out that the attribution had some accuracy to it, as Samantha did indeed grow up to exhibit athletic talent. But what I also heard in Lisa's words was that there was an *expectation* attached to Samantha's athleticism—in this case, the expectation that she would focus and capitalize on her athletic abilities and make Lisa proud while giving the two of them something to share.

Conflict was arising now because Samantha was at a point in her life when other interests besides sports were becoming important. By developing these other interests, she was threatening to defy her mother's expectations of her and, in essence, tear up the contract that Lisa thought had been agreed to ten years before.

To defuse this conflict, Lisa would first need to recognize the expectations that she had for Samantha so that she would be able to modify them in a way that made her daughter better able to live up to them.

"What would it be like for you if Samantha stuck to her guns and refused to play soccer?" I asked.

"I think it would be the biggest mistake of her life," Lisa instantly responded. "I've seen young athletes give up and they always regret it later on, wishing they'd stuck with it. I work with plenty of almost-made-its in my field, and let me tell you, they're a depressing bunch."

"But I didn't ask what it would be like for *Samantha* if she quit soccer," I said. "I asked what it would be like for *you*."

Lisa was silent for a while. I couldn't help but notice how her hands dropped back down and her eyes looked away again. "I'm not sure," she began. "I'm not sure what we'd do or what we'd talk about. I mean, she's so good at it, and I love watching her so much."

"You talk as if there were nothing else that could draw the two of you together, that could make you feel close. That's an awful lot of pressure to place on one activity."

"I just can't picture her not being on a team, not having games and playoffs and parties and pictures. It's just such an important part of our life together right now."

"But it doesn't sound as if it's feeling as important to Samantha as it is to you. In fact, it seems like she's wondering why you don't feel her other interests and talents are important as well. To you, soccer is an activity that bonds you with your daughter. To her, soccer has become something divisive, something that works against, rather than for, her relationship with her mother."

"But how can she stop something she's so good at?" Lisa wondered, her voice starting to sound more hurt than angry.

"Not everybody commits themselves exclusively to something they are good at, particularly when they are only eleven years old," I explained. "It's a time to explore, not to specialize. She'll have her whole life to do that. She may want to stop playing soccer for a while and then go back to it, or to a different sport. After having focused mostly on her athletic talents, she may want to spend some time discovering her creative gifts. She may decide to abandon sports and art altogether for a while and get involved with something she hasn't touched before, like ballet or science fiction. But that's her job at this point in her life, finding what moves *her*, not what pleases others."

"But if she stops playing soccer now, she'll never catch up," Lisa pleaded. "This is when things start to get really intense, and the girls get really good coaching and go up against really good players. If she sits out a season or two now, she won't be able to just jump back in at the highest level."

"First of all, I don't know that that's true," I commented. "Kids grow and change in such unpredictable ways that you can't presume that taking a break from soccer at the age of eleven means that she won't be able to compete when she's sixteen. For all you know, the break could do her good and *improve* her chances of doing well down the road.

"But even if your fears are on target, and she never, ever competes at the level you've been dreaming of, the fact is, she's not very happy right now and the two of you are getting along poorly. And," I added with a wink, "she's just *starting* adolescence," which elicited a slight grin and a roll of the eyes from Lisa.

I asked Lisa if she thought she could put Samantha's decision about soccer on hold, and instead try to focus on her daughter's burgeoning interest in art. Having read about a traveling exhibit on art and fashion that was currently on display at a local museum, I recommended that she invite Samantha to join her there for a mother-daughter "field trip."

When Lisa returned, she told me that their outing had worked out quite well, and that she was surprised by Samantha's knowledge of fashion. As a marketing professional, she was impressed by Samantha's understanding of current trends and how they differed from those of other periods. It turned out that Samantha had made quite a study of the sixties and seventies looks and had developed her own designs to recycle them, as Lisa discovered after their museum visit when Samantha invited her into her room to show off some of her drawings. Lisa told me that she realized that evening that she had never really paid much attention to Samantha's art before then, never understood how involved she was in it.

The knowledge that there were other ways for the two of them to have a relationship with each other was heartening for Lisa and enabled her to feel less desperately attached to the expectation that Samantha excel at sports. This in turn allowed Samantha to make a decision about soccer that was best for *her*, rather than for her mother.

After discussing it with me without her mother in the room, she decided that she would write a letter of apology to the coach and her teammates, and if it was okay with them, she would return to the team for the last month of the season.

However, she did tell her mom that she didn't want to go to soccer camp this summer, as she had done the previous three summers, and that she might like to play in a recreational league in the coming fall, which had only one practice and one game a week, rather than return to the highly competitive travel league that she had been in since last year.

Lisa's response still had an edge of warning to it. "You know that you might not be able to return to the travel league once you stop going to the camp and start playing rec league," she said. "But if that's your decision, I'll accept it."

Lisa followed up with me in the fall. Samantha had had a great summer at an arts camp that the guidance counselor had recommended. She had indeed chosen to play in the recreational soccer league, and she was enjoying it even though it wasn't as competitive as the travel league.

As for Lisa, she's still having to grit her teeth sometimes, but she's learned to step back. "I have to say there are still times when I run into parents of kids from her old league, and I feel a little embarrassed and apologetic when they ask where Samantha is and

why she didn't return. And the other day I was practically clenching my fists as I listened to one of my friends tell me how well her
daughter was doing on that team. I hung up feeling a little
depressed, and annoyed with Samantha for not having stuck it out.

"But when I see how much happier she is now, and how much
better we've been getting along, that helps me stay on course. I
realize now how crazy things had gotten, and how tense we both
were. None of that's worth it, even if it means that she would have
been a soccer star."

Because of Lisa's shift in outlook, Samantha had gone from
being a crushing disappointment to her mother to being good
enough, and the change was a great relief for both of them.

Alex was a 34-year-old engineer who consulted with me
because of the difficulties he was having with his 4-year-old son,
Alex Jr. "He never seems satisfied, no matter what we do for him,"
Alex reported during our initial session. "He never stops asking,
never stops demanding. Some days I give in to him on almost
everything just hoping to keep him quiet, but even then he finds
something else to be unhappy about. He's turning out to be a
spoiled, unpleasant little boy, and I'm afraid that when he starts
kindergarten next year, nobody's going to like him and nobody's
going to want to play with him."

I asked Alex to bring his son to the next session so that I could
spend some time with him. In his play with the toys in my office,
I noticed that Alex Jr. was certainly curious and energetic, and not
the kind of kid who took no for an answer without first pushing
pretty hard for yes. But there was not much about him that
seemed to match up with the oppositional tyrant that his father
had depicted. In fact, he engaged with me quite well, and once he
learned the rules for what toys he could play with and how he was
allowed to play with them, he was quite enjoyable to be with.

I also paid a visit to Alex's preschool to observe him and talk
with his teacher. What I saw was a cheeky boy with good social
skills who clearly knew how to negotiate, communicate, and
cooperate with peers. His teacher told me that he often talked
back to her when she needed to instruct or discipline him, and

that he was "no stranger to the time-out corner." However, she also said that he was far from the most challenging student she had this year, or any year, and that in her eyes he had matured a great deal in the first few months of this school year.

While children often behave better outside the home than inside the home, the discrepancy between how others perceived Alex Jr. and how his father viewed him was quite striking. In situations like these, and they show up quite frequently in my office, my first guess is that something from the parent's past is accounting for the bleak and negative appraisal of his child.

I brought Alex and his wife, Donna, in for a session without their son and got some background on Alex Jr.'s development. Donna's pregnancy had been normal, and Alex Jr. had been a healthy baby, but one with a very uneven temperament. He slept erratically, nursed unpredictably, and didn't handle transitions very well, twisting and crying whenever it was time for a diaper change or a car ride or a nap.

Donna recalled, "It was very hard on both of us, not knowing when we were going to get to sleep, or for how long, not being able to go out shopping or to a restaurant without him howling and whining. He seems to have grown out of the worst of it, but I don't remember those days very fondly."

"How did the two of you manage things during those first couple of years?" I inquired.

Donna continued, "Well, I have to say that as hard as it was, I really was proud of myself. I basically took it in stride. The pediatrician said that he was just a high-strung kid, and my sister was a big help, too. She said Alex Jr. was a replica of *her* son, who's now fifteen and didn't start settling down until he was nine or ten. So I just buckled down and dealt with it, and he is already a whole lot better, I think.

"But my husband—boy, that was a different story. He always seemed to take it so hard. He would always ask a question that really bothered me—still does. 'Why's he doing this to us? Why's he doing this to us?' he'd ask over and over again when Alex Jr. was crying or struggling. And I kept saying, 'He's not doing it *to* us, it's just who he is,' but it's like he always took it so personally, like little Alex was out to make him miserable."

"She's right, you know," Alex admitted when his wife was finished. "I still feel the same way, like he should know better, that he wants to get my goat, that he *can* behave better but just doesn't want to."

"But he *can't* always behave better," Donna countered, "he's four years old. Yes, he's difficult sometimes, and yes he's sort of nervy, but he's only four. You talk about him like he's a teenager trying to face you down. He's just a little boy."

Alex just shook his head, while Donna gave an exasperated sigh. "I guess that's why we're here," she said, and she was right.

I suggested that Alex make an appointment to see me alone. It was important to try to dispel the cloud of anger and disappointment that hung over his relationship with his son, and I felt that we would make more progress in an individual session. One question I often ask of parents who seem to be unable to see their child objectively is, Who does your child remind you of?

In this case, the answer was immediately clear to Alex: "My dad. He was just as stubborn, just as pushy, just as difficult to please. Nothing was ever good enough for Dad. My mom spent almost forty years trying to please him, and I don't think she succeeded more than a handful of times. And, believe me, I didn't do any better."

"You use the past tense when describing him. When did he die?"

"About five years ago, of a brain hemorrhage. It was pretty startling, actually, because he was in good health and not all that old, but one day my mom called and said, 'He's gone.' He had just collapsed on the golf course. They tried CPR but it was too late. We were all kind of stunned." Despite admitting to being "stunned," Alex spoke of this incident without a hint of emotion.

"What kind of dad was he?"

"Like I said, impossible to please. He really took me for granted. I did well in school, worked hard, played lacrosse, but he shrugged everything off. Nothing seemed to get through to him. I still remember the day I was named All-County in lacrosse. I came running in to tell them, and my mom was all excited, but all he did was look up from the kitchen table and say, 'Nice work, son' in this dull voice and then go back to his pie, like it mattered more than I did. I think I could've been elected president of the United States and he would've said, 'Nice work, son' in that same voice and then continued eating his damn pie."

"So in what ways does Alex Jr. remind you of your father?"

Alex paused for a long moment, looking as though the thought of journeying that far back in time, from my office to that kitchen table of twenty years ago, was something he wasn't prepared to do. But then, somewhat to my surprise, he answered me. "Well, there's that same sense I have of being taken for granted, and of not mattering to little Alex. However much I give him, he wants more. Whatever I do for him is never enough. And he just doesn't listen to me."

It was clear to me that the linkage in Alex's mind between his father and his son was quite strong, and that he was viewing Alex Jr. through a lens colored by the pain from his past. Clearly, to do my job, I would have to help him disentangle the image of his son from the memory of his father. That was the only way Alex Jr. could be seen, raised, and appreciated as himself, rather than as the ghost of his deceased grandfather.

What I realized in going over my notes after the session was that if Alex's father died five years ago, and Alex Jr. was now 4 years old, that meant that he had been conceived only months after his grandfather had died, something that Alex confirmed when I asked about it in our next meeting.

This was important, because I have noticed that many couples conceive a child shortly after the loss of a relative or someone dear to them. Whether or not this is a conscious decision—and usually it is not—a parent may then assign to the child the role of the individual who has departed, sometimes with disastrous results.

It was my belief that this was what was happening here. Alex didn't have the kind of relationship with his father that he would have liked, and he didn't get the chance to work this out because of his father's sudden and unanticipated death. Deprived of a chance to grieve, to say good-bye and resolve his pain, he had brought his father back to life by endowing his son with his father's qualities, such as "impossible to please" and "never satisfied."

These labels, inaccurate as they may be, and certainly inappropriate when applied to a little boy, served the purpose of resurrecting his father and the relationship he had with him. Identifying his son with his father and thus making Alex Jr. seem familiar, even though he was familiar in an unpleasant way, enabled Alex to feel connected to his son. In addition, he could now redirect the anger he felt toward his father, who is no longer alive, at his father's effigy, Alex Jr. But all of this was occurring outside of Alex's awareness, which is why things seemed to be worsening, despite his son's maturation.

As we learned above, every attribution has an expectation linked with it, and in this case, the expectation that blossomed from Alex's attribution is obvious: little Alex was *expected* to be difficult, stubborn, and defiant. The problem, of course, is that Alex will tend to see only what he expects to see, and in this case, what he expects to see is problematic. Unless Alex changed his outlook, his son would never be good enough.

One of the techniques I use in a situation like this is to try to broaden and soften the image of the relative whose spectral presence hovers so insidiously, while simultaneously amplifying the child's virtues and special talents.

I started by asking Alex more about his father, trying to get past the one-dimensional portrait that he carried so close to his heart. "You've mentioned how difficult your father was to please," I began, "but do you have any theories about what might have made him the way he was?"

"Well, I know he had a very hard life as a child, he grew up very poor, and his own father died when he was just ten, so he was always busy helping his mom take care of his younger brothers and sisters. And he dropped out of school and became a dock-worker when he was only fifteen, lied about his age and all that, to help make ends meet at home. So in some ways he had to be pretty tough to have survived all of that."

"You described yourself as a hard-working kid. Was *he* a hard worker as well?"

"Definitely. He worked from sunup to sundown, and while we weren't rich or anything, he really did take good care of us. And he also got involved with unionizing the workers on the dock and apparently was quite influential in the union, wound up being elected treasurer. I guess his persistence and his relentlessness must have served him well, because they were busting the unions pretty good back then, from the stories he would tell."

"So what *positive* echoes of your father do you see in your son?" I asked, a question that seemed to startle him. Again, it seemed as if he felt the burden of having to traverse a couple of decades in several moments' time.

"Well, I guess that business of his being persistent. I see that in Alex Jr., too, in that he never stops, doesn't give in," he said, after a pause. "But," he added right away, "it makes him such a pain in the ass sometimes."

"I'm sure it does. But I'm also sure that it's a quality that, channeled appropriately, could serve him well, just as, to some extent, it did with you on the lacrosse field and in the classroom and with your dad at work and in the union. Accomplishing anything of significance requires great persistence."

At this point, Alex smiled. It was the first time, I realized, that I had ever seen him do so. "You know, I was watching him the other day without his knowing it. He was on the floor in his room working at tying his shoes, and I was standing in the doorway. And I just loved watching him, because he wasn't getting it, but he just kept trying, over and over again. And seeing him sitting there, with his little shoulders hunched, bent over those shoes and as serious as could be, was so neat." At this point, Alex was still smiling, but his eyes were moist.

"You have great love for your son, don't you?"

"I do," Alex said softly. "I just wish I could feel it more often."

"I think you would feel more love for your son if you felt less anger toward your father."

Alex gave me another startled look. "I don't get the connection," he stammered.

I explained the ways in which I thought he was deflecting his old feelings about his father onto little Alex, making his son into a miniature stand-in for his father and heaping onto him the anger that belonged elsewhere.

Although taken aback by my hypothesis, Alex was willing to at least try it on. "So if what you're saying is true, how do I get rid of my anger toward my father, being that he's no longer around for me to talk to?"

"It's more of a challenge to work through your feelings about an important person when he is not there to participate in the process, but it's still possible. What might be a good starting point is to talk with some of the people still around who knew him well and see if there are ways to expand your perception of him."

Alex agreed to make some time to talk with his mother about his father, as well as to call his father's mother, who was still alive and lucid, and one of his father's brothers, who had moved far away, but whom he had always felt close to.

He returned for a follow-up session with a tremendous amount of energy and enthusiasm. "I sort of felt like an archaeologist, digging around to figure out more about my dad, but I was really glad I did, because I learned some interesting things. My uncle said that my dad was very well thought of at work, and that he was greatly admired for his stand in the union. And my mom said that he was very proud of me, but always felt awkward around me because he was in awe of what I was accomplishing in school and in lacrosse. She said that, not having had a father of his own for very long, he was often at a loss for how to talk with me and be with me. That makes a lot of sense now, because there were times I had the feeling he wanted to talk to me or do things but couldn't quite bring himself to do it, and neither could I.

"But I think what was most touching was that my grandmother, my dad's mom, said that my father had been very athletic too, but that he hadn't had the chance to play ball because he had to be so responsible around the house. But she said he used to call her and tell her about how well I was doing in lacrosse, and she showed me a clipping from a newspaper from twenty years ago that listed all of the All-County lacrosse players, and told me that he had brought it over to her one day because he was so proud of me, something that I didn't even know he'd done.

"And I realized that maybe I did matter to him, but he just didn't know how to show it. And it made me kind of sad, too, because I wish he could have gotten to know Alex Jr., and seen *me* as a dad. I think that would've meant a lot to him."

"And how have things been going as a dad?" I asked.

"Much better. It's not that little Alex has really changed all that much, but I keep in mind that image of him working on his shoe tying, and when he comes at me with his demands and requests, I realize he's just doing his work, going about his life the way he goes about it, with a lot of persistence, trying things out over and over again. It's like I can be fond of him now and appreciate that he's a hard worker, too, just like his father and grandfather. It's a lot easier to be with him, even when he's making things difficult."

Through the process of beginning to heal his relationship with his "difficult" and "impossible" father, Alex was able to begin releasing his son from the expectation that he be "difficult" and "impossible" as well, and liberate him to become his own person, a child who could be loved and seen as good enough.

Perhaps you are now thinking that the surest way to accept your child as good enough is to simply eliminate the attributions that lead to distorted expectations. But it's not that straightforward a path.

After all, the attributions in themselves are not bad or unhealthy. They are both *unavoidable*, because ever since Adam and Eve it has been in our nature to give the creatures in our universe recognizable identities, and *indispensable*, because they enable us to forge a bond with our child. It is that bond that enables us to invest ourselves in the hard work of parenthood—an investment that requires great physical and emotional sacrifice without offering up the prospect of any immediate or guaranteed returns. But while you can't suddenly stop making attributions, you can certainly become more *aware* of them. Once you are aware of them, you are less likely to invisibly cloud your perception of your children and distort your expectations of them in either direction.

The exercise that follows is an exercise in uncovering—a way of getting you to both identify certain attributions with which you have labeled your child, and question them.

EXERCISE TWO

The process by which we attribute or ascribe qualities to our child can be a subtle one. In this exercise, first describe some of the characteristics of your child that trouble you. Then note what negative characteristics you have typically attributed this behavior to, and follow up with an alternative explanation. The alternative may or may not be accurate— you can make up your mind about that later. For now, free your mind sufficiently to *posit* an alternative. Sometimes we get so locked into our own versions of events that simply being able to imagine other scenarios can be a liberating, and healing, experience.

Use the blank work sheet at the end of this exercise. Follow this sample from my practice. Louise was the mother of 9-year-old Gary, whose resistance to accepting responsibility had caused friction between them.

LOUISE'S CHART

Characteristic	Attribution	Alternative Explanation
Won't do his homework	Doesn't want to learn	Homework exposes his belief that he's stupid
Won't clean his room	Doesn't respect authority Doesn't care about neatness	Maybe it's the only place he can "let go" a bit and relax
Won't take out the trash without having to be reminded ten times	Doesn't respect authority Doesn't care about the rest of the family Doesn't want to be a team player	Nothing in it for him Other activities are probably more fun

Characteristic	Attribution	Alternative Explanation
Won't go to bed on time	Doesn't respect authority Won't take care of himself	Wants to prove that he's older than his younger brother Nighttime is his only time to relax without the pressure of having to do something else

Now take a look at some of the attributions that you made on your work sheet and see if you can discover their origin, what they are based upon, and how relevant they are to your child. For example, in my discussion with Louise about her chart, she revealed to me that her younger brother, a ne'er-do-well whose career rose no higher than a menial office job at a small accounting firm, had also had a difficult time accepting responsibility, and that many of the attributions that she came up with to explain her son's behavior may have been rooted in her parents' explanation of her brother's behavior—explanations that she recalls having overheard in their conversations many years before.

As we pursued this, she was able to note some differences between her brother and her son and realized that the alternative explanations that I had asked her to invent actually had more relevance to her son than did the ones that she had previously been applying to him.

Where do your attributions come from, and how well do they apply to your child? Are any of them inaccurate, more like echoes from another time, person, or place?

My Chart

Characteristic	*Attribution*	*Alternative Explanation*

THREE

Acknowledging

The best way for your dreams to come true is to wake up.
Paul Valery

Before proceeding with this chapter, I want you to agree to take whatever parental guilt that you are carrying with you and, for the duration of the chapter, dispose of it. You can picture it being stuffed into a box which is then buried, you can stoke up an internal bonfire that turns it to ash, you can zap it with a vaporizing laser—whatever works, do it.

Now that you've temporarily jettisoned your guilty feelings, you'll be prepared not only to accept, but also *to take heart from*, the statement that follows, a statement that is of supreme importance in raising a good enough child:

I contribute to the ways in which my child disappoints me and help to make that disappointment happen.

Notice that I am not saying that you are responsible for who your child is, or that it is your fault when she is experiencing difficulties, or that you are solely to blame. But it's essential to realize that the behavior of children, and of their parents, does not arise in a vacuum; it is the direct result of the influence that you exert on each other.

Understanding this in the right way can be a very liberating experience, because once we know more about the ways in which we contribute to our children's irksome behaviors and attitudes, we're more than halfway down the road to feeling less vexed and more positive and creating the climate for growth and change.

In what ways do we find ourselves creating the very family problems that so plague us? What puzzling mechanism impels us to make our children into the instruments of our unhappiness? Why do we sometimes persist in responding to our offspring in ways that so clearly make things worse rather than better? The beginnings of the answers to these questions lie in what we learned in the previous chapter: how we invest our children with qualities and characteristics that may or may not apply to them so as to familiarize ourselves with them enough to marshal the resources to raise them. Now, however, we will take this information a step further and see how we not only attribute, but also *amplify*, these qualities and characteristics to the extent that they take on a life of their own.

Becoming a parent requires of all of us what I refer to as a "reverberating journey," a pilgrimage into our swirling, murky internal world, a world that ricochets with memories, fantasies, and feelings that have lain dormant for years, regretfully or blissfully out of our awareness.

The process of taking on the life-and-death responsibility of raising a child will invariably create a widespread disequilibrium that blurs the distinction between past and present, between real and unreal, between rational and irrational, between what lurks inside of us and what lives outside of us.

This journey is a necessary and important one, because the emotional energies that are churned up through our exposure to our own children are the very energies we will need to care for them effectively. The profound upheaval that results from the detonation of the depth charge of childbearing can reactivate connections between generations, heighten our awareness of our own childhood experiences, provide greater accessibility to our subconscious, and bring to the surface strengths and qualities that had been buried for years. Parenthood is a time in our lives when we become softened, when we are unusually changeable and teachable, and because of this it is accompanied by great potential for healing and creative renewal.

On the other hand, this resurgence of buried experience will not only fuel us but haunt us. Old sorrows, hurts, anxieties, and fears flare up in all of their original potency. We are reminded of recent or ancient struggles and conflicts that we would gladly forget. Long-silent voices clamor for our attention, and the grappling hooks of our unfinished business reach out to us from the deep, pulling us back down to the disturbing psychological locales that we thought we had escaped from.

How does this affect our relationship with our child? Perhaps our most paradoxical yet common parental instinct is to re-create in our present the emotional climates and narratives of our past. We do this through enlisting our children to act in scenes that we have artfully but unconsciously scripted for them.

By casting our sons or daughters in certain roles and ascribing to them distinctive attributes, we get them to participate in a drama that, at its most elemental level, is designed to heal us. It is not our intent to exploit them, to ignore, misunderstand, or repudiate who they are, but instead to mourn old losses, to grieve old wounds, to shed old burdens, and to *rework* old pain so that it doesn't have to continuously get replayed in our relationships with those who matter to us. Through directing and engaging our children in our personal passion plays, we ultimately hope to understand ourselves and make ourselves understood—to discover and claim, or rediscover and reclaim, who we truly are.

This does not happen magically, but through the reinforcement of certain exchanges between our child and ourselves, and the avoidance or suppression of others. Through our gestures and interactions, we do what parents have always done, which is to transmit a psychological heritage, to convey to our children what we expect from them and what they are to think of themselves.

That's why D. W. Winnicott, the pioneering pediatrician and psychiatrist, used to say, "There is no such thing as a baby." Because your child is planted in the soil of your and your partner's inner world and nourished by your collective pool of memories, dreams, and fantasies, his individuality does not exist independently, but unfolds and expresses itself in a way that is profoundly altered and affected by your shared emotional climate.

Let's use language as an example. Babies are cognitively and physically wired to babble, to produce a steady stream of nonsensical sounds that eventually become the building blocks for language. One day you are bent over the changing table, diligently replacing yet another diaper while your 1-year-old stretches out his arms and watches you intently, all the while serenading you with a random assortment of phonemes.

Today's vocal assignment appears to be *d* words. As you toss the dirty diaper and start unfolding the new one, the doo-doo's and dee-dee's and doh-doh's tumble forth, until all of a sudden you hear one that sings like music: "da-da." "Da-da!" you say in response, meeting his eyes, your own eyes shining, lifted as if by magic from the drudgery of diaperdom. "Da-da! That's *me!*" you exclaim, tickling his tummy and bending your brightening face closer down to his, while he whirls his arms and kicks his legs happily.

One of the major ways (besides imitation) that babies learn language is through this kind of selective reinforcement of his primitive attempts at verbal communication. The doo-doo's and dee-dee's and doh-doh's got him nowhere, but the da-da was a gold mine. You can bet that for now he forgets about the first three, but shines up that da-da and puts it right in the glass storefront of his linguistic memory so that it can be retrieved at a moment's notice.

Of course, when your wife is bending over the changing table, she'll get jazzed when she suddenly hears "ma-ma" rather than "da-da." And in another culture, where there is a different phonemic structure for "Daddy" and "Mommy," parents will brighten and respond to, and thus selectively reinforce, a different sound. The point is that much of a baby's verbal behavior emerges through a meshing of his innate ability to express himself with his parents' response, or lack of response, to these first expressions. The language that is eventually spoken is the result of the hundreds of thousands of interactions of this sort that take place.

This analogy extends beyond the realm of language acquisition, however. *Every* behavior that a child displays is in one way or another reinforced by his caregivers, a process that contributes to the unique trajectory that each individual follows. And the nature of that reinforcement, positive or negative, is determined by the emotional strands that entangle the baby, strands that originated long before he was born, before he was even conceived.

Let's compare two women in the earliest stages of motherhood and see how this can play out. Donna loves the feeling of having a child growing in her womb. She relishes the opportunity to create a healthy and loving environment for the growing fetus, and diligently and healthfully "eats for two" while abstaining from smoking and drinking. Uncomfortable pregnancy-related symptoms, such as morning sickness and exhaustion, are experienced by her as reassuring signs that the baby is growing and doing what he needs to do. Foods that she used to enjoy but that now taste funny or create indigestion she gives up somewhat reluctantly, but without significant resentment.

As Donna starts to show, she delightedly shops for maternity clothes that colorfully call attention to her growing belly. She has a pet name for the fetus, "Big Guy," which was also the nickname of her father, a former professional football player who is now a college coach. "Come on, Big Guy, settle down," she says, laughing, when she first starts to feel him tumbling and rolling inside of her. "Big Guy's thinking about Pralines and Cream tonight," she advises her husband before he heads out for the nightly ice-cream run.

Donna and her husband enthusiastically enlist in a childbirth education class and regularly practice their breathing exercises in preparation for labor. She prepares her employer for the three-month maternity leave that she plans to take and dutifully takes her temporary replacement at work under her wing, showing him the ropes.

Labor is long and her contractions painful, but the pain is mitigated by her awareness that with each contraction, she is closer to a meeting with the beloved child who, up until now, has remained invisible. When the baby is born, she sees not the blood and mucus, the splotchy skin and the misshapen head, but her beautiful, beloved son. His insistent howls of shock play like the melodies of Mozart on her eager ears.

When the baby is nursing, Donna feels both relaxed and stimulated, confident in her ability to supply her son with what he needs, overjoyed by the limitless abundance of her milk. When he repeatedly cries out for her at night, she welcomes the opportunity to be of comfort to him, and so is able to temporarily override her own exhaustion and depletion and nurture him successfully. She wishes that he would begin sleeping straight through, as some of her friends' infants have, but she also speaks with a lactation consultant, who reassures her that nursing babies sometimes take a little longer to string together a full night's sleep.

When he is teething a few months later, he bites her breast while nursing. She howls and yanks him off in disbelief, but then quickly smiles as she acknowledges another sign of his healthy development and docks him back at her breast with a playful warning: "Better not try *that* again, buster!" Naturally, it happens a few more times, but eventually he gets the message, and she helps him learn to soothe his sore gums with pacifiers and popsicles.

When he pokes her painfully in the eye while reaching out to her from his crib one morning, she winces, but is pleased with his vitality and lovingly grabs him up anyway: "You couldn't *wait* to get hold of me, could you, Big Guy?" she tells him, chuckling, as she carries him on her hip while going to get a cold rag for her eye.

Donna has decided ahead of time, without necessarily being conscious of it, that her baby will reinforce and please her. Even when he doesn't do so in a particular moment, such as when labor is long and hard or when he won't sleep through the night or when he bites her breast or pokes her in the eye, she is able to reframe these encounters in a way that is consistent with her belief that the baby is good for her and that she is good for the baby. Everything that he does is defined by this assumption, which is why their relationship at this point is so positive, why he, for now, is the prototypical good enough child.

Such a baby experiences what psychologists call "a secure base," a trusting environment in which he can depend on his needs being met in a way that enables him to feel physically and psychologically attended to. This frees him to propel himself forward into the world and to master the age-appropriate tasks necessary to his feeling competent and whole.

Another mother, however, may have a very different response to a similar pregnancy and early childhood. After ten years of marriage, Maura and her husband decide to start a family, but it is with great ambivalence that she begins gestation. She feels that her body has been hijacked by the fetus, that an intruder has taken over her insides and is parasitically depriving her of all of her precious resources.

She alternately binge-eats, stuffing herself because she is terrified that the fetus will take everything that she has, and starves herself, hoping, at some subconscious level, perhaps, to neutralize or counteract his unstoppable expansion. She drinks constantly, as if to flush out the baby's waste products before they completely pollute her, and has to urinate frequently; in consequence, she rarely gets a good night's sleep and is irritable and impatient during the day.

Maura interprets her intermittent flatulence and heartburn as manifestations of the baby's malign presence, weapons in a murderous battle for who will claim ownership of her body. Every physical symptom that she encounters during these turbulent nine months, even those that may have little or nothing to do with being pregnant, are interpreted as dangerous components of her baby's full-scale assault on her.

Feeling under attack, she fights back, keeping up her cigarette habit despite her obstetrician's warnings about its impact on fetal health, yet simultaneously stepping up her exercise routine at the gym as a way of burning off what refuses to stop growing, to the point where one day she passes out getting off the Stairmaster.

She, like Donna, comes up with a pet name for the fetus, one that carries with it an assigned personality: "The Spy." The name suggests that the baby is somehow eavesdropping on her, privy to internal knowledge that she is trying to keep hidden from everyone else. "That's *enough*, Spy," she complains one night when his intrauterine activity is interfering once again with her sleep. "If it wasn't for The Spy, I wouldn't be going through this," she thinks to herself as her dentist fills a couple of newly developed cavities one afternoon in her second trimester.

Maura lets no one at work know that she's expecting and takes great pains to dress in such a way that her pregnancy is hidden from view. When her boss finally learns, by accident, that she is due in three months, she refuses to discuss any contingency plans, insisting that she'll be back at work "in no time." Her boss, the father of two small children himself, fortunately recognizes how unrealistic this is and convinces her to take six weeks maternity leave, with the invitation to contribute to projects that she has a hand in when she has the time to do so from home.

She and her husband enroll in a Lamaze class at the hospital where she'll be giving birth, but she sits and listens doubtfully, distractedly, and doesn't bother practicing. "If it gets bad, I'll be asking for drugs," she casually informs her sister one afternoon, explaining away her apparent indifference.

Labor and childbirth go quite smoothly, but the baby is born with jaundice, convincing her that the baby had somehow decided to exit prematurely, before his liver could function more efficiently. Meanwhile, the episiotomy that was required isn't healing very quickly: it burns when she pees, and her bowel movements are accompanied by the (unfounded) fear that her stitches will tear. All of this further supports the internal belief that she and the baby were, and are, "bad" for each other.

She tries breast-feeding but it goes poorly, and her son's inability to quickly take to her nipple results in her feeling snubbed, rejected: "He's punishing me for not taking better care of myself during pregnancy," she speculates to herself, and moves right into formula feeding a few days after birth.

The baby turns out to be quite well regulated. He gains weight nicely and is sleeping through the night by the time he is 4 weeks old, but Maura becomes very focused on the fact that he doesn't nap much during the day, giving her few breaks to get back to some of the work projects that she had hoped to reclaim during maternity leave.

His cries from the crib during naptime feel accusatory and critical, as if he knows she'd rather be working than mothering. She partially blames herself for his refusal to nap, wondering if her hectic, relentless schedule while he was in utero had somehow "taught" him not to slow down during the daytime and if he's "getting back" at her now.

Maura also begins to notice that some of her peers' children are beginning to smile, while her son, pleasant as he is, does not.

Rather than seeing him as simply lagging a bit developmentally, this data, too, gets factored into her belief that he's angry with her, and that he is expressing this anger by withholding from her.

When the baby accidentally knocks her glasses off one day while she is changing his diaper, she quickly slaps his hand, and after a moment of confusion, he begins to cry and so does she. One day when she is trying to get some work done at the computer with the baby on her lap, he accidentally falls forward, and his head bumps down against the keyboard, erasing what she was working on. She yanks him back up and screams at him, demanding to know why he can't take naps like the other kids do so that she can finally get some work done. "Why are you torturing me?" she pleads, holding him tightly against her while they both sob.

The rapidity with which she characterizes his actions as aggressive or demanding or intrusive without seriously considering more benign (and accurate) interpretations suggests strongly that she has foreseen that she will be, and perhaps *deserves* to be, the recipient of such treatment.

Not surprisingly, Maura's tendency to react to her son with sudden rage leaves her feeling guilty all the time. Because of this, she finds it difficult to set appropriate limits with him as he moves into toddlerhood. Falling into an all-or-nothing regime, she alternates between smacking his hands and hollering at him for the slightest mishap, such as a dropped fork or a crayoned wall, and indulging or ignoring the typical toddler behaviors that deserve a teaching response or some consequences, such as refusing to sleep in his own bed at night or calling her bad names when she won't do what he wants her to do. Without limits being set, he doesn't learn as quickly as he should what is and isn't acceptable for a child his age.

Unless the behavior pattern between Maura and her baby changes, over time he will come to internalize his mom's belief that he is out to punish her, and he will find that he does so without even knowing how and why. For various reasons that as of now remain out of her awareness, she has cast him in the role of her victimizer, a role that was assigned to him embryonically before he could even think about it, but that both are now contributing to his fulfilling.

Her need to see almost every departure from what she wants him to do as a symbolic statement of his need to rebuke and discipline her will lead to great conflict between them, but in reality he is behaving—and she is seeing that he behaves—in the way that she has *insisted* that he behave from the moment of his conception, if not before. By not being good enough, he is, in reality, satisfying a deep, albeit tormented, need of his mother's.

So, do Donna and Maura remain locked forever into these early-established patterns of interaction? Will Donna always be the model parent of the model child, waltzing serenely through parenthood's breezy meadows, while Maura is consigned to trudge through a desultory swamp of despair?

Of course not. Investing our children with a distinct set of personality characteristics is a part of every family process, but the dynamics of this process are never static. Like the tiny bits and shapes in a rotating kaleidoscope, these characteristics are constantly in motion, creating new narratives, new stories, and new dramas as development unfolds. With every turn of the life cycle, another configuration presents, or re-presents, itself.

Children are not wax tablets upon which their parents can write their stories, but active participants in the cocreation of the narrative of which the entire multigenerational family is a part. Their innate characteristics, tendencies, and vulnerabilities are crucial determinants in the role that they wind up performing. They may vigorously refuse to "say their lines" and sabotage the intended production, they may enthusiastically learn and cooperatively vocalize their parts, or they may come up with some compromise or combination of both responses as a result of the complex chemistry that bubbles between and within the generations.

Let's jump ahead a few years, to the point at which Donna and Maura, both with toddlers, contacted me for help, and see how these playwrights were doing.

Maura made an appointment because her son's temper tantrums were driving her mad. Convinced, as she had been all along, that

Eric's very purpose in her life had been to injure her, she was not responding well to his fits.

"Either I whack him when he starts up, and then feel horrible about it and cuddle him in my arms, or I give in just to get him to shut up," she confided, ashamedly. "I know neither one is right—I just can't get myself to do anything different."

In getting some history of her pregnancy and early parenthood, I learned how diligently Maura had gone about assuming and ensuring that Eric and she were at odds, from her interpretation of her pregnancy symptoms, to her creation of his in utero pet name, to how she chose to understand *everything*—from his erratic napping to his "late" smiles to his lack of physical coordination—as early symbols of his hostility toward her.

I also learned something else: Maura had had an abortion as a teenager after accidentally getting pregnant with her boyfriend. This was something that she had not even shared with her husband. The only ones who had known were her parents, who had carried it to the grave with them. "I told no one, and I tell no one. You're the first person I've ever told, aside from my mom and dad, and they had to know, because they arranged the abortion, and were with me when I had it. I didn't even tell my boyfriend—I just broke up with him without any explanation."

As I gently explored this issue, it was impossible for me to miss the great grief and regret that she still felt about something that had occurred literally half a lifetime ago. Because there had been such shame and secrecy, she had never had the chance to heal the wound and move on. No wonder Eric had been nicknamed "The Spy": it was as if she believed that by occupying the home of his predecessor, he was the only one who would discover the secrets of her dark past.

Instead, her abortion had become a barrier not only between her and her husband, as long-kept secrets often are within a marriage, but also between her and her son. As we spoke, she acknowledged feeling unentitled to bear the baby whose sibling she had both provided with and deprived of life during a reckless few weeks in adolescence.

"I have to say that I've carried the guilt of that abortion around forever. And I feel so bad that it's as if I don't deserve Eric, that I don't deserve to feel like a good mom when I was such a terrible mom years ago."

"Looking back, do you think it would have been realistic for you as a seventeen-year-old to keep that baby?" I asked.

She paused and then answered. "No, it would've been a disaster. My parents were older parents, they weren't prepared to take on a baby. I could've put it up for adoption, I suppose, but I think I'd be feeling the same way now. And of course I was in no position to be a good mother at the age of seventeen. I just can't get past the fact that there was life inside of me and I destroyed it."

I shared with Maura my belief that perhaps her need to expiate the guilt of her abortion was accounting for her becoming entrenched in seeing her son as her victimizer. "A lot of what you've been talking about when it comes to Eric is pretty normal stuff, from pregnancy, to infancy, to toddlerhood, but my belief when it comes to child-rearing is: 'What you see is what you will get.' If all you see is aggression and hostility, that's how Eric will come to see himself, and that's what you'll get from him."

"You mean I'm *making* him into the way he is?" she asked worriedly.

"To some extent, yes. I suspect he'd be going through a tantrum stage right now anyway, no matter what you had thought or done during pregnancy and infancy. But some of the ways in which you respond to him seem to make things more problematic than they need to be."

I recommended that Maura start making some changes by grieving for the baby who had never been born. To facilitate this process, I had her write a letter to the baby, and to express the deep sorrow she felt about having "created and destroyed" him or her. I also asked her to revisit the neighborhood where she and her boyfriend had conceived the baby, which was less than an hour from where she was living, and to plant a small flower somewhere nearby "in memoriam."

Maura completed both tasks and over the next couple of meetings appeared ready to finally unburden herself of the terrible secret that had so troubled her all these years. Eventually she decided to talk it over with her husband. Having done so, she was now ready to review her relationship with Eric. We discussed some more productive ways to handle his tantrums, such as firmly placing him in time-out and refraining from yelling at, giving in to, or hitting him. Within a short time she was pleased to report that she had been enjoying him as never before.

"He really gets it when I set a limit now, and his tantrums last half as long and occur half as often as they used to. But more important, I'm able to see the good in him, something that I wasn't able to do before. The other night he came running up from behind and grabbed me as I was taking some eggs out of the refrigerator, and I dropped them. I think before I would've yelled at him, and then felt terrible. This time, though, I caught myself, and realized that he was actually trying to give me a hug. I grabbed a towel and said, 'Let's get to work' and we cleaned it all up together. It was *such* a great feeling to be a different kind of mom."

No longer having to participate in a punishing drama, Eric was free to be seen, and treated, as a growing boy who needed some instruction in how to handle his mental and physical energies, rather than as a dangerous spy who had been assigned to exact payment from her for a regrettable decision from her past.

What about Donna? Would her son, Ryan, remain in childhood just as unremittingly adored as he was during pregnancy, infancy, and babyhood? Unfortunately for both of them, the answer was no.

Donna was referred to me when Ryan was 5 because his pediatrician was concerned about her ambivalent follow-through on his treatment for asthma. "She's clearly a bright mom and loves her son, but it's like she won't take any of this seriously," Dr. Lacroix told me by phone. "Asthma is potentially fatal, but she doesn't keep him on the inhaler when I tell her to, won't use the nebulizer when his breathing is getting tight, and hasn't even bought the peak-flow meter that you need to assess this at home. The warning signs are always obvious, and there's plenty of time to intervene, but she's not taking the appropriate precautions. The other day she brought him into my office and he was wheezing so heavily I thought I might have to hospitalize him, and she was asking if he could still go to baseball practice later that afternoon! If we get on top of this now, he'll probably be fine. If not, I fear that it's only going to get worse."

During our first session, Donna told me about what a wonderful boy Ryan had been and how "from the very first day of pregnancy, I knew that he was going to be a special kid. I could just *feel* it." She told me with pride how well she had handled pregnancy and early childhood and how much Ryan reminded her of her father: "He's big, just like my dad, always has been, and he's going to be a great athlete, just like my dad was. I can see it already—*everyone* does. We put him in a baseball league with kids one or two years older than him, and he's *still* one of the best players."

When I asked her about his history of respiratory difficulties, her tone shifted quickly and became somewhat clipped. "I think my pediatrician's good, I trust her, but I also think she's a bit on the nervous side with this asthma business. I just don't see it as a problem in the way that she does. So he wheezes some—so do I during hay fever season, so does my husband when he gets a cold in the winter—what's the big deal? Does *everything* have to be medicated? Why can't he just have a normal life instead of all of this fuss?"

I asked her more about her father, whom Ryan so strikingly reminded her of, and inquired whether he had had any health difficulties. "Well, he's an athlete and a coach, so he is usually in pretty good shape. Although he's also a smoker and has always had this horrible, racking cough whenever he gets sick. I remember sitting up in bed some nights listening to him cough and cough, it was so scary—I used to wonder if he'd ever stop. But he was hooked, and even though he was a football player, he just never has been able to give it up. It's amazing to me that he's still breathing, frankly, although he's always been into exercise, even now, and he's almost sixty."

In my mind, I started to form a picture. Donna identified her son with her father in many positive ways, such as their both having good size and physical prowess. But in linking her father and her son so closely, she must have become terrified as Ryan's breathing difficulties stirred up scary memories of her father's breathing difficulties. Not wanting to acknowledge the negative aspects of the association she had made between these two men in her life, she was stuck trying to deny the reality of Ryan's condition, a denial that, her pediatrician warned, could have dire consequences. In trying to diminish the role of asthma in his life by making believe that it didn't exist, she was actually exacerbating it.

To disrupt this potentially lethal process, I asked Donna to talk to her father about his smoking, how he had started, why he couldn't stop, and whether he ever would. Sometimes making a preconscious or unconscious issue conscious deprives it of its power and, like a wizard's incantation, releases an individual from its hold.

Donna had some interesting things to tell me after this conversation. "As I listened to him talk about his smoking, a lot started to come back to me. I had talked with you about how scared I was about his smoking, but I also started to remember how *angry* I was with him when I was growing up. I mean, here was this great athlete, cheered on by thousands every Sunday, always being lauded as a real pro, and all I saw was this guy with a graveyard cough stumbling out of bed every winter morning and reaching for his damn cigarettes. It would make me sick."

"It would also make you feel helpless," I suggested.

"Helpless, yes—*that* was the feeling. Like there was nothing I could do, nothing I could say. I remember bringing home my health book from fifth grade one year to show my father a picture of a tar-filled lung, and he didn't even want to look at it, he just said, 'Get it away from me, I know, I know.' Well, if he 'knew,' why couldn't he stop?"

"I wonder if some of the long-stifled anger that you carried toward your dad is getting misdirected toward your son?"

Donna's face grew crimson. "Do you think that could be?"

"If you were very angry with him, but buried it, and then had a son who reminded you of him in many ways, including having his respiratory problems, it's certainly possible. That might be part of why you're not following doctor's orders and taking care of him."

"That's *awful!*" Donna almost shrieked. "What kind of mother would endanger her son because of her anger at her father?"

I smiled. "Just about any kind. I wish I could say that all parents have the capacity to transcend their hurts and sorrows and rise to a saintly level of parenthood, but the reality is that we are all vulnerable. None of us is above tripping over an old piece of business here and there and goofing up."

Donna's ability to recognize the old anger that she still harbored toward her father and incorporate that into a more full-bodied portrait of him drained off the anger she felt about Ryan's temporarily twitchy respiratory system. She no longer had to avoid acknowledging his condition and was thus better able to provide him with what he needed. When Dr. Lacroix and I spoke a couple of months later, she was pleased to tell me that Donna had been much more compliant, and that Ryan was doing fine and had not had any major attacks since we had last spoken.

What I have learned in my practice from parents like Donna and Maura is that highlighting your awareness of the scripts that you have written out and pinpointing the ways in which you, without always being aware of it, maneuver your son or daughter into playing certain roles in your theatrical production is the surest pathway to change. Let's take a look at a couple of other cases in which this took place.

Carl contacted me because of his difficulties picking up and dropping off his 3-year-old son, Harry, at the day-care center he had begun to attend a couple of months before. The mornings were melodramatic affairs, with Harry sobbing, writhing, and clutching at his dad, and resulted in Carl heading off to work feeling a wretched combination of guilt and anger. The afternoons were just as bad, but for a different reason: Harry would ignore his dad, and, when Carl tried to get him ready to go, he would throw a tantrum about having to leave and continue screaming all the way home.

"I swear, it takes me two full hours before I'm able to accomplish anything once I get to work, I feel so exhausted by the morning routine. And then before I know it, it's time to pick him up and go through a whole other routine, which I need another two hours to recover from. I feel like all we do is fight and then prepare for the next one. And I hate how I feel about him. I mean, I feel bad about leaving him at day care, but there are kids younger than him there, and kids who are dropped off earlier and picked up later. And they do take good care of him, it's a really great staff. But I'm so sick of the crying and the yelling, already. It's embarrassing, and it doesn't seem fair, and I just don't get it. He should have adjusted by now. He's been there for more than a month."

"How does he seem to do at day care once you've left?"

"I've asked, and, amazingly enough, although you would never think so from how things look when I leave, he does fine. He's got a couple of little friends, and the woman in charge says they play very nicely together. She says that usually Harry will play by himself for a little while after I've left, but then he hooks up with some of the other kids and joins right in with whatever they're doing, and then he's fine for the rest of the day. Until I come to pick him up, of course. Then all hell breaks loose again."

Clearly, the problem was not with the day care or Harry's adjustment to being there. More likely, he was having difficulties navigating the separation from Carl at the beginning of the day and the reunion with Carl at the end of the day, and he hadn't yet mastered how to make these transitions smoother ones.

"How have you been handling things during the drop-off?" I wondered.

"I don't even know what to do anymore," he acknowledged sadly. "I've tried walking him over to some toys or to some of the other kids and getting him interested in something else to distract him, get his mind off of it, but it never really works. Once I stand up to get ready to leave, he starts the whining and the crying and grabs my leg so that I can't walk, and I feel just horrible."

"What happens then?"

"Usually at that point one of the day-care staff will kind of snatch him up so I can leave, and I try to give him a hug and a kiss, but then he'll grab on to my neck or my hair, and he literally has to be pried off me. So I tell him I'll sit near the door for a while and watch him play, but he doesn't play. He just comes running back to me. Finally, I'll just have to leave. The staff people are kind of pushing me out the door with the sound of him wailing as I go out to my car. It's just a disaster."

"And how about in the afternoons?"

"Well, that's what's so weird about the whole thing. I mean, you'd think after all of this craziness in the morning, he'd come running over to me as soon as I get there and jump into my arms, but he does the opposite. I'll see him busy with something, and then one of the teachers will say, 'Harry, your dad is here,' and he'll look up and see me and then go right back to what he's doing. And so I head over to see what he's doing, and he acts as if I'm not even there. And when I say we have to get going, and start getting his coat and stuff, he starts shaking his head and saying, 'No, no.' So I have to pick him up off the floor, and I can never get him to put away what he's playing with. He won't clean up, and none of the teachers give me a hard time about it, but I feel like he should be responsible. Then I'm hauling him out to the parking lot with him under my arms kicking and screaming, papers flying everywhere, trying to hold on to his lunchbox and his backpack. I'll tell you, it's a wonder I drive home safely, because he continues flailing about and hollering in the car seat the whole ride home."

"How about when he gets home?"

"By the time I get him inside, he's kind of worn out and pretty quiet. My wife's usually there around the same time on the days I do the pick-up, maybe a little later, and so she'll take over with him, while I get started on dinner, or he'll watch a video or play with his trucks, and then the rest of the evening usually goes pretty well."

"Does your wife ever do the drop-off or pick-up?"

"Not usually. She only works three days a week, and is home with him on Mondays and Fridays, but on the days she works she has to be there longer than I do. A few days a month when I have an early meeting or a dinner meeting, Susan will take care of it."

"And how do things work when she does it?"

He chuckled sarcastically. "Fine, which is one of the things that bugs me. I ask her, 'Doesn't he get upset when you drop him off? Doesn't he wig out when you go to pick him up?' but apparently not."

"What does happen?"

"She says she's usually in a hurry when she's dropping him off, and she just gets his coat off, puts his stuff in his cubby, plops him on the ground with a kiss, and off she goes. She says he seems sad sometimes, but it really doesn't bother her all that much."

"And in the afternoon, when she has to pick him up?"

"Same thing, basically. I mean, I've asked her how she does it, and she doesn't really know, all she says is that she shows up, wanders over to where he is and joins in for a while, and then they're in the car and headed home. He doesn't get particularly excited about seeing her, but he doesn't get so impossible, either."

The fact that separations were managed differently, and more effectively, when Harry was with his mom fit in with my speculation that it wasn't just Harry who was having difficulty with separations. It might be his father as well.

Carl struck me as a thoughtful, caring parent who had developed a healthy bond with his son. Whenever a parent who is well-connected with his or her child gets locked into some kind of interminable battle with that child, I usually assume that some drama from the parent's past is being unwittingly replayed. It's the only way to make sense of why an otherwise intelligent person would persist in interacting in a way that inflames, rather than mitigates, a problem.

"How did you handle separations from your parents when you were a child?"

"I don't really recall having any difficulties. I mean, I didn't really go anywhere until I was in kindergarten—no nursery school or anything like that. But by the time I started kindergarten, I was probably okay with being apart."

"How about other separations?"

"Well, I know I used to get sad when my dad would go away on business trips, which was every couple of months for a week or so. For a while, we had a baby-sitter I didn't like all that much that they'd leave my brother and me with when they'd go out on the weekends, and I wasn't very happy about being left then, either. But I survived all of that, so it couldn't have been too traumatic for me."

I was hoping that exploring Carl's own experiences with separation anxiety as a child might give me some clues to why he was having such difficulty with Harry's, but found myself without any information that would provide an explanation. For now, I'd have to proceed without having a clear understanding of what was accounting for the problem.

"What do you say to Harry in the mornings as he's getting up or you're on your way to day care?"

Carl thought for a moment. "Nothing, really. The first couple of days I tried to talk it up, telling him what a good time he'd be having, how much fun it would be, but now I don't even mention it, because I don't want him to start getting upset. He's pretty quiet—until we get in the door, that is, and then it's mayhem."

"In the coming week, I'd like you to begin talking about the leave-taking on your way to day care, before you get there. You can certainly remind him about some of the fun things that you know he'll be doing there, but you are also to let him know that you understand it's difficult for him to be left at first, and reassure him that you'll be thinking of him during the day and looking forward to picking him up in the afternoon."

"Don't you think that's just going to get him more worked up?" Carl asked, with a fretful look on his face.

"It's possible, but I think a greater likelihood is that it might help to defuse some of the tension and sadness that he feels, making it easier for him to prepare for being apart from you."

"Do you think that's really such a big deal for him?"

"Apparently so," I replied.

"Then how come all the other kids don't get so upset when their parents leave?"

"First of all, some of them probably do. They may be on a different schedule than you and get there before or after you, so you don't see it. Or perhaps they handle their upset in different ways than Harry, less dramatically. But every child has to deal with it in one way or another, and some ways are harder for parents than others."

"Then why isn't he happier to see me when I return? If he's having such a hard time with me leaving, why does he have to have such a hard time with me coming back? It doesn't make any sense." Carl looked annoyed. What parents don't feel the same way when their children's behavior is so perplexing and exasperating?

"When he sees you, he may be reminded of how angry he was when you left him earlier in the day. He expresses that by trying to hurt you back, in this case, by ignoring you. And," I said with a grin, "it sounds to me like it works."

"So what should I do about it?"

"For now, I'd like you to take your time when you get there to pick him up. Acknowledge him with a smile and a wave, but don't go right over to him. Take a few moments to talk with one of the teachers, or go over and start getting his stuff together without him."

"What am I doing, playing hard-to-get?" Carl asked.

"In a way, yes. What you're doing is giving him a chance to work through some of the mixed feelings he's having about your being back, the joy as well as the anger, so that he'll be better able to reconnect with you when he's ready to."

"I don't know." Carl sighed. "You may be right about all of this, but I'm not sure that simply talking with him about things in the morning or letting him warm up to me in the afternoon is going to help."

"It may not, but why don't you give it a try anyway, just to see? And I'd like your wife to join us next time as well, to see what light she can shed on this situation."

Carl reluctantly agreed, but returned for the next meeting even more frustrated than the week before.

"I didn't think it could get any worse, but it has," he began before he had even gotten his coat off.

"What's going on?"

"He was just as clutchy in the mornings, and unfortunately one of the teachers, the one he likes the best, was out a couple of days because her daughter was sick, so there wasn't even anyone to help me out. It took me even longer to disentangle myself from him. And in the afternoons, he was as bad as always. I really can't stand this anymore. I told my wife either she starts taking him and picking him up or I'm going to just quit and work at home or something. I simply cannot go through this all the time."

"How available are you to help out, Susan?" I asked his wife.

"Well, it's not easy. I'm able to fill in when I have enough notice, and I don't mind doing it when I can, but I have to be at work before the day care is even open, and my schedule in the afternoons is just too unpredictable. I can never be sure when I'm going to be able to take off. That's the only way I can keep my schedule to three days a week."

I turned back to Carl. "What was it like to follow through on what I asked you to do?"

"What do you mean?"

I hesitated for a second, not sure if Carl had forgotten. "We had decided that you would begin talking about your leave-taking before you got Harry to day care, and that you'd take a few moments to let him warm up to you when you picked him up in the afternoon."

"Oh, yeah, that," he replied. "I tried it the first morning when we were in the car, and he didn't have anything to say, and that morning was just as bad as the others."

"Did you give it a few more days' trial anyway?"

"No, not really. I mean, why waste my time if it's not going to help?"

"And how about in the afternoons? Did you do anything differently then?"

"It was more of the same. I guess the thing is, I don't really feel like hanging around there any longer than I have to. By the time I get there, I'm tired and just want to get home. I don't want to stand around chatting with his teacher or waiting him out."

Whenever I give parents an assignment, I listen carefully not just to the results of the assignment but to how, and *whether*, they did it. If a parent is frustrated enough to come to me for help but chooses not to follow through on an assignment that might ease the frustration, it usually leads me to think that the parent has some investment in being frustrated. In other words, why ask your doctor for a prescription to alleviate your discomfort and then refuse to take it and choose to remain uncomfortable?

If Carl had tried what I had asked him to do for several days without any positive results, I would have understood his giving up. But what I heard was that he had tried the morning talk only once and hadn't given the afternoon "warm-up" any chance at all. Something else was accounting for what was happening.

"You must be pretty fed up with this, day after day," I empathized.

"I can't believe I'm in this position of having a son who can't say hello or good-bye to me without a tantrum. We're not talking about a newborn, here. He's three years old, already!"

"Susan, why do you think things work differently when you handle this?"

"I'm not sure," she responded slowly. "When Carl is busy and I have to take Harry in, we'll often stop off and get a doughnut or a hot chocolate somewhere. But once I get him there, I kind of just shoo him over to wherever the kids seem to be playing, give him a kiss, and then take off."

"How does he seem to handle it?"

"Well, he never really looks happy, to be honest. There are some kids I see who are just dashing into the room, they can't wait to get started. Sometimes I peek in the window from the outside when I'm leaving, and I see that Harry's not really joining in, he's just kind of sitting there, staring into space. But I figure that he'll eventually jump in, and from what everyone says, it seems that he does."

"How about in the afternoons, when you pick him up?"

"I'm not sure. Usually if I'm picking him up, Carl is going to be working late, so I'm in no hurry. I'll hang out with him and his buddies, and I'm good friends with a couple of the other moms, so we'll chit-chat for a bit before we all head out. Also, I usually take Harry out to dinner from the day care, which he likes doing. I just say, 'Hey, honey, want to go to McDonald's tonight?' and before you know it, he's packed up and ready to go."

"I wish I could do that," Carl said, "but I can't possibly take him out for doughnuts every morning and dinner every night. We'd all be fat and out of money in no time."

"I don't think the solution is in going out to eat every day," I reassured him. "But it seems separation is a different experience for Susan and Harry than it is for you and Harry."

"So how can we make it better for him and me?" he asked.

Knowing that he had already chosen to ignore the suggestions I had made last time, I didn't answer that question right away. What I was thinking was that each parent was preparing for and responding to the separation in a unique way.

Susan was making it clear in the morning that she wasn't going to hang around and engage with Harry around his ambivalence about being left. She had said that she could tell he wasn't always happy, but that that wasn't enough to keep her from making her leave-taking brisk. That they usually had a special treat together on the way to day care probably helped both of them deal with the impending separation. In the afternoons, she wasn't rushing things, but was giving her son some time to reacclimate to her presence (plus, they often got to go out to eat!).

In the mornings, Carl was continually drawn in by Harry's sadness, making it hard for him to say "So long" in a quick, clear way. This, of course, elicited more clingy behavior from Harry, which in turn elicited more waffling from Carl, and before they knew it, a two-minute good-bye had blown up into a fifteen-minute tragedy. And in the afternoons, he had already rejected my proposal to allow a few extra minutes before contact was expected between him and his son so that the rest of the afternoon and evening might go more smoothly.

In my quest for a better understanding of why Carl seemed to almost willfully perpetuate this situation despite his complaints about it, I went back to his past one more time to see if I might discover some clues.

"Who in your family does Harry remind you of?" I asked.

"I'm not sure," he began. "In some ways, he seems a lot more like Susan and members of her family. He looks just like Susan, and Susan's mom as well, and his intensity is kind of like Susan's, too. He can get frosted pretty quickly when things don't go his way."

I tried again. "Anyone in your family that he reminds you of?"

"Well, he's kind of like me, I guess, in that he likes to sleep. I could sleep all day if you'd let me, and he's always been that way, too."

"Anyone else that he shares some traits with?"

"Not that I can think of."

At this point, Susan looked over at him and asked, "Does Brad know that you're adopted?"

I looked over at Carl, and noticed him almost imperceptibly nudge his chair back a few inches. "No, I hadn't brought it up," he murmured.

I hadn't ever asked, either, and there hadn't been any moments in our first couple of sessions when his disclosing this would have been unavoidable, but it sure seemed notable that it hadn't come up.

"Could you tell me some more about that?" I asked.

"What's to tell? I was adopted when I was only a couple of weeks old. I never knew my birth parents, don't know anything about them and don't really care to. I love my adoptive parents, and have always felt that they were my real parents. That's really all there is."

While adoptees vary in the extent to which they want to know more about their lineage, I was struck by how completely uninterested Carl appeared to be in his origin. Usually, there is some desire to learn more about one's birth family at some point along the developmental spectrum, even if things have gone well in one's adoptive family.

"Sometimes adoptees give new or additional thought to their birth parents when they become parents themselves. Has that happened for you?"

"I don't think so," he replied quickly.

"What about those dreams you were having while I was pregnant?" Susan offered. "The ones about the mystery woman?"

Carl smiled sheepishly. "Well, I kept having this dream when we were expecting Harry—dreams of this woman I called the 'Mystery Woman.' It was weird, because she was definitely one of those dream people—she was kind of scary but kind of loving at the same time. But she'd show up in my dreams and she'd always do the same thing."

"What was that?"

Carl squirmed. "Do I have to tell you?"

"Only if you're comfortable doing so."

"Jeez, Carl, it's not that bad," Susan said, poking him lightly with her elbow.

"Oh, okay. She'd put her finger in my belly button and wriggle it around in there."

"How did you understand the dream?"

"Well, I didn't, really, but I was telling one of Susan's friends about it once, and she said that she had learned that expectant parents sometimes have dreams about their ancestors, and maybe it was my birth mother showing up in my dreams."

"Did you figure out why she kept touching your belly button?" I wondered.

"Not really." He laughed. "That part remains a mystery."

"Not if you remember that that's the closest connection you have with her," I said. "It's the part of you that took in what she had to give you during her pregnancy with you."

"I hadn't thought about that," he said, as if in a reverie.

I let him ruminate about this for a few moments and then asked, "Can you allow yourself to feel connected with her now that you're a parent as well?"

"I guess it's never occurred to me to do so. I never felt any real kinship with her."

"You do now, however. And you may also be feeling a kinship for yourself as her son."

"How so?"

"That may be why the drop-offs and pick-ups at school are so hard—because you're replaying a painful separation that occurred a long time ago, the one between you and your birth mother."

"Oh, come on," he answered skeptically. "I was two weeks old! How traumatic could that have been. And it's not like I was sent to an orphanage. My parents were ready to adopt me, all the paperwork had been done, and they took great care of me."

"You were two weeks old, but you'd had two weeks' familiarity with your mother outside her womb, and another nine months' familiarity inside. You were intimately acquainted with her sound, her smell, her feel, her movements—yes, you were well taken care of by your parents, but you still felt, without knowing why, that you were taken away from the only person you'd ever known, your first beloved. A feeling that powerful doesn't ever go away."

"So why is it coming up now?"

"Probably because now that he's in day care, this is the first time you and Harry are having to experience a real separation from each other. Up until now, you've remained together—now, you're not. And it's hard on both of you."

"How can I make it easier?"

"Sometimes we play out scenes from our past to gain a better understanding of them. I think the scene at day care is so hard because in it you identify both with your birth mother and with yourself as an infant. In leaving Harry, you're reexperiencing what your mother might have felt in leaving you with a new family. And in interacting with Harry in a way that seems to lead to his being more, rather than less, upset, you're reexperiencing what it might have been like for you to have to say good-bye to your birth mother. It could be that just being aware of this possibility will help you to change how things go, even if you don't fully agree with me or comprehend it."

Rather than jump back into making suggestions about how to handle the mornings differently, I asked Carl to do some more thinking about his connection with his birth mother to see where this led him.

He returned with some new insights. "I think there's probably some truth to what you were saying," he began, "because I remember that I was studying biology in high school and learning all about genetics, and I was talking with my mom once and said, 'Gee, I wonder what genes I have from my birth mother,' and she got this funny look on her face and just didn't say anything. And it made me feel maybe I shouldn't think about my birth mother because it would upset my mom, so I just kind of sat on it the whole time."

"That's not an unusual response. Adoptees often feel great loyalty and gratitude toward their adoptive parents and don't want to risk another loss by doing something that might antagonize or anger them. You might have been protecting yourself by disavowing any acknowledgment of your 'other' heritage."

"You're right," he said. "I mean, it's not that I'm about to go on any search to reunite with her or anything, right now. But since we opened that door last session, I've been wondering a lot about who she is, if she's still alive, who my dad was—all of that stuff. And I realize that there's another bond there that I haven't been aware of, and that Harry has another grandmother somewhere out there, and that really blows me away."

"How have things been going with Harry?"

"Better, actually. I went back to the first idea you had, talking with him as we're driving to school, and I think that's led him to be a little more settled when I leave. And I'm not sticking around so much either. I finally got it through my thick head that hanging around and trying to comfort him was only making things harder for both of us. He survives when Susan leaves him, he'll survive when I leave him, too.

"And for the afternoons, I came up with a great idea. I bought him a special beanie baby that I only give him when I pick him up for the ride home, and once we're home I take it back and put it away. He lights up now when he sees me come in with the beanie baby and comes right over to hold it and hug it. And I make sure he's got a little time to play around before we leave."

Carl's decision to use a special doll to help Harry make the transition back to him was a touching one. To me, the doll represented both Harry and Carl as a little boy. The doll comforted both of them, and helped them to cope as they dealt with the inevitable feelings of loss that separations engender.

As he came to understand more about the ways in which he was contributing to the very problem that he was so troubled by, and the history behind why he was doing so, Carl was able to find new solutions that worked better for him and his son.

Judy called me to schedule an appointment to address the chronic sibling rivalry between her two daughters, a conflict that had seemed to be worsening over the previous several months.

Kristin, who was 12, and Denise, who was 10, had "fought like cats and dogs since Denise was born," according to Judy, but things had gotten so bad that during a recent fight, Kristin had chased Denise around the house brandishing a kitchen knife.

"Here we are with both kids moving into adolescence and I still don't feel that I can leave the two of them home alone," Judy complained. "I feel silly trying to arrange a sitter for when I go out on a date when Kristin's already old enough to begin doing some baby-sitting herself, but they really can't be trusted to be alone. The last time I tried it, all I did was go down to a neighbor's house for a party, and within an hour Denise had called me, crying, saying that Kristin had thrown a book at her and hit her in the face and her eye was starting to swell. That was the end of *that* night out."

Although I know of very few same-sex siblings that close in age who aren't engaged in some sort of ongoing warfare, it was clear that these two girls were not progressing toward some sort of mature reconciliation as they grew up, and as they both got bigger and stronger, the potential for more serious physical harm increased.

I first met with Judy, a single mother whose former husband had remarried and moved out of town, to get some background and to learn more about what she had already tried so that I didn't wind up having her repeat interventions or approaches that had already been unsuccessful. She said that from day one, Kristin was perturbed by her little sister's presence. "Kristin was like Angelica in *Rugrats*," Judy recalled with a chuckle, "constantly tormenting Denise, in her face, making her cry, and this was when she was just a baby. As she got older, it only got worse and worse. It seems like she'll do anything to get on Denise's nerves, and at this point, Denise almost expects to be tortured. I feel so sorry for her."

"What is Denise's role in the conflict with her older sister?" I inquired.

"What do you mean?" Judy wondered.

"Well, by the time children are as old as these two, each of them plays some part in a fight. What do you think her part is?"

She was quiet as she pondered this, a delay which led me to think that the drama in which Kristin played the role of unrelenting aggressor and Denise played the role of passive, blameless victim had become so routinized that no other scripts were being considered.

Finally, Judy piped up with her answer. "I think Denise just tries to avoid her sister because she knows she's going to wind up getting pounded in one form or another."

"Really?" I asked, suspecting that it had to be more complicated than this.

"Yes. I don't ever see Denise provoking a fight with Kristin. She seems to want to just keep to herself and avoid getting tangled up with her."

"How have you attempted to intervene over the years?"

"Well, I've told Kristin over and over again to stay out of Denise's hair. I've given them separate rooms, and I try to minimize their conflicts as much as possible. They were always fighting over the CD player, so I bought each of them their own. But then they started fighting over the computer, and I really can't afford to buy two computers, so I set up a schedule in which they each have different time slots in which they're allowed to use it, but somehow that never seems to work. Kristin always takes over and Denise just sort of gives in. And the same thing happens with the phone, too. We only have one line, and between calls from their friends and needing to use the Internet, there's constant arguing about whose turn it is and who gets to do what. It's really exhausting." Judy took a deep breath and sighed sadly.

"Aside from trying to help them avoid conflict through separating them, what else have you tried?"

"I've certainly punished Kristin when she's been physical with Denise," she responded. "I send her to her room and I even grounded her for a weekend after she pushed Denise into her room and Denise fell backward and bumped her head against the wall."

"Was she badly hurt?"

"Not really, as it turns out, but I was kind of worried. She was lying there with a dazed expression for a few minutes, and I thought I'd have to take her to the hospital."

"What did the grounding consist of?" I wondered.

"Well, she wasn't allowed to play with friends that weekend. Although now that I think about it I did let her go to her friend's birthday party that Saturday night. It didn't seem fair to not let her go to a party and wind up punishing her friend and her friend's parents, who had already paid for the tickets to the movie they were going to."

It was striking to me that aggression of the sort that Kristin had been displaying, such as brandishing knives and hurling books and giving forceful shoves that resulted in injuries, had not been responded to with any consequences beyond being sent to her room and an intermittent and lenient grounding.

My next step was to invite the girls to a meeting in my office with their mom. Kristin, true to form, immediately tried to take charge of the session. "Mom says we're here because I don't get along with Denise, but you don't know what it's like to live with Denise," she began.

"Tell me what it's like to live with Denise," I said.

Kristin didn't hesitate for a second. "She's just such a pain. She's always doing what I do. Whatever I watch on TV, she starts watching on TV, whatever music I listen to, she starts listening to, whatever I start wearing, she starts wearing. She's like a little clone, and I know she's doing it just to get on my nerves."

"Some find it flattering to have somebody imitate them so closely," I commented. "Your sister must really look up to you."

Kristin seemed momentarily caught off guard by my observation, but quickly regrouped. "Well, I just wish she'd get a life and stay out of mine. I don't need her copying me all the time. Somebody should tell her to watch her *own* TV shows and listen to her *own* CDs and pick out her *own* clothes. And she's always telling on me. The moment I glare at her or yell at her, she goes running to Mom, saying I'm going to hurt her. She's always hanging around watching me, waiting for me to do something wrong."

Already, in the first two minutes of the session, Kristin had provided me with another perspective on her relationship with her sister. In her eyes, Denise was not a blameless victim, but a tattletale, a subtle and insidious usurper, draining her of her uniqueness and thwarting her specialness by so diligently mimicking her.

Denise was more difficult to engage. "Tell me about some of the things that you like to do that are different from what your sister likes to do," I asked her.

"I play the clarinet and she doesn't," Denise said softly. "And I don't eat pizza all the time like she does."

"So there *are* some differences between the two of you," I affirmed.

"I guess," Denise said just as softly, then looked warily over at her sister, who shook her head disgustedly.

"What are some of the ways you've made a distinction between the two girls?" I asked Judy.

"They each have different chores to do," Judy replied. "Kristin has to set and clear the table and get the trash and recycling together the night before they get picked up. Denise has to clean the cat litter and empty the dishwasher."

"Which she never does," Kristin added quickly. "She lets the cat litter go for days at a time. You can smell it all the way upstairs from the basement."

"Is that true?" I asked.

"Well, she's pretty good about the dishwasher, but I don't really know if she's cleaning the cat litter or not since it's in the basement and we're not down there that much," said Judy.

"Trust me, she doesn't," Kristin said curtly, and I looked over to make eye contact with Denise, contact that didn't elicit any response.

"Is Kristin good about doing her chores?" I wondered.

"For the most part, yes," answered her mom. "I mean I have to remind her sometimes, and she can be pretty grumpy about it when it means stopping what she's doing to get the recycling or the trash outside, but she does okay with it."

"Is there a difference in the privileges that each of them is entitled to?" I inquired.

"Kristin has a more active social life, so I guess I let her do more things with friends. Denise just doesn't have as many friends and doesn't ask as much, so there's a difference there. I kind of wish Denise had more friends, actually. She spends a lot of her time alone."

"What about things like allowance and bedtime?"

"My sister and I have the same bedtime," Kristin snapped. "I'm in middle school and she's still in elementary school and she gets to stay up as late as I do."

"Honey, you also have to get up half an hour earlier than her. That's why your bedtime's the same," Judy interjected.

"But we had the same bedtime last year, and I wasn't in middle school then," Kristin confidently replied, clearly having thought out the injustice of the current setup. I couldn't help privately admiring her lawyerly persuasiveness.

"It's like I can't win," Judy said, tossing her hands up in the air helplessly.

What I could see almost instantaneously was that the picture that the mother had drawn for me didn't have much in common with the picture that the girls had drawn for me. Judy saw a taunting, domineering older sister looming over and threatening her innocent younger sister. But what I saw was an insecure girl on the cusp of adolescence whose mother was not recognizing the extent to which she felt intruded upon by her younger, more compliant sister and the ways in which she felt as if she was unfairly held more accountable than Denise was.

The frustration and anger that constantly simmered as a result of this situation was inevitably boiling over at the slightest irritant, making her feel even worse about herself. But nobody was making sure that she was adequately instructed in how to manage this anger and frustration in a way that was safe and appropriate, so the cycle continued, leaving all three of them feeling miserable.

In a situation like this one I often try to help find ways to distinguish the siblings from each other in a manner that elevates the older sibling, thus diminishing the need for the fights, which are often designed, at least by the eldest, to accomplish the same goal. I began by asking Judy to consider establishing a later bedtime for Kristin, even though she had to get up earlier than her sister, as a way to create some "space" between the two of them.

"But that's just going to tire her out, and Kristin can be a real bear when she hasn't had enough sleep," was Judy's instant response to my idea.

"I can understand your concern about that, but even if it's just a half-hour later, I still think it would be worthwhile in the long run. And she doesn't have to stay up that late—you're just telling her that she's allowed to."

"I'll have to think about that one," Judy said. "I'm just not sure I can sanction a later bedtime, and I'm not going to make Denise's earlier; that's not being fair to her."

"How about allowance?" I asked. "What are you giving them these days?"

"Denise gets three dollars a week, and Kristin gets four dollars," Judy answered. "Of course, that's if they're doing their jobs."

"How is that being monitored?"

"We try to stay on top of it," she replied.

"Kristin complained that Denise is not really doing the cat litter very regularly," I reminded her.

"I wish Kristin had something better to do with her time than keep track of Denise's chores," Judy said. "She should be busy enough with her *own* responsibilities, as far as I'm concerned."

"But it's sounding like she perceives things as being unfair in terms of what's expected of her."

Judy almost exploded. *"Everything's* unfair to Kristin! If I ask her to do one of her jobs over, she says I never ask Denise to do things over. If I praise Denise for something, Kristin says I treat Denise better than I treat her. I'm so sick of her complaints already! It's like she still hasn't gotten over the fact that she has a younger sister, and I really think it's time for her to grow up and deal with it."

Judy had come to me for help but did not appear at this point to be interested in accepting the help I was offering. I felt that there might be some underlying reasons why the sibling conflict was in place. Because siblings are our closest relatives, the sibling bond is a powerfully complex one and always influences our subsequent relationships in one way or another. Many times our history with our own siblings is the filter through which we view the new sibling system that we create when we have more than one child.

In obtaining some background, I learned that Judy was the oldest of three, followed by a sister and a brother. Her relationship with her younger sister seemed to be a mirror image of Kristin's relationship with Denise. "I was a very quiet kid, sort of nerdy, but both of my younger siblings were much more intense, and my parents seemed to gravitate more toward them than they did to me. My younger sister was this tomboyish hellion who was like a black hole, absorbing everybody's attention with all of her problems and talents—she was smart and difficult all at the same time. And she kind of bossed me around, because she was so much stronger. And my younger brother wasn't quite that intense, but he was my dad's favorite. My father finally got the son he wanted, so Dad pretty much focused on him and ignored me because I was quiet."

It was clear that the conflict between Kristin and Denise was at least partially an echo from Judy's past. Although the birth order was different, the situation was similar: one sibling, Judy, playing second fiddle to a sibling (actually *two* siblings) because she happened to be much quieter and more "nerdy."

The question that needed to be answered now was in what ways Judy's sibling history was exacerbating the conflict between her daughters. To my way of thinking, the current relationship between Kristin and Denise had an important function for Judy. By siding with the more vulnerable Denise against the more aggressive Kristin, she gave Denise what she wished she could have gotten from her own parents, thus symbolically redressing what she had experienced as an injustice when she was a child. In other words, Judy *needed* Kristin's aggression so that she could ally herself with Denise against an enemy and thereby right the wrongs of the past.

However, Judy's side-taking was obviously creating problems between her two daughters that might otherwise not have been there. Kristin wasn't learning to rein in her anger and was continually embodying the role of bully, and Denise wasn't learning to assert and defend herself and was embodying the role of victim. Bullies and victims always seek each other out. Until the hidden "value" of this parental approach was exposed, it was my belief that Judy would remain reluctant to make any meaningful changes—she was getting too much out of it.

With this in mind, I scheduled an individual session with her to explore these possibilities and to see if I might help to alter her perspective a bit by painting a more nuanced picture. I began by empathizing with her childhood plight. "It must have been difficult to grow up in a home in which you were relegated to such an auxiliary position."

"It was. I sometimes felt that I didn't even belong there, with all of these intense people storming around. And it was embarrassing at times to feel so intimidated by my *younger* sister."

"Do you feel that way about Kristin sometimes?"

Judy hesitated, fingering her pocketbook. "I guess I do. I mean, I wish she wasn't such a firecracker all the time. It's like she's always ready to light up and go off."

"It must be difficult to see her vulnerability, then."

"What vulnerability? I've never seen a more self-assured twelve-year-old in my life."

"Aside from your younger sister," I replied, and Judy smiled, catching my drift. "She may appear self-assured, but I don't think she'd feel so threatened by her younger sister if she was all that confident."

"Do you really think so?" she asked, in a more open tone of voice than I had heard before.

"Yes, I really think so," I answered. "Why else would what Denise does or doesn't do bother her so much?"

"I just never saw her that way," she responded, sounding a little mystified.

"You had described your sister as very intense. What is she up to now?"

"Well, she's had a pretty hard time of it, actually. She wound up going into the army, where she was quite happy, but then she left the service after a few years and has been pretty lost since then. She married but now is separated, and she hasn't really latched on to something that she sticks with, even though she's already in her midthirties. And she's got so much going for her, she's so bright and so strong."

"But despite all of her strengths and all of her bravado as a girl, and despite how intimidating she was to you, she apparently has some vulnerabilities, too."

"I guess so, based on how her life is turning out."

"So maybe you can see Kristin in the same way."

"I think I can," Judy said after a long pause. "I remember one time when I sent her to her room after she was doing her usual awful things to Denise, and I walked in and she was just lying on her bed with this incredibly sad look on her face. And I asked her for what must have been the thousandth time why she mistreated Denise all the time, and she just looked so forlorn and said, 'I don't know, Mom, I don't *know.*' It was the only time she didn't defend herself or attack me or her sister when I had disciplined her."

"So there really *is* some sadness in there—sadness that might be camouflaged by her anger."

"I guess that could be true," she said hesitantly.

"It sounds like she could really use some help controlling herself."

"But why does she always reject that help?"

"Maybe she needs more help, or a different kind of help. For example, it doesn't sound like there are any real consequences for her behavior. Even when she got grounded, she wound up going to a birthday party that same weekend. Not much of a punishment for treating her sister so violently."

"Do you think I need to be tougher?"

"I think you need to be *firmer,* and to follow through on what you say. Without positive or negative consequences to help motivate them, it's hard for kids to learn how to behave differently. We were talking a moment ago about how your sister turned out. It makes me wonder how you think you've turned out."

"I think I could've used some of my sister's strength," Judy said, laughing. "My life's okay, but I feel like I missed a lot of opportunities because I didn't have the self-confidence to pursue them. My marriage didn't work because I was such a doormat. I put up with stuff I should never have put up with, and I think my husband finally got tired of stepping on me. I never developed a career, and I could have. It's just that I didn't really believe in myself, so I'm stuck working as a classroom aide and being dependent on their dad's child support checks." She looked me straight in the eye and said, "I have a lot of regrets."

"Perhaps you'd like Denise to feel a little more self-confident than she does so she doesn't grow up with the same regrets you have," I offered.

"I'd love for her to. But how *can* she, with Kristin always torturing her?"

"You could see Kristin as providing Denise with the opportunity to become stronger and more assertive."

"How is that going to happen?" she asked.

"By refraining from rescuing her from Kristin all the time and providing her with the skills to take care of herself. And by modeling that strength yourself in your dealings with Kristin."

"I don't know. Sometimes I don't feel that we rescue Denise enough."

"I think she's rescued too much. I think that by constantly blaming Kristin and positioning her as the bully and Denise as the victim, you've inadvertently convinced Denise that she can't handle Kristin."

"I don't want *that* to happen."

"Then you'll have to accept the possibility that Denise contributes to these conflicts, too."

"How does she do that?"

"By sliding on her responsibilities, such as the kitty litter, and not being held to task. By running to you whenever there's a conflict brewing with Kristin rather than trying to solve it herself. By not developing a social life of her own and relying too much on her interactions with her sister to provide some adventure in her life."

"So you're saying that they each have some changes to make."

"Exactly. And you can help to make those changes come about by looking at their relationship in a more balanced way—following through with meaningful consequences for Kristin when she's not behaving appropriately, in tandem with building up Denise's capacity to defend her boundaries. That will be the best thing for both of them."

Sensing that Judy now had a more balanced perspective, we

went back to the drawing board to create some better ways of handling things.

In an effort to acknowledge the age difference between the two girls, Judy did agree to let Kristin have a later bedtime than Denise and to earn some "bonus" allowance money for cooking dinner twice a week. Denise, too, was entitled to some bonus money, but hers would be earned out of the house, by becoming a mother's helper in the afternoons for a neighbor who had recently given birth to her third child. That got her out of Kristin's hair several afternoons a week and also gave her the opportunity to develop her social skills.

A clear rule was established that any time either girl physically attacked the other, there would be a loss of phone privileges for one week. I suggested this because "grounding" Kristin tended to be as much of a punishment for the rest of the family as it was for Kristin and was likely to make things worse because it threw her and her sister into more, rather than less, contact with each other, something that wasn't good for either of them.

The girls were also told that for every week that neither of them complained to her mother about her sister, Judy would deposit $5 into an account be used for a joint purchase that the girls agreed upon, dependent on their mother's approval. This was designed to help Kristin think twice before she began to torment Denise and to help Denise think twice before she ran to her mother for assistance.

It also gave the two girls something to work toward collaboratively and provided them with the opportunity to negotiate as relative equals. I was aware that the joint purchase was more likely to be Kristin's preference than Denise's, but at least Denise was accorded some significance and given some say in the decision.

Not surprisingly, both girls quickly tested their mother's perseverence. Within a week after establishing these ground rules, Kristin twisted Denise's arm in an effort to get Denise out of what she (Kristin) had designated as her favorite chair in the family room, and Denise had gone running to Judy with the news. No $5 that week, and phone use was restricted for Kristin for the next seven days.

But within a month's time there was a marked decrease in the conflict between the girls. Kristin was much less antagonistic toward Denise, and while she had only cooked dinner one time, she was less combative and more helpful in general. Denise was enjoying her job as mother's helper and was significantly less whiny about her sister's bullying tactics. And the girls had decided to work together to earn a television set for the basement that would be just for them and their friends, a decision that Judy was comfortable with and that, she acknowledged, would probably help keep them all separated from each other as well.

"I finally feel on top of this situation, and it's a big relief," she concluded at our last session.

Learning more about her own contribution to the sibling struggles had helped her to find more decisive ways of managing them.

_____ EXERCISE THREE _____

In this exercise, you are going to select a problematic behavior or attitude that your child demonstrates and look at how and why you may be contributing to it.

1. First, describe how you respond to the chosen behavior or attitude and what your child's response to your response is. See if there is some cycle that gets set in motion based on your responses to each other.

2. Then see if there is something about your child's behavior or attitude that reminds you either of yourself or of someone in your present or past. Who was she named for? Whose birthday is close to his? Who looks or acts like her? Was he born close to the anniversary of someone's death? Is what she does something that you weren't allowed to do? Is what he *doesn't* do something that you were *supposed* to do?

3. Next, try to determine if some aspect of your own experience is being replayed with your child, and try to understand what is motivating you to reinvoke that experience.

4. Finally, come up with a response to your child that would be different from your more typical response. It could be something that you do more or less of, something that you add to or subtract from your parenting—it doesn't matter, as long as it is atypical. Think about what it would be like to implement this response and how it would change the reciprocal exchanges between you and your child. If it seems like it's worth a try, go ahead and do it and see what happens.

Maria contacted me because of her concerns about her 8-year-old son's interactions with his peers. "Domingo doesn't seem to play with anybody, and he gets bullied constantly. I volunteer at the playground at his school, and when they're out at recess, he's either by himself or being pushed around by somebody." Here's how Maria answered the questions in the exercise.

1. I deal with this by trying to get him to be more assertive. I've told him he has to join in some of the games on the playground, the soccer game, the football game. I've told him he's got to stand up for himself. I had him join the youth soccer team in our neighborhood, but he's not really into it, and the game just seems to go right past him. If he ever gets near the ball, some other kid takes it away in no time. His response to all that I've tried hasn't been noticeable. I don't see any change in him, and if anything, as the other kids are getting bigger and stronger, he seems to be falling behind even more, becoming more of a loner, with fewer friends

2. I don't think this reminds me of me. I was always pretty social, and while I wasn't the most popular girl, I wasn't all by myself either. And I hung around with a group of girls, so I was never singled out to be picked on. If anything, he reminds me of one of my younger brothers, Ramon.

3. Ramon was very shy and I had to defend him a lot against some of the kids who picked on him when we were growing up. I

think it was a little embarrassing for him that his sister had to stick up for him, but if I didn't, he would really get nailed by the other kids. So maybe I'm trying to toughen Domingo up so that he doesn't get taunted as much as my brother did, because my brother was pretty unhappy about it, and I don't want Domingo to be unhappy.

4. I suppose I could stop lecturing Domingo about being stronger with his peers. He doesn't seem to be listening, and it doesn't seem like it's having any impact. And I guess I could also invite just one friend over. There is one little boy I've noticed him hanging around with at recess—they don't do much together except look over Pokémon cards. Maybe I could get his name and number and invite him over.

As Maria and I went over her assignment, it became clear that her efforts to build her son's assertiveness were backfiring, making him feel less, rather than more, secure. Her recognition that Domingo was linked in her mind with her younger brother was notable because Ramon turned out to be gay, something that Maria still had a difficult time accepting. She had probably begun to associate diffidence with homosexuality, since they were both merged in her younger brother. No wonder Domingo's shyness and submissiveness made her so anxious.

Maria's instincts, however, were quite good. Domingo was not the type of kid who was going to charge out onto the soccer field and become a leader. He was most comfortable doing indoor activities with another quiet friend. Starting there and slowly building his social skills and self-confidence would be more likely to result in his ability to defend and assert himself than being lectured or forced to participate in competitive sports.

As Maria came to understand the ways in which she had burdened her son with the emotional baggage of her feelings about her brother, and as she began to create smaller but more do-able vehicles by which Domingo could develop socially, her concerns about him began to fade, and his connections with his peers began to improve.

FOUR

Understanding

All life is problem-solving.

Karl Popper

M_y first job after completing graduate school was at a residential treatment center for children and adolescents in southern Maryland. I commenced work in July, and within days was hearing from staff who had been there for some time about the increase in suicide threats and attempts that inexplicably occurred each summer and had just begun again.

Generally, these "attempts" were quite minor: one teenager was found sitting in the lounge casually scraping her forearm with scissors until it was raw and bloody, another had started telling his therapist that he was having "thoughts about killing myself," but without a great deal of emotion behind it.

As this was a state-run facility, the protocol in these situations was standard: any resident who displayed any suicidal tendency, in thought, word, or deed, needed to be taken to the psychiatric unit of the nearest hospital for at least forty-eight hours of monitoring, observation, and evaluation.

By the middle of July, it was as if there was a shuttle from our treatment center to the hospital, with "suicidal" patients being transported to the psych unit and then shuttled back once it became clear that there was not much of a risk, as was invariably the case.

Why this sudden increase in suicidal thinking and acting every summer? In staff meetings, we racked our brains. Most of us were enthusiastic and inexperienced, and naturally we set ourselves to work developing hypotheses that would explain this communal event. Perhaps there was an emotional letdown after the structure of the school year ended. Perhaps the thought of their peers and siblings being free to enjoy their vacations while they were stuck in residential treatment was so galling as to provoke the despair and hopelessness that are the typical precursors of self-destructive thoughts and actions. Perhaps this was a form of group hysteria, in which one person's emotionality infects another's, which in turn infects another's, until the entire subculture is afflicted.

One day, however, a colleague and I went to a case conference that happened to take place at the hospital where our suicidal residents were taken for observation. The weather was what one comes to expect in southern Maryland during the summer months: unrelentingly hot and humid. The forty-five-minute ride, which took us from the non-air-conditioned treatment center in my non-air-conditioned car, left us sapped and sweaty. Both of us breathed a sigh of relief as we entered the auditorium where the talk was to be held and felt the refreshing blast of chilled air. Finally—air-conditioning.

We spent the day in comfort, listening to the lecture, eating lunch, taking a tour of the psychiatric unit. The residents, unlike those at our hot, sticky facility, looked cool and relaxed as they sat in their lounge watching TV. And then all of a sudden it hit me. Maybe the shared suicidality had its origins in thermodynamics rather psychodynamics—maybe it was simply a way to get a couple of days of air-conditioned comfort during the unbearable months of summer.

I ran my thoughts by my colleague, and then presented them to our supervisor. She was skeptical but agreed to try an experiment, which was that instead of any suicidal statement or threat resulting in an immediate forty-eight-hour "vacation" at the hospital, there would instead be special staff people assigned to a "suicide watch," meaning that the resident "at risk" would stay at the treatment facility and be observed for seventy-two hours straight, even in the bathroom, and have to sleep out in the unit lounge until the "threat" had been defused.

The State Department of Health was delighted to provide

funds for the extra staff people, because it was still less expensive than a forty-eight-hour hospitalization would be. And once "suicidality" did not result in the pleasant break from a hot routine, and instead led to residents feeling irritated and suffocated by a staff person following them back and forth from lounge to cafeteria to activity room to bathroom, there was a sudden dropoff in suicidal threats, discussions, and ideas.

Of course, it wouldn't have made much sense to stop there. Once it was clear that not a lot of funds needed to be spent on additional staff, we then lobbied intensely for those funds to be funneled into the purchase of air conditioners. After all, who doesn't feel at least a little self-destructive when confronted daily with blistering heat and oppressive humidity?

This was one of my first experiences in understanding that what we define as a child's "problem" is always, at some level, an example of a child's "solution." The key to changing behavior for the better is understanding what problem the "problem behavior" is solving and then proposing a better way to solve it.

In the case of the treatment center where I began my career, suicidal behavior, hitherto designated as a problem, was actually a solution for the residents, a way to get a break from their almost unbearable living conditions. To change the problem behavior, we had to first understand what problem the behavior was solving—only then were we able to help the residents find a different, more functional solution. This was done in two ways: by taking away the solution that the problem provided (preventing them from being escorted to a more pleasant environment) and by solving the problem in a different way (providing air-conditioning).

One of the most complicated and challenging parts of parenthood is recognizing that our children are constantly problem-solving in their lives and that what we define as a problem may in fact be their solution. If we can reach this level of understanding, we can continue along the path of seeing our children as good enough, as well as help them find better solutions to the problems they are experiencing.

Sometimes the solution the problem behavior supplies is not all that difficult to figure out if you keep your eyes and ears open.

Fourteen-year-old Keith, who had been brought in by his parents because he was "too moody," confided to me that all he had to do to arrange for his parents to willingly fork over money for a haircut and new clothes was to act mopey and dress in black for a few days. "It works like a charm. I can't get any kind of good job being fourteen, so I don't have the money I need to get a haircut every month and buy the clothes I want. But if I sit out a few dinners, wear my black jeans and my black shirt, and start asking about dyeing my hair black again, they're there with the dough right away, offering to take me shopping and asking me when I'd like to get a haircut."

Once his parents became clued in to this gambit and stopped indulging him as soon as he missed a few meals or displayed a change in wardrobe, and once Keith's father was able to arrange for Keith to start earning some money of his own by helping out at the nursery a buddy of his owned, Keith's repeated periods of "mopiness" evaporated.

Seventeen-year-old Martina, who was referred because of her abuse of marijuana, said, "Everybody thinks I smoke pot to escape my problems, but the real reason I do it is it's the only way I can get to sleep at night. I hate lying there in bed for three hours with my mind racing all over the place, and then being unable to get up in time for the bus in the morning because I didn't get enough sleep. But if I get high about an hour before bed, I'm nice and calm and drop off without a hitch."

Once I taught her some relaxation techniques and suggested that she have a cup of herbal tea before bed and write down her thoughts about the day in a journal, she had much more success getting a good night's sleep, and was able to gradually relinquish her use of pot.

Rafi, a precocious fourth-grader who drove his parents mad with his casual approach to homework, said, quite offhandedly during our initial session, "When my dad plays basketball with me he gives me a few points to make it more interesting, because he's a lot better than me. I kind of do the same thing at school. I let myself fall behind and then try to catch up at the end of the quarter and surprise everyone. I used to do everything on time, but it got so boring."

When I conferred with his teachers and helped arrange for him to receive more challenging and stimulating assignments, Rafi no longer had to hold himself back from doing well in an effort to "make school more interesting." The problem that not doing his homework had solved was no longer a problem.

Eight-year-old Iden's parents were puzzled by the frequency with which she got poison ivy one summer. Then one day her mother came across her in the backyard rubbing poison ivy leaves on the inside of her thighs. When asked why she was doing this, Iden clammed up.

Her parents brought her to me for a consultation, and in analyzing the drawings she had done for me, I noticed that there was some anxiety associated with her genital area. When I asked if anybody had been touching her in a way that made her feel uncomfortable, she tearfully told me that her 13-year-old cousin, who was staying with them for part of the summer, had been coming into her room at night and rubbing his penis between her legs. He started backing off from her when she showed him that she had a poison ivy rash there. Once Iden's parents sent their nephew packing, she created no new rashes.

Twelve-year-old Sherrod was brought to me because his soccer coach had noticed that he had abruptly "lost the fire" that had regularly made him his team's high-scorer the last four seasons in a row. I learned that over the past year, Sherrod's mother had been gradually losing her vision as a result of diabetes and was now legally blind, unable to drive or read, and barely able to make out shapes.

As we explored the impact this was having on Sherrod, he blurted out, "My mom has always come to my games, but now she'll never see me score another goal," and started to cry. It became clear that he believed that by willfully choosing not to score at all, he was sparing his mom the anguish he was sure she would feel if he scored a goal she could not see. Once I helped his mother explain to him that she would always be able to experience the thrill of his scoring by listening to the crowd and by using her memory and her imagination, he was free to restoke his competitive flames and lead his team once again.

Even toddlers will sometimes be able to explain the basis for their problem behavior in solution-based terms if you're tuned in enough. Three-year-old Melissa, who was brought to me because of her tendency to bite her preschool classmates, joined me on the floor of my office to play with my dollhouse. When I moved one little plastic baby up against another little plastic baby and had the first pretend to gnaw on the second's leg, Melissa stopped what she was doing and said sympathetically, "Oh, his teeth must hurt! He's helping his teeth feel better!"

It appeared that biting might be a way for her to discharge some tension or relieve some tenderness in her mouth. I recommended a dental evaluation, which she had not had yet. The dentist confirmed that her gums were becoming inflamed and prescribed more regular brushing and an antiseptic mouth rinse. A few weeks later, her gums were healed and the biting had stopped.

I wish that all children's "solutions" were as consciously conceived, as quickly revealed, and as rapidly accompanied by more adaptive alternatives as in the several cases I've just discussed, but, alas, such is usually not the case. Often, the problem behaviors that lead us to be disappointed in or angry with our child seem to be just that—problem behaviors, without any redeeming or as-yet-unrevealed value for the child. Instead of seeing our child as struggling valiantly to meet a need or resolve a dilemma, we feel fed up with him, convinced that he "wants" to create problems and make us unhappy, or that he has some immutable personality flaw like "laziness" or "selfishness" or "immaturity."

But if you remain patient and continue to look for the solution embedded within the problem, you will almost always be rewarded with a greater understanding of your child's behavior, and thus be in a better position to help modify it in a constructive way.

One aid in doing this detective work is to consider whether the solution is addressing an *internal* problem or an *external* problem.

An *external problem* is one that resides "outside" of the child, but one that he feels compelled to address or resolve because it affects him so profoundly. The children described above were mainly dealing with external problems, whether it was hot weather, the need to repel a cousin's sexual advances, or the desire for a better wardrobe. *Internal problems* have to do with a child's interior life, her emotional conflicts or battles, and can be harder to identify. And because life is not as well-ordered as we would like it to be, internal and external problems sometimes overlap; as parents, we have to look both inside and outside to learn more about the problem our child is trying to solve.

Let's examine a problem that had its roots in an internal dilemma. Ten-year-old Nathan regularly tormented Victor, a boy down the street who was the same age, but somewhat bigger and stronger. Naturally, Nathan just as regularly got beat up by Victor, returning home with an assortment of bloody noses, cut lips, and bruised appendages. Nathan was otherwise a fairly well-behaved fellow, and his provocative behavior didn't extend into any other relationships.

In fact, he had a surprisingly good connection with his younger brother, whom he was quite protective of. Nathan's parents naturally had tried everything to get him to stop getting beat up—lecturing him, talking to the other boy and his parents, trying to prevent Nathan from heading down the street—yet month after month he wound up eliciting still another assault from his apparently happy-to-oblige neighbor.

In talking with Nathan, I suggested that it was almost as if he was punishing himself for some undetermined act. "Do you enjoy being beat up?"

"No."

"But you're smart enough to know that if you start calling Victor names he's going to come after you. It doesn't sound like this guy has a lot of patience for that sort of thing."

"Well, he deserves it."

"He might, but I wonder if you feel that you deserve to be beat up."

"No," Nathan said sullenly.

"Well, either you're not yet mature enough to see how these things work"—at this, Nathan glared at me—"or you feel deserving of being punished. I can't come up with any other explanation."

"I'm *mature*," he insisted angrily.

"Then why do you deserve to be punished so often? What crime have you commited?" I insisted back.

Nathan folded his arms and studied the floor.

I brought Nathan's folks in to join us and asked about the history of his relationship with Victor.

"This is what kind of surprises us," his mother said. "He and Victor were never all that close, but until recently they always got along okay. They've been in the same Boy Scout troop for a couple of years, which his dad and my husband lead, and that has been a lot of fun for them. And they both play trumpet in the band at school, and there haven't been any problems there, either."

Nathan's father spoke up, too. "When I have them in the Scout troop together, they are actually pretty tight, they'll sometimes pair up on their own to do some projects here and there. But I've noticed that since Victor's little brother got hurt on the bike, Nathan hasn't wanted to team up with him anymore."

"What happened?" I asked.

"It was very scary, although it turned out all right. A bunch of neighborhood kids were riding their bikes together, they were doing some kind of race or something, and Nathan's bike bumped up against Markie's bike. I'm sure it was an accident, but Markie spun out of control and his head hit the curb, and he was unconscious. We had to call 911, and they had to medevac him to shock-trauma. It turns out that he only had a concussion, there wasn't any fracture or brain damage, but I know that Nathan felt awful about it."

Nathan, who had been silent while his parents spoke, blurted out, "*It wasn't my fault!* He should have been wearing a helmet, or this wouldn't have happened! Neither of them wear helmets, their parents don't make them like mine do. I didn't mean to bump him, we were all just racing together down the street." His face was red and his eyes were filled with tears.

"We know, honey," his mom reassured him, but he didn't look all that reassured.

"Nathan, you and I were talking a few moments ago about the possibility that you were punishing yourself by taunting Victor until you get beat up. How much of this might be a way of making up for his brother's having been hurt in the bike accident?"

"It wasn't my *fault!*" Nathan shouted at me.

"I believe you," I said, "but I'm not sure that *you* do. It sounds like you're still feeling blamed for the accident, and still feeling angry that Victor's brother wasn't wearing a helmet, which might have prevented this from becoming as frightening as it did."

"So is that why he insists on bugging Victor until he gets hit— because he thinks he was at fault for the bike accident and has to make up for it?" Nathan's mother wondered.

"I think Nathan may believe that if he gets beat up enough times by Victor, perhaps it will make up for having been involved with Victor's brother's having been hurt."

"So what can we do?" Nathan's father asked.

"Well, that's partially up to Nathan," I responded, "since he's the one who seems to feel so guilty. You could decide how many more times you need to be beaten up by Victor before you've officially been absolved of guilt," I said, with a little wink at Nathan, who didn't wink back. Turning to his parents, I added, "But I think it would be a good idea to come up with a better way for him to relieve himself of his guilt without his having to get pummeled by someone that he likes, someone who might still like him if Nathan wasn't continually provoking him."

Nathan and his parents returned a week later with some ideas. They had decided that Nathan would write a letter of apology to Victor and Markie's family for having "been a part of" the accident that had been so worrisome. And they also decided that since he had to come up with a science project at school, he would do it on the importance of wearing bicycle helmets.

Nathan wrote his letter to Victor's family, who graciously thanked him for it, and he also got very involved in his project, which included educating his fellow students about head injuries and brain damage and setting up a booth at a local bicycle store stressing the importance of purchasing a new, properly fitted helmet with every bike.

Having found a better solution to discharging the burden of guilt he had felt so intensely, he was then free to terminate his self-punitive interactions with Victor and relinquish his problem behavior. Nathan and Victor did not become best friends, but the fights stopped, and by the end of the year, Victor was feeling trusting enough that he decided to invite Nathan to his birthday party.

In a follow-up session, when I asked if he was going to go to Victor's party, Nathan replied, "Yes I am. I've even gotten him the perfect gift—a bicycle helmet."

Now let's take a look at a problem that had its origins in the world outside the child but was disturbing enough to demand some kind of solution from her. Tara's parents called me because she still soiled her pants at age 8, even though she had been successfully toilet-trained five years before. She would maintain good control of her bowels for months at a time and then go through periods where she would, almost on a daily basis, make bowel movements in her underwear.

Her pediatrician had tried every intervention he knew of, from dietary to behavioral, but nothing had met with any success. The periods of encopresis seemed to disappear as mysteriously as they would appear, and her poor parents were completely mystified about what caused them.

Tara's mother, Bea, reported that toilet training had been on time and unremarkable, and her pediatrician reported that there hadn't been any evidence of gastrointestinal difficulties or physiological abnormalities, as there sometimes are in cases such as these.

When I asked her parents if there was any pattern that they were aware of that would explain the comings and goings of this symptom, they threw their hands up in the air. "If I knew that, Doc, I wouldn't be here," her father, Mario, said, shaking his head. "It's got us completely baffled."

It was also completely absorbing this whole family's attention. The periods of encopresis were characterized by frequent fights and great tension, as Tara's parents would insist that she sit on the toilet on a regular basis, something that she would refuse to do, or do quickly, without producing anything. They would put her on a high-fiber diet, which she would fight by simply refraining from eating what was put in front of her and sneaking snack foods at night.

"When she's in one of her soiling periods, our whole life revolves around it," Bea complained. When I hear a statement like that, and in one form or another it comes up quite often, it alerts me to the possibility that it may be the child's *intent* to elicit precisely that kind of response—total attention.

Sometimes parents will mistakenly assume that this means that their son or daughter wants more attention than she's getting, which often creates resentment, particularly when parents feel as if they're already being generous with their time and energy.

In my experience, however, children's efforts to get family life revolving around them often has to do with their desire to *distract* the family from something scary, pressing, or worrisome. Children are ingenious at becoming family lightning rods, trying to protect their parents and siblings by drawing off the intense emotional charges that may be circulating dangerously through the family system. On most occasions, they take on this role without being aware that they are doing so.

Sticking with this possibility, I tried to pinpoint with more precision the timing of Tara's encopretic episodes, believing there was something going on outside of Tara that was creating the problem everyone had assumed was located inside.

"When did Tara most recently begin soiling again?" I asked her parents.

Bea and Mario looked at each other quizzically for a bit, and then Bea spoke: "I think it was probably at least two months ago."

"Does that sound right to you, Mario?"

"Yeah, I guess so. I'd say two months ago is about right."

"And what was going on at that time?"

Both were quiet, and then Mario spoke up. "Like I said before, I'm not sure why this keeps happening. She seemed to be doing fine, and then all of a sudden one night she's sitting next to me on the couch watching TV, and I smell something, and I tell her to go take a bath, and she won't, she says she smells fine, and I know she doesn't, and that's how we know we're back into it."

"Bea, does that ring true for you?"

"Basically. I think I noticed it at dinner one night, something smelled funny, and I thought, 'Oh, no, here we go again,' and the same thing happened. I said, without trying to embarrass her in front of her brothers, 'Tara, why don't you take a bath tonight, honey?' and she just sat there, not moving. I can't stand fighting with her about taking a bath. She's eight years old, for god's sake. If she's going to poop in her pants, can't she at least wash herself so that we all don't have to suffer?"

I couldn't blame them for being so frustrated. Once you're done toilet-training your youngest child, you think you're done with dirty diapers for good. Who wants to have to continue dealing with this so many years down the road? Is it possible to see an 8-year-old girl who regularly smells like feces and won't take a bath as "good enough"? I was also frustrated because I couldn't understand what value Tara's behavior could possibly have, and I closed the session without being able to shed any light on their problem.

They returned the following week with Tara present, and Mario opened the session with a request. "I wrote a check for today's session," he said, "but was wondering if you could hold it until next week."

"That's not a problem," I replied, "but is there some financial stress right now?"

"Definitely," he said. "I was laid off again a couple of months ago, and I had a decent amount in savings, but we're starting to run dry. By next week, however, my unemployment checks will start coming in."

"Do you have any job leads?" I inquired.

"A couple, but nothing solid just yet. I've been e-mailing my résumé all over the place, but the work that I do is pretty specialized, and there aren't a lot of openings if I want to be paid what I'm worth."

"You mentioned that you were laid off 'again.' Have there been other periods recently without employment?"

"Yes, this most recent job I only had for about eight months. Before that, I was unemployed for a few months as well. That's one of the reasons we're in such bad shape financially."

I looked over at Bea, who was sitting with folded arms, pursed lips, and narrowed eyes, and asked her what impact Mario's job losses had on her.

"It's been quite hard," she said pointedly. "And I don't think he's going about his job search the best way. He's sitting around the house all day, hoping the Internet's going to come to the rescue, but I think he's got to get out there and meet people, and network, and talk himself up. He doesn't get dressed some days—he just sits at the computer in his pajamas, drinking coffee. Half the time, I think he's busy looking up sports results and playing solitaire, rather than checking into job sites."

I looked over at Tara, who was shifting uncomfortably in her chair. "How much do you know about your dad's work situation?" I asked.

"I know that he's not working right now, because when I leave the house he's still there, and Mom's already left for her job. And I know he's busy trying to find a new job. I hope he does."

"What's it like when your mom's working and your dad isn't?"

She darted a look at her mom before proceeding, and her mom shrugged her shoulders, as if to give her the go-ahead. "They fight a lot," she said softly.

"What happens when they fight?"

"My mom yells at my dad for not doing anything all day, and my dad yells back at my mom telling her he's trying."

"Do the fights scare you?"

This time she looked at her dad. He held his palms up in the air and raised his eyebrows, as if wanting to hear her answer, too.

"Yes. I'm afraid they're going to get divorced."

Mario jumped in right away. "Sweetie, we're not going to get divorced. It's just a very hard time for us. I'm sorry there's been so much fighting."

I looked at Bea to see if she was going to join in with her husband in reassuring their daughter about the future of their marriage, but she was watching Mario without saying a word. Not a good sign, I thought.

I asked Tara to leave the room for a while and spent some time talking with her parents. Without her mollifying presence in the room, their anger at each other exploded.

"I find it embarrassing that we have to come in here and ask Dr.

Sachs to hold the check because you're out of work once again," Bea yelled.

"I'm doing everything I can," Mario yelled back. "I never stop trying, but it's not as easy as you think. I'm not just going to take any job that comes along. We've got a mortgage to pay and college education to fund. I can't exactly take any job I get for twenty-five thousand dollars, like you do."

"That's not fair! I'm making that because I took ten years off to stay at home with the kids. If I hadn't done it, I'd be making twice that. And either way, I'm making a whole lot more than you are right now!"

"That's it, rub my face in it," Mario muttered. "She doesn't know how hard this is on me," he said, burying his face in his hands. "She just doesn't know."

"I'd *like* to know, but you never tell me! If I ask what you've done or what progress you're making, you don't respond. You just tell me you're working on it."

Mario lifted his face out of his hands. "Why should I bother telling you? You're never satisfied anyway! If I send out a résumé, you say I should've gone there in person. If I get ready for an interview, you don't like the way I'm dressed. If I tell you about a job prospect, you're right away telling me why it's not a good job for me. You've been telling me I've gotten it wrong for fifteen years now, whether I've had a job or not! What's the point of telling you *anything* when you're going to criticize me?"

Two things were quickly becoming clear to me. Bea and Mario's marriage was teetering perilously as they endured another round of his unemployment and the consequent financial stress and uncertainty. And Tara was extremely worried about the state of their marriage and frightened by the intensity of their conflict.

There was a third thing, too. Mario had lost his job two months ago, and both parents had agreed that Tara had begun soiling about two months ago. I couldn't help but wonder if there was a relationship between the two events. And since Mario had a history of employment problems and there were clearly fractures in his relationship with Bea, it seemed plausible that previous encopretic periods might also have occurred during stressful times in their marriage.

Going back to the description of how the whole family "revolved around" Tara during those periods, I wondered if the encopresis was Tara's unconscious attempt at a solution to the problem of her parents' anger with each other. By deflecting that anger onto herself and unifying them in their attempts to deal with her, she was perhaps trying to save their marriage.

When I presented this possibility to Mario and Bea, they were both taken aback. Then they reacted as parents typically do when I believe a child's problem is in actuality a desperate attempt to find a family solution—with a mixture of skepticism, fascination, and incredulity.

"Does she really think that?" Bea asked, eyes wide.

"I don't believe that," Mario said, looking at me as if I were from another planet.

Already they seem more unified, I said to myself, with a silent chuckle.

"No, I don't believe she really *thinks* that," I said. "I doubt that she has any awareness that that's what she's up to. But children are very, very astute when it comes to family dynamics—not a lot gets by them, although they can't always put it into words.

"And she is clearly upset by your fighting and worried about whether or not you're going to stay together—with good reason, based on how angry you are with each other. So I do think we have to consider the possibility that, without being conscious of it, she has chosen to bring the two of you together during a difficult time by creating a difficult problem which attempts to solve a much bigger problem—the erosion of her parents' marriage."

Bea and Mario seemed dumbstruck. Eventually, Mario spoke up. "Well, if you're correct about this, what do we do?"

"The best thing to do would be to demonstrate to her that your marriage is not at risk and find a better way to navigate this crisis than by pointing fingers at each other."

"You mean, if we fight less, maybe she'll soil less?" Bea asked.

"It has to start there," I said, "but there needs to be more than just the absence of fighting. You need to demonstrate in other ways that the two of you are a cohesive pair, willing to put your resentments and differences aside for the sake of the family bond."

"How do we do that?" Mario asked, sounding a little more interested than he had before.

"One place to begin would be around how you handle Tara's soiling. I don't think it's enough to simply allow her to soil herself and then refuse to take a bath, without there being any consequence."

"What should the consequence be, though? I don't want to punish her and make her feel bad. She probably feels bad enough already," said Bea.

"Who does the wash?" I asked.

"Usually me," Bea replied.

"Who pays for her to get new underwear when she runs out because they're too dirty?"

"We do," Mario replied.

"What happens if she refuses to take a bath?"

"She gets sent to her room so we don't have to smell her," Bea answered, with a laugh.

"And what happens there?"

Both looked at each other. Bea finally said, "I guess she listens to her radio or reads."

"Doesn't sound too unpleasant to me," I commented.

"I think I see what you're getting at," Mario said seriously. "She's not really paying the price for her behavior."

"Exactly," I agreed. "She experiences your anger and your frustration, but that's actually her *goal* right now. Your anger and frustration tell her that she's succeeding in detouring your anger away from each other and rerouting it toward her. At some deeply unconscious level, she believes that's best both for your marriage and for the stability of your family."

"So if we fight less and show some unity in our approach to dealing with her problem, she'll start to realize we're going to stay together?" Bea said.

"That's what I would like to test out. Let's see what happens when you try."

Bea and Mario worked out a plan whereby they would instruct Tara in how to use the washer and dryer, and from that point on she would be in charge of her own laundry, for which they'd pay her fifty cents a load. However, she would also be responsible for purchasing her own underwear, using her birthday or allowance funds. And if she refused to take a bath when asked, she was denied TV privileges for twenty-four hours.

In the meantime, I also scheduled separate sessions with the two of them to address their conflicts around Mario's work history and to find some ways to get along better until he could once again get on his feet. Mario agreed to contact at least five potential employers a day until he found work and to summarize his progress, or lack thereof, for Bea at the end of each day. Bea agreed to listen attentively and without criticism, offering feedback or advice only if asked to do so.

By the time we met again a couple of weeks later, Tara had regained control of her bowels, and while Mario had still not found a job, there had been a drop-off in tension between the two of them.

"Tara's actually enjoyed doing the laundry herself, and now wants to do our laundry if we pay her fifty cents a load for that, too," Bea reported, laughing. "Which I'm happy to agree to."

"But when I took her shopping and showed her how much a pack of underwear cost, that got her goat," Mario said. "She said, 'Dad, I'll be spending my whole allowance on underwear,' and I said, 'That's right, sweetie. Think about it.'"

By taking care of the underlying family problem and by addressing Tara's reaction to that problem in a way that both demonstrated their unity and held her responsible for her behavior, Tara's parents enabled her to relinquish her role as family distracter and grow back up.

Sometimes, the behavior that is making our child seem as if she is not good enough is a combination of internal and external problem-solving. David and Melinda contacted me because of their daughter's apparent inability to function responsibly on her own. Cindy, 15 years old and in the tenth grade, was indifferently meandering through school without any real initiative and getting by with C's, mostly by relying on her excellent memory rather than through studying. She had recently begun smoking and had already been caught lighting up at school, resulting in a suspension.

A fine athlete, Cindy was just getting by in this realm, too. Even with her coach promising her the opportunity to start on the varsity softball team in the spring, Cindy did little to prepare. She showed up for the first week of practice out of shape, and as a result she was consigned to the junior varsity once again. Not that she appeared to mind: "JV, varsity, I don't really care," she said when I asked her how she felt about not making the varsity squad. "In some ways, I actually prefer playing on JV because that's where most of my friends are."

Her parents weren't quite as accepting, however. "This is just what I'm referring to," Melinda snapped. "She's got this great coach on her side, with this great opportunity to start on the varsity team, for a school that went all the way to the state finals last year, and what does she do? She blows it! I kept telling her all through January and February to start working out, to jog and go out to the batting cage, but she just kept putting me off, telling me that everything would work out. And lo and behold, it didn't."

"But it *did*, Mom," Cindy countered. "I'm still on the team, I still get to play, and I have another two years to play varsity anyway, so what's the big deal?"

"The big deal," said her father, "is that you've let your coach down. She was counting on you to show up in shape and you didn't."

"She wasn't counting on me," Cindy replied. "All she said was that I had a chance to start on the varsity. So now some other girl will, and I'll be fine. I can't see why this is such a big deal for you when it's not such a big deal for me. Why won't you lay off already!"

Melinda gave me a look of pure exasperation. "It's this way around everything. When her grades are C's, she tells us C's are fine. We think she could get A's in at least half of her classes if she would just do her homework and turn it in. When we say her room is a mess, she says that her room is fine, that she can find everything she needs to. When we talk to her about the dangers of smoking, she says that she's only smoking a few cigarettes a day and can stop anytime. How many times have you heard *that* one?

There's just not the kind of maturity that we would like to see in her. She says she's not even sure she wants to go to college. But there's only a couple more years of high school before she's on her own—and then what?"

Cindy's being "on her own" in a few years had more drama to it than it did for most tenth-graders, however. In the course of our initial interview I learned that her mother had been suffering with colon cancer for the past five years, and although she had responded to chemotherapy, tumors had continued to grow once the treatment had been completed. While originally Melinda had been optimistic about her recovery, she knew enough to know that with each recurrence of cancer, the odds of her surviving were diminished.

"I've done everything the doctors have told me to do and more," she told me later on in the session, after I had asked for some time with Cindy's parents alone. "Not only did I go in for surgery and continue with chemo, but I started meditating, and recently began a new organic diet that is supposed to retard the growth of the tumors. However, I have to tell you that, after five years of this, I am prepared to die if that's what happens. There's an experimental radiation treatment that I might qualify for, and I'll give that a try, but no more surgery. If I don't survive, I don't survive, but I've got to have some quality of life left to me or it's just not worth living."

"What do you think about Melinda's decision, David?" I asked.

"Obviously I want her to do everything she can to fight this, and she's really shown great strength throughout the whole ordeal. As far as I'm concerned, I have to say that I'd like her to consider the surgery if the experimental treatment doesn't work. I don't want her throwing in the towel. . . ."

But before he could complete his thought, Melinda burst in: "I'm so *sick* of people deciding that I've thrown in the towel, that because I don't want any more surgery I've lost my will to live. Who are you to say? Who is anyone to say? Do you want to be sliced open? Do you want to feed yourself through a tube when we're all out at a restaurant? Do you want to lose all control of your bowels?"

David sat silently as her barrage of questions continued. When she had finished, he said apologetically, "I know it's not my place to tell her what to do. It's just that I'd like to have her around as long as possible."

"And *I'd* like to be around as long as possible, but only if being around means I can live my life with some semblance of dignity, not like some disfigured, emaciated skeleton who's hanging on waiting for the next miracle cure to come around the bend."

"Have you asked Cindy what her wishes regarding your treatment are?" I wondered.

"Actually, no," Melinda replied hesitant, sounding a little puzzled by the fact that she hadn't.

"Would you like to?" I inquired.

"I guess I would," she answered after a short pause.

I invited Cindy back into the room and had Melinda lay out for her her dilemma. "So I guess what I'm wondering, Cindy, is if this experimental treatment doesn't work, what you think about the possibility that I might choose not to do anything else and just take my chances on surviving without doing any more from a medical standpoint."

Cindy's answer was immediate. "I want you to do whatever you want to do, Mom," she said, reaching out to touch her mother's arm. Melinda's eyes filled with tears, and she leaned over to kiss Cindy lightly on the head. Cindy started to tear up as well.

"What has this been like for you, Cindy?" I asked. "Most young men and women your age don't have to deal with their mother or father having a serious, life-threatening illness. How have you handled it?"

"It's been pretty hard, I guess," she began. "I mean, I don't think it's ever *not* on my mind. Just last week I came home from school on a day that Mom's usually there, and she wasn't there, and the first thought that went through my head was, 'I wonder if she's at the hospital again. I wonder if something's the matter.' "

"So how do you deal with the fear and uncertainty that you're up against?"

"Well, I have a couple of good friends that I talk to, although it's not always that helpful, because they're always trying to make me feel better by telling me my mom will be fine—but nobody knows that for sure. And I guess I try to distract myself with other things, like going out or listening to music. Sometimes I write poetry, too," she added a little sheepishly, looking down at her lap.

Clearly Cindy had found some ways to cope with the fear and unpredictability that had been her constant companions during the years since her mother had been diagnosed with cancer. As is often the case, the activities that her parents might have preferred that she invest in, such as academics and sports, were not in fact the activities that were most meaningful to her as she struggled to contend with the possibility of her mother's death.

I decided to schedule the next session with Cindy alone, and I asked her to bring some of her poetry with her. When she came into the room, she handed me a thick sheaf of papers and said, "Well, here you go. . . ." I was astonished by the depth and quality of her work. Only two of her poems dealt directly with her mom, but every single piece addressed the theme of love being lost or endangered in some way. It was clear from reading what she had written that Cindy was greatly preoccupied with the prospect of losing her mother to cancer, and her fear and pain were most freely expressed through her poetry.

"Have you shared your work with anyone else?" I asked, after letting her know how moved I was by the power of her words.

"Not really. A couple were written for assignments in English, but mostly I keep them to myself."

"What would it be like to show them to your mom?"

"I doubt that she'd like them all that much. She's so critical of everything I do. If I ever get a B, it's 'Why wasn't it an A?' If I clean the kitchen, it's 'Have you vacuumed yet?' I worked incredibly hard on this essay on abortion for social studies, and she didn't even get what I was saying, she was so busy pointing out the spelling mistakes and punctuation errors. It was a rough draft, for god's sake! She's always on me for something, and whatever I do is never good enough."

"Is your relationship with your dad any different?"

"Yeah, it's very different. At least my mom talks to me, even though she's usually upset with me. My dad doesn't even do that. He's always at work, and when he's not at work, he's home doing work or on the phone. He wonders why I don't say good morning to him when he says it to me, but why bother? He doesn't really care, and he's never around for the rest of the day anyway. Like saying good morning means we have a good relationship or some-thing—it's ridiculous."

"Have you given much thought to what your life would be like if your mother dies?"

Cindy looked at me hesitantly for a moment, as if to gauge whether it was safe to answer this question, and then proceeded: "All the time. *All the time*. And I don't like the way things look. I can't imagine living at home with just my father, he's so out of touch with me and who I am. And my mom got to see my older sister graduate high school and go off to college, and she was so proud of her, and sometimes I think about walking across the stage for graduation without my mom being there to see it, and it feels awful. And it makes me angry, *so* angry, that she got to see my older sister graduate and go off to college, but maybe she won't be able to be there for me. It seems so unfair."

Through further discussion, it became clear to me that what David and Melinda were designating as Cindy's "problems" were actually her solutions to her problems. She was feeling profound anger about her mother's illness and the possibility that Melinda might die and desert her before she had completed her childhood, but her mother's hypercriticalness and her father's remoteness were making it difficult to articulate these feelings and move through them.

The anger was instead being expressed in indirect and less pro-ductive ways, such as through underachieving at school and sports, which deprived her mother of the pleasure of seeing her succeed, or through smoking, which was making her parents worry about her as much as she worried about them.

There was also another solution embedded in her self-sabotage. This emerged when I asked her again, but this time privately, to share with me her thoughts about her mom's decision to not con-

tinue pursuing extensive medical treatments if her tumors continued to grow. Her response was a good deal less circumspect than
she had been with her mother in the room the week before.

"Sometimes I think my mom has given up. I mean, I know it's
been a real ordeal for her, but I wonder if she cares anymore. It's
like she's not living her life. If I knew that I was going to die, I
would be doing all kinds of things to make my remaining days as
full as possible. I'd be going places and doing things. But she
doesn't really do anything except sit around, maybe do some knitting or reading."

"Does she have enough energy to do much more than that?"

"I know what you're saying. I'm sure a lot of it's due just to her
fighting cancer as long as she has. But I still kind of wonder if she
wants to fight it anymore."

"Maybe she doesn't."

"I guess not. But I wish she would. I mean, if nothing else, just
to see me graduate high school. That would be enough, I think, if
she could just survive until then . . ." Her voice trailed off, and she
sighed, staring sadly at the floor.

Cindy was not quite as ready to relinquish her mother as she
appeared to be in front of her parents. It occurred to me that perhaps Cindy was unconsciously declining to grow up out of the
fear that if she appeared too autonomous, her mother might interpret that as a sign that it was okay for her to die. She wanted her
mother to feel the necessity of sticking around long enough to
give her the mothering she needed—especially since she felt
abandoned by her father.

"Have you let your mom know what you think about her having 'given up'?"

"I actually did one time, a little while ago. She had just come
back from a doctor's appointment, and she was looking very
down, and I told her that she should do something to pick herself
up, that maybe we could go out to a movie or something, but she
just wanted to stay home. And I really yelled at her and got on her
about needing to do more than just feel sorry for herself."

"How did she respond?"

Cindy laughed for the first time in our meetings. "She yelled right back at me and told me I'd be better off cleaning my room and doing my homework than going out to a movie with her, and it was about time I stopped worrying about her and did what I needed to do for myself, and that if I kept smoking I'd be joining her in the grave in no time at all."

"What made you laugh just now as you were remembering this story?"

"I guess the thought of it is kind of funny—I'm busy yelling at her and she's busy yelling at me, and we're both so frustrated with each other."

"What was the outcome?"

Cindy thought for a moment and then smiled. "Actually, it was kind of interesting. I went stomping upstairs to my room, and she came up a few minutes later and just sat on my bed, and we talked for a while. She told me that she didn't want me to have to take care of her, but that she also didn't want to die without knowing that I could take care of myself. And I told her I didn't want her to die whether I could take care of myself or not. It was the first time in a long time that we really talked. And then all of a sudden, she said, 'Pick a movie, we're going out.' And we did."

The argument had temporarily cleared the air for the two of them and enabled them to get their feelings out in the open and join with each other during a difficult time. But when Melinda told Cindy, "I don't want to die without knowing that you can take care of yourself," it was easy to imagine how this might have reinforced Cindy's subterranean feeling that she might be able to keep her mother alive by *not* taking care of herself. Giving her mother something to live for by creating enough problems for her to focus on might be Cindy's way of motivating her mother to "fight the good fight" long enough that she could see her graduate.

I decided next to schedule separate sessions with Cindy and her mother, and Cindy and her father, so as to bolster each of those relationships during this precarious time and create the possibility that Cindy might find some better solutions.

My session with Cindy and her father focused on helping him to understand more about what she was needing, and what she was going through at this point in her life. David was quite receptive to what I had to share with him and surprised Cindy with his capacity to empathize with her plight.

"I know this isn't easy for you, and I know I haven't been around all that much to help out, and I'm really sorry for that. I guess that's kind of how I deal with this, by burying myself in my work and shutting everything else out."

"But you've shut me out, too, Dad," Cindy complained.

"What is it that you'd like from your dad right now?" I inquired.

"I don't know. I guess just paying attention to me besides that stupid 'Good morning' every morning, or 'Did you get your homework done?' It's like that's all we have to say to each other."

"What parts of your life would you like him to pay attention to?" I asked.

"Anything! Come up and listen to the music I listen to! Ask me what I did when I went out with my friends!"

"Oh, come on, Cindy," David answered quickly. "Anytime I've tried to ask what's going on, you just give me the cold shoulder and act as if I'm not worth talking to."

"You don't act interested at all, Dad! When was the last time we sat down and talked?"

"I don't know, but I know it wasn't very recent." He turned to me with his hands turned up. "How do I let her know I care?"

"Probably by finding some things to do with her that you might both enjoy. What interests do the two of you have in common?"

"That's a good one," Cindy said. "I don't think we have a thing in common. I don't even know what Dad's interested in besides work."

"What do you think, David? What do you like to do when you're not working?"

"Well, I like music, too, although from what I can tell, not the kind that Cindy listens to. And I like to read, mystery-type stuff. And I like sports. I try to get to Cindy's games whenever I can, and I play racquetball with a friend every week."

"So what might the two of you do together that would be enjoyable?"

David sat mutely, while Cindy stared at him with her arms folded and her jaw jutting out. After a few moments, she said, "This is what I mean. Why bother? He's just not interested."

David spoke up, but to me rather than to Cindy. "I just don't know how to relate to her. I never had any sisters, and my mom died when I was in high school, and I really have no idea how to connect with a teenaged girl."

"How did your mom die?"

"Cancer . . . ovarian." He fell silent again. I looked over at Cindy, whose face had suddenly softened.

"How much have you shared with Cindy about your experience of losing your mother at such a young age?"

"Nothing," Cindy interjected before he could answer.

"She's basically right," David added.

"Do you think this might be a good time to open up to her?" I asked.

David looked up at me again and smiled shyly. "I guess that's what you're thinking, huh?"

I spent the remainder of the session asking David to share some of his memories of his mother's death, and I couldn't help but notice Cindy's rapt attention as he talked about this lonely and helpless period in his life.

"I can't believe we've never really talked about this before," he concluded, as we were finishing up the session. "Maybe Cindy and I have more in common with each other than I had thought."

"Evidently," I said. "You might want to continue this conversation outside of here and see if there are some ways to help each other through this difficult time. Maybe that will open some other doors in your relationship as well."

"Plus, Dad, you used to smoke, too, you know," Cindy added abruptly, as they were getting up to leave.

David admitted that this was true.

"When did you pick up the habit?" I asked.

"In high school, just like Cindy," he replied. "But it took me years to quit. I didn't stop completely until I turned thirty, and finally got sick of having bronchitis for three months every winter."

Children will always find a way to identify with their parents, and often it is a hidden or surreptitious part that they choose to imitate. Because David had shared so little of himself with Cindy over the years, it was as if she had no choice but to connect with a part of him that had gone underground, but was real nonetheless. To my way of thinking, her making it a point to mention that smoking was something they had in common revealed this bond.

"Perhaps that's another thing the two of you might want to do some talking about," I suggested.

It was touching to notice David put his arm around Cindy's shoulders and give them a squeeze as they walked out of my office into the waiting room, the first time I'd seen any physical contact between the two of them.

My session with Cindy and her mother was also fruitful. We began by addressing Cindy's feeling that Melinda was too critical of her.

"I don't think I'm being unreasonable," Melinda began. "Asking a girl as bright as my daughter to earn a few A's, clean her room, focus on sports, and give up the damn cigarettes is not asking for the moon. We're talking about things that she's quite capable of doing."

"But, Mom, the list is endless. If I get a couple of A's, then you'll want me to get *all* A's. If I make varsity, then you'll wonder why I'm not All-County. I honestly don't think you'll ever be satisfied with me. That's why I don't even bother trying to please you."

"It's not for me, dear, it's for you. It's your life, you're the one who's going to have to live it."

"Then why don't you let me live it, already? If it's my life, then why do you keep telling me how it's supposed to go?"

Melinda sighed. "How would you answer Cindy's question?" I asked. I received no answer.

I probed gently. "Can you think out loud?"

Melinda began slowly. "I guess I'm just not convinced I'm going to be around all that much longer. I know what I'm up against here. I know what the chances are. And I feel that I've got to get all of the parenting in that I can while I can, because there's such limited time left for me to do it."

"Oh, Mom," Cindy said, shaking her head, "don't think like that. You're going to be here for a while." She sounded like she was trying to convince herself as much as her mother.

"Cindy, I don't know that, and neither do you," Melinda said bluntly.

"It's like you've designed some kind of crash course in life for Cindy and are trying to jam everything in before the final exam," I commented.

"I think you're right," Melinda agreed. "There's so much that she needs to know, and I don't know how else she'll learn it."

"I think you may be neglecting the most important learnings, however—which are taking place right now—and have been for some time."

"Which are . . . ," Melinda said, waiting for my reply.

"Which are the lessons of courage and tenacity that you've been teaching her every day since you've had this illness, lessons that will serve her far more than any lectures you give her on what grades she should earn or how clean her room should be."

It took a few moments for this to register with Melinda, but Cindy caught on right away.

"He's right, Mom. I think I've learned more from watching you fight this than I do from all the talking you do about my grades or my sports or my room. In our social studies class the other day we were talking about who we admired most, and I thought that if I had to answer that with one name, it would be you."

By now, Melinda had gotten it. She reached over and hugged Cindy, who warmly hugged her back.

"But it still doesn't explain why Cindy doesn't do better than she does." (Her tenacity was showing up again.)

"I think that Cindy has been so preoccupied with worrying about and coming to terms with your illness, she just doesn't have enough energy left over to take on tasks that aren't that inherently appealing to her, like cleaning her room or excelling in classes, when she can do decently with minimal effort."

"But I haven't asked her to worry about me. I'd rather she stop worrying and take care of her responsibilities."

"Without her feelings about possibly losing you being openly addressed, however, they remain bottled up inside her, where they get in the way. How can you ask a young woman not to worry about her mother's life-threatening illness? Does that seem realistic to you?"

"I guess not," Melinda concurred. "But are you saying I shouldn't care how she's doing, that I shouldn't have standards?"

"Not exactly. I'm saying that if you give her a chance to explore and share more of what she's feeling, and join with her rather than fight with her around her struggles, she'll be more likely to become the independent young woman she needs to be if she has to do without you."

I knew at this point that it would be necessary for me to help them find some way to join, since they had been adversaries for so long and were in a rut. I remembered Cindy's complaint that her mother didn't do anything but "sit around knitting and reading," and followed up on that to see if it might lead them anywhere.

"What kinds of things do you knit?" I asked Melinda.

"I'll show you," she said proudly, and bent down to pull out of the bag at her feet a child's sweater, with fanciful colors and designs running through it.

"Mom's amazing at knitting," Cindy said as I took a closer look. "She can pump these things out in a week or two."

"Do you have an interest in learning to knit?" I asked her.

"Kind of. I mean, Mom's got her circle of knitting friends. They get together once a week to knit and talk, and it seems like a neat thing to do."

"Would you be willing to give your daughter some lessons, Melinda?"

Her eyes brightened immediately. "I'd be delighted! You can come join me some evening at our group. The other women would love to have you, and we could use some new blood."

"If your mom is going to share her knitting expertise with you, there's one thing that I'd like you to share with her in return," I said to Cindy before we finished up.

"What?" she asked warily.

"I'd like you to show your mom some of the poetry that you have been writing."

"Do I have to?" Cindy asked, with a not entirely convincing display of reluctance.

"I think you know what I'm going to say," I replied, and she grinned.

At a follow-up meeting with all three of them, there was a distinctly different interaction. Melinda began by telling me how powerful Cindy's poetry was. "When I read her stuff, I realized how much my illness has been on her mind, and it's like I understand all of a sudden why a bed isn't always made or a project isn't always top-notch."

Cindy told me that she had begun her first knitting project and had enjoyed being included in her mother's knitting group the previous week. "They really treated me like a grown-up, and I felt like one, although I don't know that I'll ever be able to knit like they do."

"Oh, you will," Melinda said, "it's just a matter of time and practice," and I realized that her comments about the poetry and knitting were the first positive ones directed at her daughter that I had heard her make since we had commenced treatment.

David told me that he and Cindy hadn't spent a lot of time together since our meeting, but that he had asked her, on the spur of the moment one evening, if she wanted to keep him company while he went to pick up some computer parts he had ordered. The half-hour ride each way had given them an opportunity to elaborate on some of the issues we had opened up several weeks before in my office.

When I asked Cindy what this had been like for her, she said, "It was okay. I mean, I liked hearing more about his mom, what she was like, since I never knew her."

David added, "Cindy was also asking me about how I stopped smoking, and I told her some of the various tricks I used, and she says she might give them a try."

"Yeah, we were talking about it in health class the other day, and the teacher said the sooner you try to quit, the more success you have, so I might try to convince a couple of my friends who also smoke to give it up. I think that might make it easier."

As I saw it, now that Cindy had found another, healthier way to connect with her father, she was free to let go of the destructive behavior she had come up with in her efforts to find some linkage with him.

In the following months, the level of combat continued to drop significantly, and the three of them began to enjoy one another's company a great deal more. Cindy did decide to give up smoking and got down to "one or two cigarettes a day—some days none at all." And she had a fine season in softball, convincing herself and her coach that she would be ready for varsity next year.

One problem remained, however. She finished up the school year with C's and D's and even failed a couple of her finals. "Things seem to be getting worse, not better, when it comes to school," Melinda said with a sigh at our end-of-school-year session.

I discussed this with Cindy privately, who was more distressed about her grades than I had ever seen her be. "I don't know what's happening. It's like everybody else is getting it but me."

"You had said that one of the reasons your grades were low was because you weren't turning in your homework. Why haven't you been?"

"I don't know. It's like I have no energy for it at night, after a full day of school and after practice. By the time I'm done with dinner, I just don't have anything left."

Cindy certainly did have a full day, and I knew what a load she had been carrying from an emotional standpoint these past several years, but I still couldn't help wondering if something else was interfering with her success in school. For her to be feeling so much at sea, to be avoiding her work so much, and to have the sense that "everybody else is getting it but me" suggested the possibility of a learning disability.

I recommended to her parents that they arrange for her to be tested, and the evaluation revealed that my hunch was correct. She had a good memory and was able to take information in, which is why she had gotten by all these years. But her inability to process the information and express what she knew in writing, which is a crucial task in the high school years and beyond, had become more noticeable and more problematic now that she was a sophomore.

For example, writing an essay, even on a topic that interested her, was an ordeal, an uphill climb from beginning to end. I remembered her talking about how hard she had had to work on her abortion essay and how disappointed she was when her mother focused only on her grammatical errors. No wonder she "sat out" so many assignments or backed away from having her projects evaluated altogether. It was too painful and too embarrassing.

The psychologist who had done the evaluation referred them to a tutor who specialized in working with bright students with learning disabilities, and Cindy worked with him weekly throughout the summer, telling me, "Now that I know I'm not stupid, I feel like I can give school a try again."

Although there wasn't any need for us to meet anymore, Melinda called me after the first quarter of the next school year with an update. "I'm holding my own with the cancer for now, but I've decided that if things take another downturn I'm going to seriously consider getting the surgery."

"What changed your mind?" I wondered.

"Well, a lot of things, one of which was my doctor telling me about a new kind of surgery that would be less radical. But part of it was because Cindy's been doing so well. She got all B's and an A on her first report card this year, and she's just so thrilled. Not only that, she's decided to take an SAT course this winter—this from a girl who wasn't even sure she was going to go to college. I don't want to lose the chance to see all of our hard work together pay off." Interestingly, the signs of Cindy's increasing competence and self-reliance had enhanced, rather than diminished, her mother's will to live.

For Cindy, her lack of achievement and focus initially resulted from her attempts to solve both an *external* problem, the impending loss of her mother and her distance from her father, and an *internal* problem, a previously undiagnosed learning disability. Once she learned that these problems could be dealt with in ways that did not work to her disadvantage, she was able to develop some more satisfying solutions to them.

_____ EXERCISE FOUR _____

One of the key elements in seeing your child's problems as solutions is understanding your own way of problem-solving. We all develop our individual approach to solving problems based on the strengths, attributes, and resources that we have at our disposal, as well as the nature of the problem and the environmental response to our problem-solving attempts.

Even babies do this. An infant who is cold, for example, might cry out in the hopes that one of her parents will come and hold her and warm her up. As her physical and expressive abilities begin to develop during her first couple of years of life, she won't always have to cry but will be able to do other things, like crawl or walk over to her father and snuggle up on his lap or tell her mother that she's cold.

But if her cries as an infant tend not to result in receiving that kind of care, she may shift to a different problem-solving mode. She may begin to shiver or curl up so as to independently raise her body temperature. Her initial experiences with problem-solving may set the tone for her subsequent attempts, and she may grow up to feel that, in general, it's best to withdraw, "curl up," and rely on herself, rather than depend on others when she's uncomfortable.

Many times our children are not good enough in our eyes when they choose to problem-solve in a way that is different from what we think is best, based on our own experiences. You handle criticism from others by firing up your efforts, for example, while your daughter handles criticism from others by appearing to give up and shut down. You manage your feelings of being stressed out by going to the gym to work out, but your son manages feelings of being overwhelmed by holing up with his Gameboy.

For your child to be good enough, however, his or her method of problem-solving needs to be recognized for what it is. Only then will it be possible to help the child address the underlying problem in a better way. For this exercise, pick a problem that your child has and answer the following questions:

1. What internal or external problem could his problem be solving?

2. Have I had a similar problem in my life? If so, how did I solve it?
3. How is my method of problem-solving similar to my child's? How is it different?
4. What are the advantages and disadvantages of my chosen method of problem-solving?
5. What are the advantages and disadvantages of my child's chosen method of problem-solving?
6. What other solutions are there that might address this problem in my child's life?

One of my patients, André, was the father of 13-year-old Peyton, an excellent violinist who had decided he wanted to quit after five years of lessons. André thought it was a mistake for Peyton to stop when he had such potential and had had so much success. Peyton said he was sick of practicing more than an hour a day and wanted time for other things. After nights of fruitless discussion they had a blowup that resulted in Peyton hurling his violin bow at his father in frustration and walking out of the house threatening never to return. Here is how André answered these questions.

1. By saying he wants to stop taking lessons, he's solving the problem of having to do something he's grown weary of, that's obvious.
2. I don't know if I've had a similar problem in my life. I do know that there were times I was tempted to quit something, and didn't, and was glad that I stuck it out. A couple of years ago, my boss paid for me to take a course on leadership, which I didn't really like that much and which was eating up a lot of time, but I stuck with it, and I think that it's probably paid off. I have more responsibility at work now, I learned a lot, and he gave me a bonus at the end of the year.
3. I don't think there are a lot of similarities between my approach to the course and Peyton's approach to the violin, because he's planning on quitting and I didn't.
4. The advantage of my sticking with stuff I don't always like is that I see the light at the end of the tunnel, and sometimes it pays off. The disadvantage, I suppose, is that I get locked into staying

with things that might not pay off. Like our first house. It was a disaster, and we just kept sinking more and more money into it, trying to turn it into our dream house. I should've given up on it a long time—and thousands of dollars—before I actually did.

5. The advantages of Peyton's quitting violin is that he'll get a break from it and he won't have to do something he's getting tired of doing. The disadvantage is that he may regret it when his fellow violinists continue and get even better or start receiving awards or scholarships that he won't earn.

6. Another solution would be for us to give him a break from violin without having to actually quit. Or maybe it's time for him to consider trying a new instrument for a time, because he's so musical. He might like that.

Initially, André envisioned himself as someone who always persisted, and who succeeded because of that persistence. As he continued the assignment, however, he acknowledged that persistence didn't always pay off for him, as, for example, when it came to their first house.

By the end of the assignment, he had gotten out of a binary continue-or-quit debate and begun to entertain other options, which, as it turns out, were quite acceptable to Peyton. They agreed to a six-month hiatus from violin, and a few months later Peyton expressed an interest in joining the choir at his church.

By examining his own approach to problem-solving, and respecting his son's approach rather than criticizing him for it, André was able to work with Peyton to arrive at a new and better solution.

FIVE

Forgiving

> There are open wounds, shrunk sometimes to the size of a
> pinprick, but wounds still.
>
> F. Scott Fitzgerald, Tender Is the Night

One of my favorite jokes is about a farmer who enters a hardware store and buys a chain saw advertised as being guaranteed to cut down fifty trees a day or your money back. He eagerly pulls one down from the display out front, pays for it at the cash register, takes it home, and gets right to work, but finds that he is only able to cut down twenty-five trees.

Thinking that maybe he was just getting used to it, he's in the woods out back the next day as well, but once again doesn't come close to the promised fifty trees. The third day he gives it one more good, long try, but, alas, no better.

Upset, and feeling that he's been hoodwinked, he gets up the following morning, marches right back to the store with his disappointing purchase, and demands his money back. "You said this chain saw could cut down fifty trees a day, and even though I'm a big, strong guy and I worked from sunup to sundown, I couldn't ever cut down anywhere *near* that many," he announces angrily to the clerk, who goes and gets the store manager.

"Let's take a look," the manager says after hearing the farmer's complaint, and the farmer disgustedly hands the chain saw over to him. The manager pulls the cord to start up the chain saw's shrieking engine, at which point the farmer's eyes suddenly grow wide, and he asks, "What's *that* sound?"

Trying to parent effectively without practicing forgiveness is like trying to cut down trees with a chain saw that isn't turned on: it can be done, but it is unnecessarily wearing to do so and destined to be an arduous, joyless ordeal.

But the idea of forgiving a child may at first seem like a foreign concept. After all, isn't forgiveness something we are asked to extend to those who have hurt, betrayed, violated, or wronged us? Can we really think of a *child*, particularly a small child, as someone who is responsible for having injured us in these deep, enduring ways? How can it be necessary to learn to forgive your child, difficult as he may be to raise?

If you think of forgiveness as a healing act, however, the answer to these questions may seem much clearer, because forgiveness helps you to heal not only when there has been an injury, but also when there has been a loss. And what is often lost when we become parents is a sense of personal justice, a belief that there will be a healthy balance between what we feel compelled to give and what we feel entitled to receive.

All of us grow up with some internal sense of what is just in our relationships with others, a sense that the philosopher Immanuel Kant referred to as "the moral law within." The emotions that we experience are a reliable gauge of how balanced and fair we perceive our relationships to be. For example, we feel guilty when we believe we're getting more than we're giving, or angry when we believe we're giving more than we're getting.

In a balanced partnership between two people, there will be an ebb and flow between giving and getting that evens out over time, and creates a sense of relational balance. But when we feel we have consistently given more than we have received, a feeling of entitlement is born within us which motivates us to try to achieve justice by finding some sort of compensation that will redress the imbalance.

This search for compensation may be a constructive one. For example, over the last few weeks you've been feeling neglected and unloved by your spouse, and you arrange for a sitter so that the two of you can go out and have some time together. In discussing this in a pleasant, calm setting, your spouse has the opportunity to realize how much pressure there has been at work because of an all-consuming six-month project, and over dessert the two of you develop some ways to manage this pressure more successfully until the project has been completed.

You agree that each night, as of ten o'clock, you will both stop using the computer and the telephone and set aside the half-hour before bed to brew a pot of tea and play a game of Scrabble. You also decide that once the project has run its course, the two of you will go away for a weekend to the charming country inn that you read about in the paper last month. Your evening out has taken the edge off the tension, and you both return home feeling like balance has been restored.

Or, you are starting to feel taken advantage of by having to run your son over to the library for the fourth time this week so that he can come up with an appropriate science fair project. You decide to inform him that before he goes again, he needs to fold the two baskets of laundry that have been on the floor of your room since the weekend. Later that night you tell him that you're willing to transport him to his many activities, but only if he starts shouldering more responsibilities around the house. The two of you agree that you'll continue to provide transportation, but that in return he'll be in charge of folding laundry, and in addition he'll take over loading and unloading the dishwasher on Saturdays and Sundays. You wind up feeling proud of his growing sense of maturity, pleased, rather than annoyed, that he's taking his schoolwork so seriously. He winds up feeling a greater sense of self-respect as he discovers some concrete ways of contributing to the family enterprise and learns some important lessons about reciprocity.

Of course, the process of constructive entitlement does not have to take place only in the relationship that is feeling unbalanced. There are all kinds of ways to restore a feeling of justice. For instance, while your partner is going to be so immersed in work for the next six months, you might decide that you're going to pick up the e-mail correspondence with your favorite cousin that had been dropped the year before, or you finally sign up for the volleyball league that your best friend has been trying to drag you to. You successfully turn to other relationships so that your emotional needs can be met, rather than depending on one temporarily less available individual and then feeling resentful when these needs cannot be fulfilled.

Or instead of just dropping your son off and then returning home, obediently waiting for him to call you for the pickup, you take along your gym clothes and work out at the athletic club while he's at the library, even if it means he might have to wait a bit for you to get back there. The rides back and forth feel less burdensome because you're now using them for you as well as for him. In fact, you wind up appreciating the time in the car because you actually get to have a conversation with him without any distractions.

Sometimes, however, the search for justice when you feel a relational imbalance becomes a destructive one, one that winds up amplifying, rather than diminishing, the injustice that you are feeling. For example, instead of letting your spouse know that you're feeling unloved and neglected, you angrily retreat and staunchly avoid giving or receiving physical affection; this, of course, engenders less loving behavior and more of the neglect that helped spur the initial imbalance.

A cold war begins, and the marital ship lists treacherously as each of you strives in your own way to correct the balance by withdrawing more angrily and neglecting more vengefully. Your partner feels justified, rather than ambivalent, about focusing exclusively on work, since there's not much at home with you but tense silence, and you feel no choice but to distance yourself even further, and the chasm between the two of you quickly widens.

Or instead of letting your son know that you're tired of being his chauffeur without his taking some responsibility around the house, you blow up at him the next time he asks for a ride. Then you feel guilty about having lost your temper—after all, he's going to the library, not the mall, and it is schoolwork that he's doing, not hanging out. So you wind up apologizing for your loss of temper and drive him again anyway, without asking anything of him but his acceptance of your apology. Of course, this reinforces his belief that everything is fine, that there is no imbalance in your relationship with each other, that he's free to continue taking without giving. In fact, he concludes that the relational ledger book is now in his favor, because you were the one speaking and acting inappropriately. In other words, now you owe him!

Meanwhile, you drive him over once more, but inside you're still bedeviled by a feeling of being taken for granted. This expresses itself in the negativity with which you respond to the proposed science fair project that he eventually, and proudly, runs by you—"After five trips to the library, that's what you came up with?"—and you feel like the worst parent in the world as you watch his face fall. To stave off your guilt, you then offer to take him back to the library one more time, without his even asking, which keeps the cycle of resentment and imbalance alive.

As with constructive entitlement, the process of destructive entitlement does not have to take place in the relationship where you are feeling the imbalance. In fact, the entitlement that is often the most destructive is misdirected entitlement, born in one relationship and carried over into another.

You remember your own mother's self-absorption when you were growing up, her unwillingness to give up her card games and her phone calls and her luncheons to listen to you, to be with you. But you can't turn back the clock—your mother is no different today than she was thirty years ago, and with a host of medical problems she is even more self-absorbed than ever before—so you look to your spouse for the time and attention that you were deprived of decades before, and overreact when it's temporarily not there by dumping into the marital present all of the hurt from your personal past.

Or your father never appreciated how hard you worked at school and simply assumed that you would come home each quarter with sterling report cards, barely raising an eyebrow, rarely voicing his praise. So your own son, without his even knowing it, is somehow supposed to offer you the gratitude and commendations that you conscientiously earned but were never the recipient of long ago. And when he doesn't deign to come through, he winds up shouldering the blame that really belongs elsewhere.

If we are instinctively going to try to create relational balance one way or another, how can we make sure that we maintain this balance in appropriate and effective ways? The answer is: through pursuing forgiveness, a concept that has many different meanings for people. It's important in this context that forgiveness not be confused with any of the following: enabling, indulging, acquiescing, making excuses for inappropriate behavior, forgetting, pretending things are fine, passivity stemming from fear of a confrontation, capitulation, tolerating abuse, trusting without thinking, pitying, admitting defeat, or self-righteousness.

Forgiveness, to my way of thinking, is the process of releasing ourselves from the grip of our anger and disappointment in others so that constructive, rather than destructive, entitlement is the result. When we forgive, we do not minimize those other feelings; rather, we acknowledge them so that we can move forward into love and healing.

Embarking on the journey of parental forgiveness does not mean that we will never again be upset with our child. In fact, the most positive result of the forgiveness process may be our ability to express our hurt and anger more straightforwardly. Instead of repressing or misdirecting these feelings, we will reveal them in a way that helps to resolve conflicts and problems rather than exacerbating them.

Whenever we forgive, and in whatever way forgiveness is ultimately experienced, we become motivated to be more understanding and generous in our relationship with our offspring, and to repair whatever relational injustice we experience guided by our feelings of love and compassion rather than by our feelings of disappointment and anger.

As you probably already know, the parent-child relationship is a rich breeding ground for feelings of relational imbalance. This is partially due to the great sacrifices of time and energy that child-rearing requires, sacrifices that result in the understandable desire for a child who reflects well on us, who validates our chosen parenting style, who realizes our hopes and makes manifest our dreams. When our child has not agreed to fulfill this matrix of expectations, we are likely to experience a feeling of injustice. "How *dare* he be reading below grade level when I have read to him every day of his life from day one, and I can't remember *my* father reading me a single book?" or "I scrimp and save to buy a brand-new two-thousand-dollar computer system, and all she does is waste her time in chat rooms and download pictures of her favorite rock stars!"

But a relational imbalance with our children may also remain in place because of our inevitable tendency to take our quest for fairness and justice to them, and to insist that they redress imbalances that *did not* originate with them and may not even have anything to do with them.

In either case, whether these imbalances have their roots in the present or in the past, our attempts to secure emotional compensation from our children will be doomed to failure. Only through embarking on the journey of forgiveness can we truly come to see our children as good enough and respond empathically and helpfully when they don't give us what we insist that they should.

OUR UNSPOKEN EXPECTATIONS

The process of forgiveness can be accelerated by learning more about some of the ways that we expect our children to compensate us. And we can learn more about this expected compensation by examining some of the motivations, conscious and unconscious, behind our desire to have children. Each of the following unspoken expectations can subtly but powerfully affect our capacity to see our child as good enough.

1) Our Child Must Help Us Come to Terms with Our Parents

Becoming a parent is the most potent and profound way of announcing the end of our childhood and the commencement of our adulthood. As part of that process, it changes forever our relationship with our own parents, as we establish an identification with them that we have never had before.

That identification can express itself in different ways, however. Sometimes, for example, it manifests itself as a successful competition with our mother or father, a desire to see ourselves as better than, or at least as good as, our mother or father. Denise, for example, an expectant mother in one of my workshops, commented, "Now I can finally become my own woman. Now I get to raise a child the way a child is supposed to be raised, rather than inflicting on a child what my mother inflicted on me."

The challenges inherent in raising a particular child may, however, also leave us feeling less, rather than more, competent, as if we're on the losing end of our rivalry with our parents. Lamont disclosed these feelings during a session: "I'm talking to my son exactly the way my father talked to me. I'm telling myself I know better than to belittle him like I do, but the identical words just keep pouring out whenever I get another call from another teacher that he's not doing his work. He's making me into the same man my dad was." In Lamont's eyes, his son is depriving him of the triumphant transcendence that he has yearned to experience for so long, and he is enraged with his son for doing so.

Another way this identification with one's own parents can express itself is in experiencing gratitude and a wish to "give back" to our parents out of our feelings of indebtedness to them for having raised us. For instance, many new parents appear to be "offering" one of their children to the grandparents, as if the child were a gift or repayment on a loan.

"I make sure my mother sees my son every weekend," said Elise. "Come rain or shine, I'm over there with him, giving her a chance to enjoy him, because I know how important he is to her, and I know that she isn't going to live forever."

And that's great if everyone enjoys those weekends. But sometimes a grandchild isn't particularly agreeable to being the immensely pleasurable package that his parents are presenting as a gift to their parents, and confounds this supposedly satisfying transaction. When Ivan was 6 months old, for example, he appeared to stubbornly refuse to smile at his grandmother no matter how hard she tried to engage him. Now 4 years old, he cries and squirms when his grandmother tries to hug and kiss him and will not say thank you when she brings him a cookie or good-bye when she is leaving.

Ivan's father, Rod, then has to bear the brunt of his mother's disappointment—disappointment that he has not been unfamiliar with over the years. "All of my other grandchildren love it when I come over," Rod's mother admonishes him. "He could at least say thank you when I bring him something. He reminds me of you when you were that age."

Rod, of course, is mortified by his son's intransigence and by being reminded that he was similar—similarly awful, that is—at the same developmental stage. Feeling bad that he hadn't been a "good son," he angrily insists that Ivan "show some respect for" and "be more affectionate with" his grandmother, which of course results in even less cooperation on Ivan's part, since respect and affection cannot be mandated but instead can only emerge gradually and naturally. As long as Rod needs to have his son make up for what he himself couldn't do for his mother, Ivan will continue to be seen as a source of displeasure to everyone.

2) **Our Child Must Replace a Loved One**

One of the most natural ways to respond to a loss is to "find" something or someone to conceal, ease, or erase that loss. When the loss involves a loved one, creating a new beloved brings with it enormous healing potential.

In my work with adolescent parents, it is hard to ignore how frequently an "unplanned" pregnancy occurs within a short time after the loss of a significant person in the young father or mother's life. Sixteen-year-old Daryl, whose older brother died suddenly of complications related to diabetes a year before, and whose girlfriend was now six months pregnant, revealed this connection to me without even being aware of it: "I didn't think I would ever get over my brother's death. I was crying every night, it seemed. But with all that's been going on since my girlfriend got pregnant and all that has to get done, I haven't really been thinking about him all that much."

Daryl may or may not be able to summon the resourcefulness to become a good father in the coming years, but the pregnancy has "done the trick" and enabled him to release himself from the paralyzing grip of his grief for his brother.

However, no one person can ever truly replace another. Delia, whose first child, Darnell, died from the sequelae of a congenital heart ailment at the age of 10 months, became pregnant again six months later. Her insistent expectation that her secondborn, Maiesha, successfully measure up to her deceased firstborn would never be met. Every flaw, problem, and idiosyncrasy that Maiesha displayed was another mark against her, another declaration of her being second-best, and another stage in her predecessor's canonization.

"Darnell, he was really such a perfect baby. But Maiesha, now, she's another story. Darnell was sleeping through the night at three weeks of age—three weeks! Maiesha is almost two years old, and she's *still* up in the middle of the night—I want to throttle her sometimes! And Darnell, well, he was already beginning to talk. Even though he was only ten months old, he was saying Mama and Dada, while Maiesha doesn't even say a word, she just looks around and stares all the time."

Anticipating that Maiesha should somehow be an adequate replacement for Darnell was only leading Delia to feel more and more intolerant of and annoyed with her. For Maiesha to develop a positive self-concept, she will have to be forgiven for not matching up to the child she was expected to replace.

3) Our Child Must Enable Us to Relive Our Childhood

Nostalgia is one of the most compelling emotional vistas in our lives, and nostalgia for our real or imagined childhood is particularly fragrant and seductive. We all dream of the halcyon moments of our youth, moments when time appeared to stand still, when love and hope and joy were woven together in a wondrous braid.

Our desire to re-create, or to create for the first time, an idyllic childhood is one of the primary motivations for having children of our own. Through our child's birth, we seek to go back in time and become reborn ourselves. In connecting with our child, we hope to connect with our childhood and recapture its finest, most delectable flavors.

Devin remembers countless hours spent in the woods behind his home as a youth, trapping snakes, studying grasshoppers, scouring the banks of a muddy creek with his trusty net for new additions to his prized insect collection. Now a father, he would excitedly take his 5-year-old son, Mitch, out to the woods near their home, hoping to share his delight in nature as only a father and son could, but Mitch would get bored and distracted in no time and yearn to go home.

"Why would he rather stay inside and watch the same stupid Teletubbies tapes over and over again?" Devin asks me impatiently. "By the time it's the weekend, I'm so sick of having been cooped up in the office all week that all I want to do is get outside, but he doesn't seem to get with it. And if I insist, he just whines the whole time, so why bother?"

Sometimes it's the image of the childhood we *wished* we had had, rather than the one that we actually had, that beckons us, thereby creating difficulties between our child and ourself. As the little girl confides to a friend in a cartoon: "Sometimes having to have the happy childhood my parents never had is just too much responsibility."

Nancy grew up in a household that did not really believe that women and men should have equal academic and professional opportunities. In fact, money was put aside for her two older brothers to go to college but not for her. "I was told that secretarial school was good enough, and that my job was to marry someone who would support me well. There was no need to save thousands of dollars for *that*," she complained sarcastically. Her family's double standard didn't stop her, however. She went to college by paying for it herself and eventually earned a master's degree in library science.

Naturally, she made it clear from the beginning that her daughter, Christina, would find every possible door open to her. So it's a particularly bitter pill for her to swallow when she sees that Christina, now 13, couldn't care less about school and spends most of her evenings on the phone talking with her friends about the best place for a manicure and the cheapest tanning salon in town.

"I busted my tail in every class I had, from elementary school through graduate school, because I knew I'd have to excel to make it, and here she's got a mother who's behind her every step of the way, and all she cares about is how long she can grow her nails and how to repair them when they break."

Expecting her daughter to capitalize on all of the opportunities that she was not privileged to have when she was a young woman is making it hard for Nancy to see that Christina's preadolescent concerns are both typical and transient.

4) Our Child Must Erase Our Flaws and Failures

By the time we have become parents, we have usually had more than enough chances to experience disillusionment. The grand and seemingly invincible dreams of our childhood have been mugged by the realities of adulthood, and it no longer seems as if every wish can come true, as if every fantasy can be fulfilled, as if unlimited beauty, talent, power, and accomplishment are right at our fingertips if we just choose to reach for them.

For all of us, parenthood holds forth the promise of personal redemption, a resurrection of failing hopes and a reversal of the tide of setbacks that we seem to have so relentlessly suffered.

Sometimes the expectations for our children that emerge from such a universal desire are only too predictable—the never-quite-made-it-in-show-business mother who relentlessly drags her reluctant daughter to every audition she can find, the baseball star wannabe who forces his exhausted son to field two hundred grounders a day in his vicarious pursuit of the major leagues. Sometimes the expectations we foist on our children are less obvious, however.

Vince had been coming to see me with his wife, Julie, and his daughter, Sarah, to help them deal with the score of medical problems that Sarah had been afflicted with since birth. When Julie became pregnant with their second child, he confessed, "You know, Sarah has been a medical disaster from day one. She's already been operated on five times and she's not even four, and I know there's more to come. My wife and I have spent a lot of time feeling guilty about this, wondering what we did wrong that led to such problems. But I'll tell you, I'm excited about having another child because I know that this kid is going to be healthier than Sarah. The odds have just got to be in our favor."

Feeling like a failure for having created an unhealthy child the first time around, Vince is certain that his secondborn will compensate him for all the guilt, fear, and worry that his firstborn has forced him to experience, and finally enable him to feel like a more successful father. Should that turn out not to be the case, Vince is likely to become impatient and disenchanted with the child who inadvertently refuses to redeem his self-image.

Sometimes it is a flaw or defect within our family, rather than within ourselves, that we look to smooth away. Adrian consulted with me because of concerns about his 4-year-old son's "lagging" cognitive and physical development, even though neither the preschool teacher nor the pediatrician were noticing anything awry.

In hearing about the kind of father Adrian was, and watching him and his son interact, it was clear to me that he was overwhelming and overstimulating his son with a steady barrage of mental and physical activities. Every hour seemed to be structured and focused, devoted to flash cards or gymnastics or computer games or soccer practice.

While obtaining a family history, I learned that Adrian's younger brother had been mentally retarded and sent away to a group home at an early age, where he still remained. In discussing this with Adrian it became evident that his brother's handicapping condition was a source of great shame and guilt for both Adrian and his parents.

It occurred to me that Adrian may have been unable to recognize or adapt to his own child's needs because he was so assiduously trying to reassure himself, and perhaps his family as well, that he could create a son who wasn't retarded.

Demanding that his child be not only "normal" but "super" was one of the ways that Adrian was hoping he and his family could shed the legacy that they had felt as such a shameful burden for so many years, even if it meant pushing his son beyond the boy's mental and physical limits.

5) Our Child Must Heal Our Marriage

In an age of accessible birth control, deciding whether and when to have a child can be one of the most gripping dilemmas that a couple will encounter in their marriage. Many times that decision is affected by the status of the marriage itself.

Couples in a solid marriage may decide to have a child to further solidify their commitment to each other and make it feel more permanent. Couples in a shaky marriage may fantasize that parenthood will provide some much-needed stabilizing, and that the joys of parenthood will help them conquer the forces that have led to marital mayhem. Couples who appear to have successfully come through a difficult time may attempt to put the past behind them and begin defining a different future by starting or expanding a family.

The child born into this matrix may not have the same understanding of his responsibilities, however. In the case of Cliff and Deena, the first eight years of their marriage were characterized by tremendous turbulence, with both of them having affairs and abusing cocaine on a regular basis. With tremendous effort and courage they had finally emerged from this dark period with their relationship intact, and, after much debate, they decided to have a child together to celebrate their marital recovery.

Their 3-year-old girl, Missy, however, was not the darling daughter they felt they had earned. She was a real pistol—willful, high-strung, and pugnacious. Her relentless insistence on challenging authority threatened to throw Cliff and Deena's marriage right back over the fearsome precipice that had only recently ceased to threaten them.

"She's *destroying* us," Deena lamented in her first session with me. "Cliff and I can't agree on a single thing, and if we do agree, she pushes us until we're exhausted. I thought we'd already been through hell and barely made it back. Now it feels like we're going through it again. I don't think Cliff and I can handle this, not after all we've recovered from. If only we could give her back!"

Missy's almost alchemical transformation from desirable fantasy child to undesirable reality child has disrupted their hard-won equilibrium, and it is not yet clear if they will be able to forgive her for not upholding her end of a bargain she never made.

6) Our Child Must Decontaminate Us

All of us are aware that there are parts of ourselves that seem so scandalous or unsavory that we strive to disavow them because they make us uncomfortable. Deep down—or perhaps, to our great embarrassment, not so deep down—we really are the vain or selfish or vengeful or petty or critical individual that we struggle so valiantly not to be. We may try to deal with our discomfort by pretending these dark, indefensible facets of our personality do not in actuality exist, but in one form or another, they will always emerge.

Sometimes we resolve this problem by assigning these sinful qualities to somebody other than ourselves. For example, we choose a marriage partner who embodies the very qualities we detest so they are then symbolically discharged onto someone else and we are finally free of them. The result is that we wind up feeling cleansed and can then spend our energy lambasting our spouse rather than taking responsibility for acknowledging, incorporating, and modulating what it is about ourselves that we find so reprehensible.

The same process can occur when we have a child. It's as if we look to parenthood as an opportunity to pass on not only our positive genetic heritage—our good looks or our intelligence or our sensitivity—but also the traits that we'd prefer not to have to recognize and deal with. Our child, then, becomes a tiny caricature of the person we feel so dangerously close to becoming.

From as far back as she can remember, Kona had to take care of her alcoholic mother and her younger sister. Unable to tolerate the pain of constantly having her own childhood needs ignored, she buried whatever self-centeredness existed and aspired to sainthood instead.

Now a clinical social worker, she specializes in developing outreach programs for treating the mentally ill who inhabit homeless shelters, and two evenings a week she volunteers with members of her church to bring blankets and hot meals to street people.

But when she had her first child, she found herself unable to summon any empathy when her daughter howled with hunger, discomfort, or pain. "She's *insatiable*, she expects me to drop everything and show up at a moment's notice, and I think she's just manipulating me," Kona complained during our first session.

Women who drive around the city on cold winter nights with

blankets and tureens of hot soup clearly do not lack for compassion, so her intolerance of her daughter's distress could not be easily explained away by insensitivity.

What emerged in our work over time was the fact that her daughter's cries stirred in her the ancient longing for comfort and care that had never been fulfilled when she was a child. Rather than acknowledge the unspeakable pain of having had to relinquish this desire in the service of others, Kona preferred to pretend that she had never had these longings, and instead blamed her daughter for daring to have longings of her own. That way, she could continue to preserve the image of herself as selfless and virtuous without having to acknowledge any hypocrisy.

Forgiving both herself and her daughter for their very human neediness was the process that ultimately led her to being able to care for her daughter in a more beneficent way.

Now that we have a better idea about the meaning and importance of forgiveness and how it can transport us from the land of destructive to constructive entitlement, let's take a look at a couple of cases in which parental forgiveness resulted in a child's being transformed from disappointing to good enough.

Valerie called me feeling "completely baffled" by her 11-year-old son, Tony. "He's just not doing much of anything with his life, and I'm kind of wondering where he's headed. His grades are mediocre, even though he's very bright. He doesn't really stick with anything, and he's not really interested in any of the sports or musical activities most of his friends are doing."

"How does he spend his time?" I asked.

"Mostly avoiding homework, or at least doing as little as he can get away with without getting a detention or an E. He's not much for doing his chores, either, I might add. The only thing he *really* does is build model airplanes, and he talks about wanting to maybe learn how to fly one day. But that's going to be years off, and I don't feel comfortable with him dawdling his way through the rest of middle school on into high school. And if he wants to actually go on to the Air Force Academy or some place like that one day, he's going to need something besides C's on his report card."

In interacting with Tony, I was surprised by the discrepancy between what I saw and how his mother portrayed him. I had been expecting a passive, lethargic preadolescent who would sit slumped in his chair, expressionless, making barely intelligible comments (I've seen plenty of them over the years). Instead, I found myself talking with a handsome young man with a quick wit and a delightful manner.

"Your mom had mentioned to me over the phone that you're interested in flying. How long has that been the case?"

"Oh, as far back as I can remember. I used to dive-bomb the other kids in my nursery school. I don't think they liked that very much."

His father, Ruben, chuckled as he joined in the reminiscence: "I think I heard airplane noises coming from his room when he was still in the crib! And as soon as he could walk, he was pretend-flying all over the place, using his arms as wings and knocking stuff off all the furniture."

"Hey, Dad, remember the time I tried to fly off the top of my bunk bed and broke my wrist?"

Ruben laughed again. "He was only four years old, and the whole time he was in the emergency room he was busy telling the doctor and nurses about needing better "lift-off" next time. I couldn't believe he was using that word.".

This humorous interchange between father and son continued for another few minutes, during which I couldn't help noticing Valerie's tight-lipped, wintry smile.

"Valerie, what do you remember about Tony's interest in flight?" I asked.

"I know that was always his thing. I'm just concerned because that seems to be his only thing. He's not very well rounded if all he does is think about airplanes all the time. His room is like an airplane museum, filled from top to bottom with models and flying magazines and posters. What about playing sports? What about picking up his grades? What about learning how to play an instrument and joining the band at school? He can't spend every minute of his life on airplanes."

"Ruben, do you share your wife's concerns about Tony?"

"Sort of. I sure would like to see him get something above a C on his report card. He doesn't seem to put much time or effort into school, and it shows in his grades. But I don't think he should have to play a sport or an instrument if he doesn't want to."

"But that's the problem, Ruben. We never push him to do anything else, and you never back me up on anything, so it always comes back to airplanes, airplanes, airplanes."

"That's not true, dear," Ruben protested. "We had him start piano lessons a few years ago, but he just didn't take to it. And he played baseball in third grade and fourth, but he didn't seem to enjoy it, so we let him quit."

"The idea of standing around in the heat waiting for someone to hit a ball for me to chase wasn't my idea of a good time," Tony commented wryly. "And as for the piano, my teacher didn't teach me what I wanted to play."

"What did you want to play?" I asked.

"Anything written by someone who's not dead," was his droll reply.

"Honey, we could've done that, but the teacher said you had to learn your basics first."

"By the time I was done with 'basics' I would've been dead myself."

"This is pointless," Valerie snapped, directing herself back to me. "He's got to do something besides dream about flying."

"Why?" I asked, a question that seemed to shock her.

"Why? Because you can't go through life putting all of your eggs in one basket, that's why. What if he doesn't get to be a pilot? What if he doesn't make it to the Air Force Academy? What if his vision goes bad? Then what? There's nothing else that he'll have thought of doing, nothing else he'll be prepared for."

"What do you think, Ruben?" I asked.

"I don't know. Like I said, I'd feel better if he was doing better at school, but I'm not convinced that there's much wrong with his being so single-minded right now. Flying's what he likes. Nothing else seems to appeal to him. He's only eleven—it's not like he's leaving home tomorrow."

"You say he's only eleven, but that's what you always say. 'He's only eleven,' or 'He's only ten,' or 'He's only nine.' Soon you'll be saying 'He's only eighteen' and he'll have graduated from high school with no real plans and no real future," was Valerie's counter-argument.

"At least then I won't have to explain why I don't play baseball or the piano, anymore," Tony said, with the first hint of anger that I had heard from him. Despite his good-naturedness, his mother's vigilance was apparently taking a toll on him.

Because Valerie seemed to be more upset about Tony than Ruben was, I began by exploring some of the expectations she brought to parenthood. In asking about her family of origin, I learned that she had one sibling, a brother two years younger named Clark, whom she perceived as her mother's favorite.

"Clark could do no wrong, and my mother just spoiled the hell out of him. Nothing was too good for Clark. He was always the golden boy, and I always felt like I was superfluous, the older sister who existed simply to cater to my younger brother."

"How were you expected to cater to him?"

"Believe it or not, I was appointed to be his cook! I mean it. By the time I learned how to handle things on my own in the kitchen, when I was just starting high school, my mom would give me recipes to make that Clark liked, and I would go ahead and make them! She never asked me what I liked—she just made sure that he had what *he* wanted."

"What was that like for you?" I asked.

"Sometimes it was okay. I mean, for one thing, I did like to cook, and still do. And in general, I wasn't the kind of kid who wanted to be in the spotlight, anyway. But there were times when I got a little resentful. For example, Clark was a terrific pianist, and the whole extended family would come to his recitals. They'd be a really big deal, and then there'd be a big party afterward, and I'd feel invisible. And he was a very good runner, and my parents made a shrine in the den with all of his ribbons and medals and all the articles that were written about him."

"Were your interests supported?"

"Sort of, but not in the same way. I remember when I was around twelve, I was in the choir at our church, and one Sunday we were going to be in a concert at a big cathedral downtown.

And I was hoping that everyone would come for that, just like they did for Clark's recitals, but it turned out to be only my parents. Clark didn't have to come, I can't remember why. My parents were proud of me, I know that, but I still remember wondering why there wasn't much fuss being made of it. And afterward we just went home. We didn't go out to dinner, or anything like that, like we'd always do after one of Clark's performances."

When there is more than one child in a family, there will always be times when one child is preferred by one or both parents over the others. This usually has to do with the stage of life the child is in, what interests or activities he pursues, what personality he displays, and how well all of these mesh or clash with his parents'. In a healthy family, these periods of preference will even out over time, and children will be able to experience what it's like to feel special and unique, as well as learn to tolerate life when they're not the center of attention.

When one child is given ongoing preferential treatment over his siblings, however, it's often because the preferred child is basking in the glow of someone important from a parent's past. The preferred child comes to embody nothing but positive qualities or attributes, and the remaining siblings feel irrelevant, neglected, and resentful.

This seemed to be the case in Valerie's childhood. The phrases she used to describe him—"could do no wrong," "my mother just spoiled the hell out of him," "nothing was too good for Clark," and "the golden boy"—all suggested that her younger brother had been anointed king from the moment he was born, and from that point on, her role was to faithfully devote herself to his service.

I inquired as to the circumstances of Clark's birth, and learned that it occurred at an exquisitely painful time in the family's life. Valerie told me that Clark had been conceived about a year after her maternal grandfather had died. She also said that while she didn't know it at the time, she had learned much later on that her mother had had a miscarriage a couple of months before becoming pregnant with Clark.

So Clark had arrived on the scene shortly after two profound losses had occurred, setting the stage for his coronation. Valerie told me that her grandfather, whom she remembered faintly, had been the family patriarch and still held a place of honor in the extended family's heart. Valerie's mother had also told her that she had had a very difficult time after the miscarriage and spent days in bed crying, something that Valerie did not actually remember but surely had to have been affected by.

While Valerie found it useful to learn more about why Clark had become the favorite, she still wasn't able to make the connection between the recollections of her brother and her frustration with her son.

"Why are you so interested in Clark, anyway?" she eventually asked, with a mixture of curiosity and annoyance.

"Because I'm thinking your relationship with him might have something to do with your relationship with Tony."

"How could that be?"

"I'm wondering if perhaps your becoming a mother, and having a son of your own, might have been seen by you as an opportunity to raise yourself from servant to queen in your family's eyes."

"I never thought of that," Valerie mused, "although now that you mention it, the nicest thing about my pregnancy was that it brought my mom and me closer together. It was as if we finally had something to share, something in common, and she really was a big help and a big support. There was actually a point early on when I was spotting, and I called her in tears because I knew she had miscarried, and she came right over and went with me to the doctor's. Obviously, it turned out to be nothing, but I felt very special in her eyes all of a sudden."

"How about after Tony was born?"

Valerie took a moment to gather her thoughts. "I think there was kind of a drop-off, then. She was very helpful during the first few weeks, but I have to say she never really fussed over Tony all that much. Even now, she's very kind and warm with him, she buys him birthday presents and Christmas presents, but . . ."

"But what?"

Valerie's eyes filled up with tears. "But it's not how she treats Clark. I mean, he doesn't even have kids, he never married, but she and my dad will still go out of their way to see him. It's the same story. Like when it was Grandparents Day in Tony's kindergarten, my in-laws, who live more than an hour away, came in for it, but my parents, who live only a few miles from the school, couldn't make it because that was the same day Clark was moving to a new house, and they wanted to help him out. They could have taken a couple of hours off to go to Tony's school, but no, they had promised Clark they were going to help him, and that's just what they did. They're still at his beck and call."

"Were you hoping that would change once you gave them a grandchild?"

"Yes. And it seemed like it did during pregnancy. But Tony just doesn't interest them in the way Clark does."

What I was thinking was that Valerie was having such a difficult time appreciating Tony's strengths and seeing him in a positive light because she was so angry at him for not having been the kind of child who would finally wrest her parents' attention away from her brother. This seemed to have happened briefly, during pregnancy, but then things went back to the old status quo, and Clark once again reclaimed the crown.

Tony didn't excel at music, as Clark had, and he wasn't interested in sports, as Clark was. What he was fascinated by—flying—was, unfortunately for Valerie, something that had very little positive valence for her parents. She couldn't help but feel resentful that a golden opportunity to finally match her brother in importance had been lost because her son refused to follow in his uncle's regal footsteps.

Tony's dad was less troubled by Tony's single-mindedness and lack of commitment to school, sports, and music not because he was a better parent but because he had been pretty much the same when he was growing up, and because it appeared that he wasn't entering parenthood expecting his child to redress an injustice from his childhood.

"What were you like when you were eleven?" I asked Ruben.

He laughed. "Not all that different from Tony. I was a gearhead. All I wanted was to look at cars, read about cars, work on cars. If I could somehow get my head inside somebody's engine, I was happy."

"How did you do in school?"

"Lousy! I got through it the best I could, and as soon as I was eligible I transferred over to the vo-tech program the city had, and I was in hog heaven. I graduated in the top of my class, and the garage where I had started working part-time paid for me to get some additional training, and before I knew it I was rolling. I've got two garages of my own right now, and a towing service, too. I believe I make more money than just about every one of my customers, even the ones with the fancy suits and the Lexuses."

"What did your parents think of the choices you made?"

"I think they're pretty pleased. I mean, they knew I wasn't happy in school, and they saw how happy I was under the hood of a car. We grew up pretty poor, and I've got more money now than they ever dreamed of having."

Ruben couldn't get all that worked up about Tony's mediocre grades and lack of "well-roundedness" because it basically mimicked his own life and because his own life had turned out to be pretty satisfying, in both his and his parents' eyes.

It was time to get back to Valerie and see if we could help pry Tony loose from the grip of her belief that he needed to equal or surpass his uncle for him to be a good enough son.

"I think it's time to forgive Tony," I began.

"Forgive him? For what?"

"Forgive him for not having elevated you to your brother's stature in your family's hierarchy."

"I don't expect that of him. I just want him to do something with his life."

"He's going to do something with his life. He's already doing something with his life. But you're not able to see it because you're still too angry with him for not having been the child that Clark was."

"What is he doing? Getting C's and avoiding reading anything besides flying magazines?"

"He's doing exactly what he should be doing, which is to cultivate his passion. His passion is flying. That's where his heart is. That's where he feels at home, where he feels most complete, most soulful. And you need to be able to see this, and rejoice in it, because that's where his beauty is shining most brilliantly."

"Don't you think he's just looking to get out of doing anything else?"

"No, I don't. I'm sure he's not crazy about school, but I think that, right now, everything else in his life is eclipsed by his great passion for flying. If you can find ways to enhance and support this interest, he'll develop other passions, and other skills and responsibilities as well. If you *don't*, he'll always feel as if he's disappointed you, and that will diminish his capacity to derive joy from pursuing his passion, whatever it is."

"So how can I learn to appreciate him?"

"By forgiving him."

"And how do I forgive him?"

"There are lots of ways. You might want to start by writing or saying something in your head about forgiving him, something that gives you a chance to reflect upon the very notion of relinquishing your fantasy of who he should have been."

"What could I write or say?"

"You might write simply, 'Tony, I forgive you for not being the son that I thought I would have.' Or, 'I forgive you, Tony, for not being the son that made me the equal of my brother in my parents' eyes.'"

"Do you think that can help?"

"I think it's worth a try."

Valerie came back for our next session sounding much more positive. "I actually took a pad of paper and just wrote the words 'I forgive you, Tony,' and sort of sat with it for a while to see what would come up. And then I just started writing all kinds of things. At first I wrote that I forgave him for some of the stuff that you and I had talked about last time, for not being the pianist that Clark had been, for not being athletic. But then I started writing about forgiving my mother for favoring Clark, and forgiving Clark for being the favorite, when it really wasn't his doing that he was born when he was born, after the miscarriage and after my grandfather had died.

"And it's like something got freed up for me. I started realizing that Clark, for all of his being the favorite, doesn't really have what I have. I mean, he's done well professionally, but he had a really bad marriage that seemed to go on forever, and now he lives alone and dates here and there, but he isn't close to having the kind of family that I have with Ruben and Tony. And I thought, 'Why should I be expecting Tony to live up to him? What turned out so great about him being the favorite?' "

"How has this led you to feel about Tony?"

"A lot better. I did this writing right after dinner, and then I went into his room to say good night, and I realized it had been months, if not years, since I had really looked at some of the models he has been building. And I asked him to show them to me, and he was so pleased, and so eager, it was the closest I'd felt to him in a long time. I saw how incredibly intricate some of what he's working on has been, and I couldn't believe that I've missed how wonderful this is, because I'm always so busy wondering about his grades or questioning why he won't pursue sports and music."

The idea of forgiving her son for turning out differently from what she had imagined and moving from destructive to constructive entitlement was a liberating one for Valerie and changed the way in which she saw and treated him. Once she got past her resentment and anger, she was better able to join with him in his passion and spur him on to a deeper involvement.

At what turned out to be our final session, Valerie said, "I was talking with this friend of mine at work who's involved with the Civil Air Patrol, and apparently they have a program for preteens who are interested in flying. And I asked Tony if he wanted to do it, and he jumped at it, so he's going to be starting that next month. It'll be on Sundays, and he's just so excited, they take them up in planes, and everything. What's interesting is that to qualify for the program, you have to maintain a C average in school, and I told Tony that, and he smiled and said, 'Oh, I can do that.' And I realized he had just been kind of idling, waiting for some reason to get into gear."

About six months later Valerie called to tell me that Tony had been doing a little better at school and was loving the Civil Air Patrol program. She also said that she had continued feeling much better about who he was and what he had chosen to pursue. She was much less concerned about his future and his single-mindedness, and as it turned out, her forgiving him had literally enabled him to soar.

Sam and Tovah called me about their 8-year-old daughter, Doralina. Her yearly medical checkup revealed that her weight was once again off the charts, as it had been when she was a year old, and now her cholesterol was inching up as well.

"We've really lost control of this situation, and her health is going to be endangered if we don't do something soon," Sam said.

"We adopted Doralina from Mexico," Tovah added, "and she was chubby from the day we first saw her in the orphanage, when she was just eight months old. We kept hoping or assuming that she would grow out of it, but she really hasn't. Some years she gains more than others, but overall she's always above the ninety-ninth percentile. Now that her cholesterol is high, too, we're really getting scared."

Since this had been a longtime problem, I invited them to tell me how they'd been trying to deal with it up until now.

Tovah responded, "Our pediatrician has been no help at all. All he's done is refer us to a pediatric endocrinologist, and she didn't have anything to offer, either—that is, after charging us $250 for blood tests that concluded that her metabolism was fine."

"Whenever we try to get her to cut back on what she eats, she finds a way around it," Sam continued. "We try to give her moderate portions at mealtime and not let her have seconds, but then we find her sneaking food from the kitchen between meals when we're not looking.

"I pack her lunch each day for school so that she's got good stuff in there and appropriate serving sizes, but her teachers have said that she's a real scrounge in the cafeteria, always trying to bum leftovers and extra treats from her classmates. And the other day, when I happened to be in her closet because she couldn't find her shoes and I was helping her look, I found a whole stash of food hidden away in the back—a big bag of chips that we'd been missing, some candy bars, a couple of soda cans, even some stale bagels. I was really upset when I saw that."

"It's as if the harder we try, the more clever and insistent she gets," Tovah said with frustration. "We had told her to stay away from that bag of chips and even put it on a high shelf so she wouldn't see it and be tempted, but somehow she got it anyway. The soda cans were probably from the basement, where we keep drinks left over from parties. I don't even know how she found them—I'd forgotten we had them. I guess the candy bars were from kids at school. But it's ridiculous—we can't put a leash on her or chain her in her room when she's in the house, and even if we could, she plays at other kids' houses a lot, and gets invited to birthdays and sleepovers, so we don't have any control over what she eats when she's somewhere else."

"In what ways have you spoken to her about your concerns regarding her weight?" I asked.

"I tell her that I love her very much, but that she needs to watch what she eats because we want her to have a long, healthy life," Tovah replied. "She gets teased about being fat, although I must say she generally handles it pretty well. But a couple of times she's come home crying, and I've told her that if she doesn't want to be teased anymore, she'll have to control her eating better. And I'll notice some changes for a day or two, but then she's back to wanting more and more to eat, and finding ways to get it."

Sam added, "Sometimes I'll make a suggestion, like when she's smearing a ton of cream cheese on her bagel, I'll say, 'You know, Doralina, it would probably taste just as good with *half* that amount.' Or when she's just dumping the dressing onto her salad, I'll encourage her to use a little less. But she'll just glare at me and continue doing what she's doing. In fact, it seems like she'll put even more on, just to spite me. She simply won't accept any of our advice, and meanwhile she's getting heavier and heavier and heavier."

It was clear that the more Sam and Tovah tried to exert control over Doralina's eating, the more she rebelled against that control and ate in a way that was worsening the very problem they were concerned about. But why had food become such an issue, I wondered.

"How about exercise? Does she get out much and move around?" I inquired.

"Amazingly enough, she's really quite active, though you wouldn't know it to look at her," Sam said. "She's not a star athlete or anything, but she's not one of those lazy fat kids, either. She loves to be outside, riding her bike, running around with the other kids in the neighborhood. I'm a big bike rider myself, and sometimes we go out together, and she really hangs in there. The only team sport she's taken to so far is basketball. We signed her up for a league this past winter, and while she was definitely the slowest kid on the court, she caught on to the game. She really seemed into it and got along with the other kids pretty well."

I then brought Doralina into the room and spoke with her for a time. Dark-haired and bright-eyed, she conversed easily as we discussed her home, school, and social life. When we got to the issue of her relationships with friends, she did comment that she gets "made fun of" by the other kids for being overweight.

"Do you let that get to you?" I asked.

"Usually not," she said with conviction, but then her face grew sad. "But I wish I didn't have to hear some of the nicknames sometimes—you know, 'Dumpy Doralina' or 'There goes the Pillsbury Doughgirl.' "

"If you could change anything about your physical appearance, what would it be?"

"I guess I'd like to be thinner."

"How much thinner?"

"Thin enough that I wouldn't be teased so much," she replied with a slight smile.

I asked her if she knew her cholesterol level was high, and while she was aware of this, it was clear she didn't understand the ramifications. Once I explained to her how high cholesterol might affect her as she got older, she responded, "So I guess that's another reason I've got to eat right, huh? But I love to eat so much!"

"I think it's great that you enjoy food, Doralina," I answered, "and I want you to always have that pleasure. But maybe we can work on some ways that you can really enjoy your food and still eat in a way that's good for your body."

"I'd like that," she said eagerly.

Whenever you can help children feel that a goal is actually *their* goal, you're more likely to have an active participant in any plan intended to meet that goal. Feeling convinced that Doralina herself, not just her parents, had some investment in her eating more sensibly, I asked her to leave and brought Sam and Tovah back in the room to develop a new approach.

"Your first step, I believe, should be putting Doralina back in charge of her food," I proposed. "It seems that the more you try to stay on top of her eating, the more anxious she gets that she won't have enough to satisfy herself. Some of this may be residual behavior from her first year of life in the orphanage, when her individual nutritional and emotional needs probably couldn't be fully attended to."

"You mean let her decide how much she's going to eat?" Tovah asked incredulously. "She'll be up at the two-hundredth percentile by next year! I think the only reason she's where she's at now and not completely obese is because we really monitor her."

"I'm not sure," I responded. "We also have to consider the possibility that when she knows she'll be able to have as much as she wants, she'll gradually moderate her intake. The danger here is not only her weight and her cholesterol level, but also her risk for developing a serious eating disorder, and she's already displaying the initial signs of doing so. In the long run, she's much better off at a moderate to high weight but with a healthy body image and good eating habits than being thin and suffering with anorexia or bulimia and their attendant nutritional problems. Those disorders are much more perilous and life-threatening for a child or adolescent than having above-average weight or borderline-high cholesterol."

Sam was skeptical as well. "Let me get this straight. You're saying to let her eat whatever she wants, whenever she wants? I agree with Tovah—she'll eat herself sick in no time."

Realizing I needed to clarify, I added, "I'm not saying she should eat whatever and whenever she wants. When I say that I want you to put Doralina back in charge of her food, I mean that the two of you continue to decide what she eats and when she eats, but she gets to determine how much she eats."

"I can't believe this is going to work," Tovah said acidly, shaking her head. "She's already showing us she can't control herself. It's up to us to teach her how to eat the right way. I was a little heavier than I wanted to be when I was growing up, and I learned that I really have to control what I eat and exercise regularly if I'm going to stay slim."

"It is up to you to teach her the right way to eat," I agreed, "but you wouldn't be here unless the ways in which you have already tried to do so weren't working so well."

"Let's just hear what he has in mind," Sam urged his wife, looking at me with not a little of the same annoyance his wife had displayed.

"I'd like you to designate eating times to be whatever works for the family. For most families, it's three meals, and a couple of snacks, one after school, and maybe one before bed. At mealtime, she's to decide how much goes on her plate, and she's allowed to have seconds as well, but only if she waits *ten minutes* after finishing her first plateful—you can set a kitchen timer if necessary. That will give her enough time to know if she's truly hungry or wants to eat for other reasons. She can decide on the amount for seconds, too, but she's to be told that that will be all for that meal.

"At snack time, she should be given some freedom as well, except that there are no seconds. And you should encourage her to have healthy snacks, like fresh or dried fruit, or low-fat granola bars, because these have some nutritive value. But you should also have some regular junk-food treats available for her as well from time to time, because if you don't, that'll jack up her cravings for these and spur her to search them out in school and at friends' houses, and begin bingeing on them when she finds them. You should make sure that it's stuff like sorbet or light ice cream, however, or snack packs of low-fat cookies, since these are already portion-controlled."

"But I still think that if we leave the amount she eats entirely up to her, she'll gorge herself until she gets sick," Tovah said emphatically.

"It's certainly possible that she will. This will be new for her, and she may experiment with eating too much at first. But I believe that over time she'll gradually develop the ability to recognize when she's had enough, and if she trusts that she's always allowed to have more, she'll eventually learn to have less."

"I guess we'll give it a try," Sam said, "but I have to say that I'm not very hopeful either."

"I'm not asking you to be hopeful," I replied. "I'm just asking you to try something different. If it doesn't work, we'll try something else. In the meantime, observe Doralina's behavior as you implement the plan and let me know what you notice."

Sam and Tovah returned two weeks later, not very pleased with the results. "It went exactly as I thought it would," Tovah began. "We laid out the plan for her, and she was actually very excited about it. But the very first dinner she loaded her plate up with food, it was an obscene amount, and she was so happy, and Sam and I just looked at each other. I mean, how can we sit there and support her eating that amount of food when she's already so overweight?"

Sam added, "And then, as soon as she was done, she wanted seconds, and I had to say, 'Honey, don't you think that was *enough?*' but she just glared at me and said, 'You said I could have seconds,' and off she went for another plateful. If we had cooked a second chicken, I'm afraid she would still be eating."

"How'd the rest of the meals go after that first one?" I asked, with the funny feeling that I knew what the answer was going to be.

"Pretty much the same," Tovah said. "I mean, at breakfast the next day, she wanted a second bowl of cereal, and she never asks for a second bowl of cereal. The only reason she did so was because she knew we were trying this plan. I don't think she even wanted it, but she went up and got it."

"How did you handle that one?" I asked.

"That's kind of where I put my foot down, and then we had a big fight, with me saying, 'No more seconds!' and her saying, 'But you promised!' I hope you've got some other ideas up your sleeve, because this one sure didn't work."

I agreed that it hadn't worked, but mostly because nobody had given it a chance to work. It sounded like it had taken exactly two meals for my recommendations to be ditched, and even during those two meals, they hadn't followed through in the way I had asked them to. For one thing, they hadn't asked that she wait a full ten minutes before having seconds at dinner and breakfast, which probably would've slowed her down both times.

I was also becoming increasingly aware of how angry Sam and Tovah appeared to be. They spoke angrily about Doralina, they spoke angrily to me, they had spoken angrily about the ineffective medical care they had received. To really get somewhere with this family, I was going to have to back up and find out more about their anger and where it came from.

"How did the two of you make the decision to adopt a child?" I began.

"We tried for many years to conceive," Sam responded, "but we just couldn't. And then we finally did conceive, but Tovah miscarried, and this happened two more times. By then, we were both past forty, and it was enough already."

"I'm still upset because I feel that we were misdiagnosed for a long time," Tovah interjected. "It turns out that I had endometriosis that was never picked up on by my gynecologist, so we really wasted a lot of time. We thought about suing, but eventually decided it was time to move on."

"How do you feel about your decision?"

Sam said, "To be honest, I don't see Doralina as an adoptee, I see her as our daughter. People are always saying to us, 'Oh, she's so lucky that the two of you rescued her from the orphanage and gave her a real chance,' but, really, I think that *we're* the lucky ones, not her."

Tovah nodded in agreement. "You know, I don't even look back anymore to all those years we spent meeting with doctors, going to fertility clinics, grasping at straws trying to get pregnant and stay pregnant. Three miscarriages is a nightmare, let alone all the time and effort it took to conceive in the first place. It's like it's in the distant, distant past for me. In some ways, I do kind of wish we had made the decision to adopt earlier, sometime before we were in our forties, so that we could've had a better opportunity to adopt a second or third child as well. It would've been nice for Doralina to have a brother or sister."

"Have you ever thought that if you had been able to have a child by birth, he or she might not have had the problem with weight that Doralina has?"

That question was the first one I had asked that seemed to stop them in their tracks. There was a long, uneasy pause as they both looked at each other, almost as if they were hesitant to answer and daring the other to go first.

"Yes," Tovah eventually said, emotionally. "I don't regret having her for a second, but there have been times when I've looked at her, seen her naked in the bathtub or how she looks in a bathing suit, and I'm just filled with disgust. I hate myself for it. I wish I didn't feel that way, but it's there, and I know it's there. After all, look at Sam and me—neither one of us is overweight. If we'd had a daughter by birth, it's unlikely that she would have been as heavy as Doralina."

Sam was watching Tovah attentively as she spoke. Then, seeming to have finally been given permission to share his own discomfitting thoughts, he chimed in. "It's occurred to me, too. And I guess some part of me blames her for not looking like the child we would have produced. I've had dreams in which I'm watching Doralina eat and eat, and I just scream at her, '*Stop* it already—you're a fat pig!'—things I would never say out loud to her in a million years."

When Sam and Tovah finally had the courage to reveal these private and forbidden thoughts, it was as if a valve had been turned that suddenly released all the tension in the room. They both loosened up measurably, and I could feel myself begin to relax with them for the first time since we had met.

"You may be unaware of it, but your belief that you wouldn't have this problem if you had had a child by birth may be coming across to Doralina," I said carefully.

"How? We haven't even shared it with each other until now, let alone with her," Sam replied with disbelief.

"It may not come out directly, and I know you would never want to say it in a hurtful or inappropriate way, but it could be expressing itself in your efforts to control her eating and force her into being and acting and looking like someone she's not," I said.

"You mean we're kind of letting her know that we don't accept her for who she is by trying to control what she eats?" Tovah asked.

"That's along the lines of what I was thinking," I said.

"But how can we sanction her overeating when we see how unhealthy it is and how much pain she's in?" Tovah inquired.

"I'm not saying that you should sanction her overeating. The plan I'm proposing is designed to empower Doralina so she feels confident that she'll get what she needs, which will make her less, rather than more, likely to overeat."

Sam jumped in: "But what if you're right? What if we are mishandling Doralina because we secretly wish we had had a child by birth? We can't make those feelings disappear."

"You can't—and what you said earlier is absolutely true: she's not just blessed to have the two of you, but the two of you are blessed to have her. But it doesn't mean that there's still not some old pain from the infertility and miscarriages the two of you had to endure. And that pain may poke through the surface when Doralina reminds you, in the way she looks and the way she eats, of the child that you didn't get to have through no fault of hers or your own."

"So what do we do now?" Tovah asked.

"I think it's time to forgive yourselves and Doralina."

"For what?" they both said, almost simultaneously.

"I think you need to forgive yourselves and each other for not having been able to have a child by birth. And I think you need to forgive Doralina for not being the fantasy child you strove so hard to conceive but were unable to bring forth into this world."

"And how do we do that?" Sam asked, as he moved his chair closer to Tovah's and laid his hand on hers. I could see that the process of forgiveness was already taking place.

"People forgive in different ways. One thing that's often helpful in facilitating forgiveness, however, is creating a ritual that helps us to relinquish the feelings of hurt and anger we're still imprisoned by, so we're freer to move forward."

"Got any ideas?" Sam queried.

"You might start by finding something that symbolizes or captures the valiant efforts you made to have a child by birth, and then do something with it that finally puts those efforts to rest."

After bouncing some ideas around between the two of them, Tovah came up with a suggestion: "I still have a picture from the sonogram I had when I was pregnant for the last time, because that miscarriage didn't occur until late in the first trimester—the other two were in the first couple of weeks. I've kept it in a drawer in my night table, in a little envelope, and I know it's always there because that's where I put my watch and keys at the end of the day."

"I'm sure that that photograph has great meaning for the two of you," I said, "and I'd like you to think of some ritual involving that picture that would help the two of you to acknowledge your having become parents in a different way than you thought you might, by raising a different child than you thought you would have."

Tovah and Sam returned a week later and filled me in on what they had done. "I think this was the hardest thing I've ever done in some ways, harder even than dealing with the infertility," Tovah began, "but we decided to have a little ceremony, just Sam and me. I took the photograph from the sonogram and put it in a box, and we went out back and buried the box, right near where our old cat and Doralina's gerbil are buried." She began tearing up as she spoke.

"And Sam and I each said good-bye, both to that baby and to all of our wishes for a full pregnancy and a birth child. And then I got a new envelope, and I put a picture of Doralina in it, and I put the first tooth that she lost in there, too, and I put that in my night table drawer instead. And it just feels more right to have her picture there, close to me at night, rather than the picture of a baby who we'll never know or care for."

"How did it feel for you, Sam?" I asked, touched deeply by their great grief and courage.

"I didn't realize how hard it would be to let go, but I think it was necessary. Part of me, I know, was still somehow believing that we might have a 'real child' someday, even though Doralina is very real, and we've gotten very old, at least in the childbearing sense. But I guess I had underestimated how much we've both held on to our old dreams, and how maybe that's been making it hard for me to treat Doralina in the way she deserves to be treated."

Having begun to dissolve the sludge of anger that had impeded their capacity to more effectively address Doralina's difficulties, they went back to trying out the plan I had proposed initially. This time it turned out to be much more successful.

"You were right," Sam reported to me in a follow-up visit. "Doralina really took advantage of things at first, and we had to sit on our hands as she loaded her plate with these very hefty portions. But we stuck with the ten-minutes-before-seconds rule, and that actually made a big difference, because she's too restless to just hang around talking to us, so she usually just asks to excuse herself and doesn't even get seconds anymore.

"And I've made sure she has some cool treats in her lunch, but ones that don't have too much fat, like fruit rollups, stuff like that. Her teacher says she's been less grabby at lunchtime, too."

"Plus, I was really shocked," Tovah said, "when one night she didn't even want her snack before bedtime—she said she'd had enough at dinner! I think it was the first time she's ever turned down an opportunity to eat. I've checked her closet a few times on the sly, and I haven't seen any food or wrappers back there, either, so I don't think she's hoarding anymore."

When the family returned a month later, Doralina proudly informed me that she had gained only one pound since her last checkup two months before, less than the two-pounds-a-month increase that they had been used to seeing, and her cholesterol had dropped a little as well. "And when I got on the bus yesterday, this kid said, 'Make way for fatty,' but I didn't even say anything back to him because I knew I was starting to eat right." Sam and Tovah positively beamed with pride as she related her anecdote.

Doralina and her parents met with me a few more times to fine-tune her new eating plan, but clearly they were already moving in the right direction. Over the next six months, as Doralina grew in height her weight gain continued to slow, and she began to look a little less chubby. Her cholesterol continued to drop as well, to a level that her pediatrician considered more acceptable.

About a year after I had finished working with them, Tovah

sent me a letter, telling me that she had had a business meeting in California and Sam and Doralina had tagged along to sightsee. At the conclusion of their trip they decided to rent a car and drive down to the village where Doralina had been born, the first time they had all been back there since they had met almost a decade before. I was particularly moved by the following paragraph:

> What struck me was how many of the women in this village seemed to have the same body shape that Doralina has. They weren't obese, but *none* of them were thin. They were all very round and soft, and I realized, seeing all of these women, that her body is part of her heritage, too. We are her "real" parents, but she also has birth parents, and they will always be a part of her and express themselves through her as well, even if they never rear her or get to know how special she is.

The experience of learning more about Doralina's lineage helped to deepen Sam and Tovah's forgiveness and acceptance of their daughter and allow her to be the daughter of all four of her parents, rather than just two.

EXERCISE FIVE

Forgiving is ultimately an experience that is completed internally, with or without the knowledge or participation of the individual we are trying to forgive. Try having someone you trust read the following guided-imagery exercise or make a tape recording of it yourself using the appropriate gender for your child. Then take a few moments to observe how you feel after you've taken yourself through the various steps of the visualization.

> Find a comfortable position, close your eyes, and take some deep breaths, in through your nose and out through your mouth. Keep breathing in this way until you find yourself in a slow, peaceful, effortless rhythm. *(Pause for a minute.)*

In your mind, place yourself in a setting that feels very safe and very pleasurable. It may be real or imaginary, from your past, your present, or in your future. *(Pause for a minute.)*

Once you have located yourself there, invite your child to join you. As the image of your child forms in your mind, gaze at her with as much love as you can summon, putting gently to the side any angry or negative thoughts or feelings about her. *(Pause for a minute.)*

And as you are gazing, imagine that she is now able to talk to you about all the things that she has never spoken to you about before: her pain, her fears, her vulnerability, her sorrow, her grief—all the ways in which she aches.

Imagine as she speaks that you are able without any effort at all to open your heart up to her, to listen plainly, quietly, lovingly, attentively. And imagine that in the process of listening, you naturally begin to feel within you a very deep and profound bond with your child, a bond filled with mercy, understanding, and kindness. *(Pause for a minute.)*

Now tell your child that you forgive her for all of her flaws, defects, failures, and imperfections, for all the ways in which she has disappointed, angered, hurt, and disillusioned you.

And, in your mind, extend your arms to your child and bring her toward you, and feel her melt and give in to your warm embrace. Feel yourself melting, too, aware of the pain that you each bear, each of you letting that pain bring you closer, ever closer to each other. Feel the reassuring grace that comes with inviting her into your loving arms and the freedom that comes with forgiveness. *(Pause for a minute.)*

Release her from your embrace and thank her for having met you here, for having unburdened herself to you, and in doing so helping you unburden yourself as well.

Allow her to leave, and watch her depart with new eyes, seeing her as bound to you, part of you, yet as her own person, radiating a unique, indescribable beauty as she moves away from you and forward into the world.

Continue breathing deeply and quietly for a few moments, cherishing the feelings of forgiveness and compassion that you have begun to discover and invite into your life. Promise to hold these feelings close to you as you awaken and move through the rest of your day.

—————————————— EXERCISE SIX ——————————————

The process of forgiveness can be a conscious, cognitive one as well. Take some time to reflect upon or fill out the questionnaire below, and, once you have done so, see how your feelings toward your child begin to soften:

1. In what ways does your relationship with your child feel imbalanced or unjust?
2. Think back to some of the hopes and wishes you had about parenthood. Which of these have been fulfilled? Which of these have not?
3. Take another look at the material in this chapter that focused on some of the expectations that parents have of their children (pages 149–158). Which of them apply to you and your child? What other expectations of your child were or are you aware of having?
4. What imbalances and injustices from relationships with individuals other than your child have existed or still exist? In what ways are you asking your child to make up for those imbalances and injustices? Is it truly possible for your child to do so?
5. What do you hope will happen if you are able to relinquish your resentment and disappointment and forgive your child for not being who you expect him or her to be? What do you fear will happen?
   What is likely to happen if you refuse to forgive, and instead cling to your resentment and disappointment?
6. What other relationship in your life would change for the better if you could forgive your child?

Greta was consulting with me because of her frustration with her 14-year-old son, Mack, who had decided not to attend a prestigious magnet high school that he had been selected for as a result of his high standardized test scores and stellar achievement in math and science classes. Mack had originally been interested in this alternative, but as his eighth-grade year came to a close he had gradually begun changing his mind, and he was now saying that he didn't want to have to make the forty-five-minute commute to and from the magnet program. He was reluctant to be separated from his friends as they finished middle school and prepared for high school.

"I know it has to be his decision," she admitted to me, "but I am just so convinced it's the wrong decision. He has this wonderful opportunity to participate in an experimental curriculum that would be perfect for him. He can take classes at the local university, intern at laboratories in the area, work with college students on their independent study projects. Instead he wants to go to the neighborhood high school, which is an okay school, there's nothing wrong with it, but it really pales by comparison.

"But I just haven't been able to let go of this, and I'm making both of us miserable. I keep asking him to reconsider, and of course all that's doing is just cementing his refusal. I'm just so angry that he's willing to give up this golden opportunity just so he can be with his buddies and avoid a long bus ride. What kind of reasons are those?"

Here is how Greta answered the questions I gave her to reflect upon.

1. Things between Mack and me feel unbalanced and unjust because I feel that I've always gone out of my way to give him every opportunity to be a success. I've always been flexible. I've spent countless hours sitting in parking lots or waiting rooms while he had his lessons and practices and doctor's appointments. And now, when I'm asking him to consider doing something that will really be better for him in the long run, he's shutting me out and choosing to look at this decision through a very narrow lens. Why won't he be as accommodating to me as I've always been to him?

2. I think that a lot of my wishes and hopes about parenthood have been fulfilled, at least by Mack, because he's such a wonderful kid, so accomplished. His older brother, Will, who's now twenty, developed schizophrenia three years ago, and has been

in and out of psychiatric hospitals since that time. He never even got his diploma. He is very bright, like Mack, and also very scientific, but because of his illness I've lost hope that he'll be the kind of success he could have been, and that really breaks my heart.

3. I guess the two expectations that stand out the most for me are "Our Child Must Replace a Loved One" and "Our Child Must Erase Our Flaws and Failures"—in both cases because of what happened to Will. Maybe I am asking Mack to be the standout that Will was on the road to becoming but probably never will be. And maybe I'm expecting Mack to be such a success that it will negate all the shame and horror I feel when I think about Will having spent most of his early adulthood in a psychotic state.

4. I'd answer this one just like the one above. Now that I think about it more, I realize how many hopes I've pinned on Mack since Will got sick. It's not fair to him, but it's also not fair that I have to watch my oldest son struggle so hard just to find some sanity.

5. I hope that if I relinquish my resentment and disappointment, we'll get along better, stop making each other miserable, and—this would be a miracle, but I can dream—Mack will change his thinking and decide to attend the magnet school after all. I fear that if I relinquish my resentment and disappointment, I'll no longer be motivated to fight him, and thus lose any chance I have of convincing him to do what I think is best for him. If I refuse to forgive, I run the risk of continuing to make Mack feel bad, and of remaining so angry that I don't appreciate all of the great things he's still likely to do with his life even if he goes to the regular high school.

6. Other relationships that might change for the better if I were able to forgive Mack: I think my marriage would improve, because I'm also angry at my husband for not pushing Mack as hard as I am in this, and he's angry at me for pushing *too* hard. And I believe my relationship with Will could improve too, because even though it wasn't his fault, and he didn't ask to become schizophrenic, I still look at him sometimes and won-

der why he's not improving. I know that's a terrible thing to say, and that he would probably do anything to go back to thinking normally, but sometimes, like when he stops taking his medication and gets psychotic, or when he doesn't show up for his therapy appointments, I feel like he's insisting on staying mentally ill, and I hate him for that. I know he needs to be forgiven too, and maybe starting with Mack would help get me there with Will.

Through the process of completing this exercise, Greta gradually became more accepting of Mack's decision to attend the local high school rather than the magnet program. She was able to talk with him for the first time about how her dreams for him had become so inflated once his brother had been diagnosed with schizophrenia and about how much she wanted to unburden him from the expectation that his successes make up for his brother's illness.

As it turned out, Mack did not change his mind, but his relationship with his mother improved significantly as she relinquished her belief that she knew what was best for him. Greta was able to acknowledge and celebrate Mack's very positive adjustment to high school, and she and her husband resumed their good relationship once they no longer needed to argue about Mack's future.

Interestingly, Mack expressed an interest in meeting with me a couple of times midway through his freshman year. He used some of the time to think back about the decision he had made. I discovered that Will had also been accepted into the same magnet program when he was in eighth grade, and that his first psychotic episode occurred while he was a junior at that school. We discussed some of the unspoken fears Mack must have had that the same frightful fate awaited him if he entered those doors.

I also learned that Mack felt terribly guilty about Will's illness, a form of survivor's guilt, it appeared, and that his fealty to his older brother made him reluctant to surpass him by succeeding at the program that Will had not been able to complete. "I know I was thinking that it would be embarrassing for him to have his kid brother make it through the magnet school when he couldn't," Mack thoughtfully explained.

Talking about the ways in which his loyalty to his brother influenced his decision about his own academic direction was a big relief for Mack and led to a greater likelihood that he would allow himself to accomplish what he wanted to accomplish without feeling like he was betraying his brother.

SIX

Changing

If there is anything that we wish to change in the child, we should first examine it and see whether it is something that could better be changed in ourselves.

Carl Jung

I always chuckle when I recall a telling moment that occurred a few years ago in my family life. I had had a particularly frustrating day with all three of my children, leaving me feeling strung out, depleted, and disappointed with them and with myself. None of us had met my expectations: one had once again forgotten to get the recycling box out of the garage and out to the curb in time for it to be picked up; one had once again forgotten his math book at school and needed me to hustle over and get it before the building closed so that homework could be completed; one had talked back to me in a somewhat brazen manner when I had asked her to finish cleaning her room; and I had responded to all of them in a distastefully critical and short-fused way.

With only a meager cadre of brain cells still functioning after finally having gotten everyone off to bed, I grabbed a parenting magazine from the stack on my night table, lay back, and leafed idly through it until I came to an article about the problem of overreacting to your children's bad behavior.

"Remember that they're usually not intending to make you feel wretched, and that when they're at their most obnoxious, they're also at their most fearful, needy, and insecure," it advised. I sighed sadly to myself, wishing I had been able to keep that thought in mind throughout a day in which we had *all* misbehaved.

And then, reading on, I got to the attribution for that quote: "Dr. Brad Sachs, author and family psychologist." *It was my own "expert" advice I had been reading,* months after I had so sagely and confidently proffered it to the writer who had interviewed me— and at the end of a day in which I had been a monumental failure at following it!

I share this anecdote because I believe that parenting is probably going to be, for most of us, the most demanding, complicated, and bewildering endeavor we will take on over the course of a lifetime. Even if you have carefully read the previous chapters, conscientiously worked on the exercises, and gradually increased your awareness of the unconscious sources that fuel the parent-child dynamic, for better and for worse, you will still have numerous days like the one I described above, days when the comment on a bumper sticker I recently spotted—"My other car is a broom"—fits all too well.

With this reality in mind, I offer a compendium of specific recommendations, many of them based on my own experience, for how to make life with children both easier and more rewarding. As I note below, it will be up to you to pick and choose which strategies seem most relevant to your particular situation.

BEWARE OF ADVICE

Before we proceed, it's important to remember that nobody knows your child better than you do. The parents who come to me upset because they "don't know what to do" often find that they do, in fact, know what to do—it's just that it's difficult for them to tune into this instinctive frequency and act on it because they're so distracted by all the information they're letting in from other broadcasts.

Parenting is such a challenge because there are so few absolute rights and wrongs or goods and bads. No text can provide all the answers, there can be no recipes for surefire success, no catechistic set of responses to your most vexing child-rearing questions, no mathematical formulas for calculating the exact amount of stimulation, reinforcement, and frustration your child needs. It's simply one gray area after another.

And not only does your own mother or father or sister or brother or best friend or neighbor not know best, but a lot of expert advice isn't so hot, either. I have read and reviewed numerous child-rearing books over the years, and I have found many of them to be quite useful as long as you meet the following criteria:

1. You have only one child.
2. Your own childhood was stable, safe, happy, and carefree.
3. You are *never* sick, tired, lonely, dissatisfied, worried about money, dealing with a failing car or a broken appliance, or trying to lose weight, stop smoking, or make some other significant change in your life.
4. You have responsibilities to no one other than your child.
5. You don't need to have a job outside the home to make ends meet.
6. You are happily married to a spouse who also meets these criteria.

I'm sure you get the point. There's nothing worse than reading a self-help book that offers brilliant suggestions that can never be realistically implemented. You wind up feeling even more disappointed in yourself and your inability to make significant headway than you did before you started. And as a sometime purveyor of such advice, as well as a person who has on occasion been unable to follow it, who would know that better than me? There are many ways to grow, but there can be no growth without errors, self-doubt, confusion, and uncertainty—the handmaidens to any progress.

So as you read on in this chapter, keep this disclaimer in mind: If what I am recommending seems to fit, use it. If not, ignore it and trust your gut—you're more aware of the unique characteristics of yourself and your child than I can ever be, and ultimately you can only do what you are comfortable with. And if you feel my advice is on target, but have lapses in your ability to follow it, forgive yourself and move on.

DEFINE YOUR DIRECTION

My mother does not hesitate to share Yiddish proverbs with me when she believes I am floundering and in need of maternal advice. One of her favorites is *"Me ken nit tantsen oif tsvai chassenes oif ain mol,"* which can be loosely translated as "You can't dance at two weddings at the same time."

As with much folk wisdom, there is great insight embedded in these simple words. You, as mother or father, need to decide the direction you want your family ship to head in, because without a destination in mind, you will never get to where you want to go. But you can only choose one direction to go in: trying to go east, west, north, and south all at the same time will leave you going nowhere at all. In the words of Bill Cosby, who on occasion seems to know as much about the ways of the world as my mother, "I don't know the key to success, but the key to failure is trying to please everybody."

What beliefs do you want your children to take into adulthood with them? What is it that you want them to value, to embody? How do you define a successful child? A successful parent? A successful family?

All parents need to have a core agenda based on answers to these questions, a *platform*, if you will, that guides them as they make significant child-rearing decisions. You can't expect one child to excel in every realm of life. If your daughter is going to invest her energies in her burgeoning dance and dramatic abilities, and good grades at school are a priority, too, she may not also be able to hold down that part-time job you thought would teach her a sense of responsibility. If you want your son to continue to have an important role in student government, and maintain an A average while participating in the after-school program for gifted math students, then his energy and enthusiasm for getting chores done at home may wane, and he may be not be able to be as patient with his younger sisters as you would like.

Above all, remember that cultivating the qualities that successful families possess—regularly conveying affection and appreciation, developing a sense of spiritual well-being, viewing challenges and crises as opportunities to grow closer and stronger—all require time. And I'm not just referring to the elusive "quality" time, but a certain "quantity" of time, too, during which there is opportunity to talk, share, laugh, weep, play, walk, or simply hang out.

Pam and Donald, for example, had orchestrated an extremely efficient way of life for their two children, an 8-year-old and a 10-year-old who followed a tightly mapped-out schedule that enabled them to participate in numerous activities but left little room for any kind of simple family time. As Pam laid out their weekly routine for me, I was impressed both with how neatly coordinated their logistics were and how suffocated I felt just hearing about the precision timing required to make it all happen.

They had come to me because, while things seemed to run smoothly during the week, weekends tended to be disastrous. "By Sunday night, there's always been some horrible fight, with one or both of us shrieking at the kids and sending them up to their rooms. It's just a terrible way to end the weekend and begin the week, but it happens at least three out of four times a month." These were two people totally devoted to their children but with no time to enjoy them.

It did not surprise me to learn that their weekends were, in some ways, even harder than their weeks. Instead of ratcheting down the intensity and allowing themselves to sleep in once or twice, or take an evening to go out together as a couple or as a family, they were up and running Saturday and Sunday, flung like comets through a matrix of children's lessons, practices, and games while trying to slog through their own housekeeping and bill-paying chores. No wonder their weekends usually ended with a blow-up—it served to vent the tremendous amount of tension that built up over the course of the tightly constrained week. Indeed, it was the only opportunity for an unscripted, unscheduled, unstructured interaction to take place.

Pam and Donald at first questioned my recommendation to cut back on their children's activities, as though I'd suggested a cut-back in love. But when I asked them when they had last sat down to a family meal together and the answer was Thanksgiving— three months before—they saw my point. They were so busy "doing" family, they'd forgotten to *be* a family. Realizing that they'd lost sight of what mattered most to them, they decided to observe a family Sabbath each weekend, hearkening back to an ancient religious anchor as restorative now as it was when it was first prescribed thousands of years ago, and perhaps more needed than ever before.

A couple of months later, they reported that they now make it a point to spend Friday nights at home together—"dinner and a video"—and to reserve Sunday afternoons, after religious school, for a family walk. "And if the weather's bad, we play a game or work on a puzzle." Saturday nights they try to go out, leaving the children with a baby-sitter or allowing them occasional sleepovers with their friends.

"There's enough going on that we still have to get up early both days, which I'm not crazy about," Pam remarked, "but it's much easier to tolerate knowing that we have some other quiet times later in the day to fall back on. And since we've started doing this, we haven't fought at all. In fact, instead of dreading the weekends, I actually look forward to them again."

Creating the necessary time for their family to once again *feel* like a family was all that was necessary for Pam and Donald to immeasurably improve their relations with their children.

LOOK FOR THE EXCEPTIONS

No matter how frustrated we are with our child's problematic behavior, we have to remember that it doesn't always occur. Searching for and discovering what the family therapist Michael White refers to as "unique outcomes" helps us not only to feel more optimistic but also to amplify or augment parenting behaviors that are more likely to create changes.

For example, Ida complained to me that her 12-year-old son Grant was "always doing the opposite of what we want him to" and wondered if he had the "oppositional-defiant disorder" she had read about in a magazine, since "he fits *all* the criteria." Hearing her words "always" and "all" made me think that perhaps she was not looking as closely as she could at Grant's behavior.

I asked her to take out an imaginary magnifying glass, and over the course of the week to scrutinize Grant's behavior and see if there was any evidence of compliant or cooperative behavior on his part. She returned for the next session sounding much more optimistic, reading off from a three-by-five card the numerous times when Grant had been helpful or responded positively to requests of hers: "Some of them were as small as 'Please pass the ketchup,' which he did without even thinking. But when I really looked carefully, I noticed there were lots of other times, too, like when I asked him to give our neighbor a hand jump-starting her car, or when I e-mailed him from work asking him to run the dishwasher because I had forgotten to."

Realizing that there was more to Grant than his defiance and looking for the patterns that seemed to enhance the likelihood of cooperation, Ida quickly got past the complaining stage and was able to come up with a better way of engaging Grant. "I've learned that if I write stuff down for him to do, or even e-mail it to him, he's more likely to do it than if I just tell him, and that if I make it clear that following through on something will be of help to myself or someone else, he's actually quite eager to help out."

MEASURE PROGRESS IN BABY STEPS

Paying closer attention to when a problem does not occur often puts the problem in perspective and yields new ways to mitigate it. But it's also important not to ignore the "baby steps" that are already being taken in the direction of positive change.

Markus, 14, consistently earned low grades in most of his classes, not because the material was difficult for him but simply because he didn't complete or turn in his homework. I asked his parents to rate, on a scale of 1 to 10, how diligent he was about getting to work on school assignments when he got home, and both quickly agreed that he was a 1.

When I asked what would make him a 10, they said that he would have to "finish, and *make sure his teachers receive and give him credit for*, every single one of his homework assignments." However, when I asked what would bring him from a 1 to a 2, they were so slow in coming up with an answer that Markus himself finally chimed in: "How about if I write down all my homework assignments in my assignment book, but don't actually *do* the homework?" Though his parents did not see the point of this, I asked them to agree to an incremental 10-step program, to which they reluctantly assented. Markus promised to follow through on his idea and see what happened.

They returned in a couple of weeks, reporting that every night Markus had indeed shown them a completed homework assignment book but had declined to actually do any of the work. I could see that they still saw very little point to this exercise, but I persisted.

First, I congratulated Markus for beginning to turn things around, and then I asked the three of them to agree to an additional increment in responsibility which would increase Markus's rating by another notch. To go from a 2 to a 3, they decided that he had to "bring home all books, worksheets, and materials necessary for homework to be completed." This he did during the week between our sessions.

During each of the following weeks, I got them all to agree on a further increase in Markus's commitment to schoolwork. To go from a 3 to a 4, he had to "be in his room from 3 to 4 P.M. without any distractions." To go from a 4 to a 5, Markus had to complete one subject's homework assignment successfully.

By our tenth session, Markus was completing and turning in his homework on a reliable basis, and his grades had quickly risen in response to his efforts. By highlighting and reinforcing even the *smallest* changes, Markus's parents laid the groundwork for bigger changes to finally come about.

MAKE YOUR CHILD YOUR PARTNER

Many of the parents who come to me are inadvertently ignoring an invaluable resource for establishing a better relationship with their child, and that is the child himself. As with Doralina, whom we learned about in the previous chapter, children are always more enthusiastic about doing things differently when they're invited to participate in the development of new plans, and they will come up with surprisingly useful and creative suggestions of their own.

Tim came to me frustrated by his 10-year-old daughter, Ginny, who regularly said that she needed help with her homework but within minutes would reject the very help Tim tried to provide. "As soon as I make the slightest suggestion, or point out as gently as I can where her mistake is, she blows up, starts scribbling all over the paper, throwing her books on the floor, and telling me I don't understand, that the teacher taught it differently in school. So I don't know what to do anymore—if I *try* to help, she goes bonkers. If I say I'm not going to help her, she insists she needs my help and can't get it done without me. Where do I go from here?"

I asked him if he had brought this dilemma up with Ginny, and he told me he hadn't. I recommended that he give it a try, looking for a calm opportunity to tell her how stuck he feels and wondering out loud if she might have some advice for him so that they could both work to prevent repeated explosions of this sort.

Tim reported back to me that their "conference" had gone quite well. Ginny had said, with great insight, that sometimes she asks for help before she's sure she needs it, and then she gets frustrated because once he starts to help her she realizes that she might have been able to figure it out by herself and wishes she had given it more of a try.

Taking his cues from his daughter, Tim suggested that whenever Ginny asked for help, he would set a timer for fifteen minutes, during which time she was to try to figure out the problem for herself. If she was still lost when the timer went off, he would try to help.

But if she then began to display signs of help rejection, he was to tell her calmly that this must be a sign that she needed more of a chance to make some progress on her own, and he would set the timer for another ten minutes.

The plan was implemented successfully. Tim's asking Ginny to join him in problem-solving instantly led her to feel more pride and self-sufficiency, and this in turn enabled Tim to tolerate her temporary distress and give her the chance to develop her own skills and resources without relying on him. In addition, the use of the timer lent a gamelike quality to doing homework, and Ginny enjoyed trying to "beat the clock."

In another situation, Jackie reported to me that she and her 11-year-old son, Troy, were at an impasse regarding the role of tutoring in his academic life. She had arranged for him to get tutored in math halfway through sixth grade, when he went from a B in the first quarter to a D in the second quarter, and with this outside help, he was back up to a B by the end of the fourth quarter.

Now she wanted to start him off with a tutor at the beginning of seventh grade, while Troy, who was never crazy about the idea of a tutor in the first place and had frequently moaned about having to go, said he no longer felt he needed any extra assistance. Interestingly enough, however, even though they had had numerous discussions about this issue over the summer as the school year neared, it appeared that Jackie had never asked Troy what grade *he* would like to get in math.

When I asked him that very question, he replied that he'd like to get a B, maybe even an A. I asked him to make a plan for how he would achieve an A or B in seventh grade without a tutor, and he said that he would try to pay attention in class, make sure he did his math homework first, before he got tired or distracted, let his mother go over his homework and correct whatever mistakes he had made, and let her quiz him the night before a test.

With this commitment in place, Jackie and Troy agreed that he'd begin the school year without tutoring, and as long as his grade remained at an A or B level, it would not be discussed any further. However, if his grade dropped below B, he would have to agree to work with his tutor for at least the subsequent quarter, until the next report card came out and he was earning an A or B again.

In the first quarter, which was mostly review, Troy's commitment to following through was strong, and he actually got an A in math. But in the second quarter, when new material began to be presented and his work habits began to falter, he earned a C. When Jackie, according to plan, reinstituted the tutoring, she was able to point out that *he* was the one who had wanted to be achieving at least a B level or higher, and that the tutoring was designed to help him do so.

This led to his more readily agreeing to work with the tutor, since he was able to see it more as his idea than something that was being imposed on him by his mother. Within another quarter's time, Troy was back up at a B level, and he surprised his mother by wanting to continue working with the tutor halfway through the fourth quarter as well, until the beautiful spring weather cast its spell on him. However, he had enough good test grades in the bank by then to finish off the school year with another B. Only when Troy felt that his own expectations were being factored in could he buy into his mother's efforts to support him.

A child's natural creativity can also be effectively tapped if you take the right approach. Six-year-old Kara was still sucking her thumb, even though the dentist had warned her and her parents that continued thumb-sucking would interfere with the growth of the "big teeth" that were beginning to come in now that she was starting to lose her baby teeth.

Kara was a big fan of Winnie the Pooh, and we spent much of our first session looking over the Pooh books and trinkets that she had acquired over the past couple of years. First, I was able to get her to agree (without much difficulty) that it was time to give up the thumb-sucking, since, as far as she knew, none of her friends still had this habit and she'd been teased about it several times in school. I then asked her what advice Winnie the Pooh might offer Kanga if Kanga came to him with similar concerns about Roo.

She excitedly churned out a list of Winnie's suggestions, including, "suck on candy instead," "have Roo sit on her thumb when she wants to suck it," "give Roo a ball to play with so her hands are busy," and "make her thumb taste bad by putting it in pepper." I asked Kara and her parents to transcribe Winnie's ideas onto a chart that they would keep in her room. Kara experimented with these ideas, and within a month's time, she had finally kicked the habit, to her, her parents', and her dentist's great relief.

Nine-year-old Gary was plagued by a persistent facial twitch that embarrassed him and elicited much teasing from his classmates. Because he was a big Harry Potter fan, I asked him to imagine that he was a wizard, and that "evil spirits" who had taken over his face needed to be lured away. He came up with the idea of creating an open box filled with candy that he would place in his room at night to draw out the spirits, who loved sweets.

In the morning, he would awaken, pad quietly over to the box and quickly seal it, trapping his nemeses inside. He'd then take the box outside and empty the candy and the hapless spirits into a trash can. Gary's ingenuity enabled him to exorcise these demons, and begin to regain mastery of his facial muscles.

DELABEL OR RELABEL

Every one of our flaws and weaknesses is, or can be under different conditions, a strength. When you label your child, or when you see her as no more than a disorder or diagnostic category, you are greatly narrowing her possibilities. It's important to pay close attention to the language you use, because words are very powerful and have great influence on how we perceive our children and how they perceive themselves.

Many times a parent will report a problem to me in a very limiting way. "My son is ADHD," for example, suggests that this diagnosis comprises all that he is. "My daughter's just plain lazy" locks her into a personality type that will, over time, become an inextricable part of her identity.

Take the time to listen to the phrases you use to describe your child, phrases that, even if they are not spoken aloud and only remain part of your interior conversation, are still being communicated in your actions and attitudes. When you find yourself labeling, try to delabel or relabel in a more positive and open-minded way, to see the strengths embedded in the apparent weaknesses.

The child who becomes prickly and irritable whenever he feels he's losing control over a crafts project might be better understood as one with an "artist's temperament." The child who is stubborn and single-minded may also be the child who refuses to bow to dangerous peer pressure in his adolescent years. The child who is withdrawn may actually be carefully and thoughtfully reflecting on important issues. The child who is so concerned with his looks and having the latest (and most expensive) designer clothes may be better understood as vulnerable and insecure—or perhaps creative, gifted with a great visual sense—rather than vain and spoiled.

Redefining your children doesn't mean that you are ignoring the need for some changes, that they couldn't stand to be a little less irritable, or stubborn, or withdrawn, or fashion-conscious. But by refusing the easy call of negativity, you give your child room to grow, to make changes that will be pleasing to you both.

As we have seen earlier, if you are having difficulty delabeling or relabeling, it is important to determine if your child has become a prisoner of your past, a stand-in either for yourself or for someone else. If your memories of your mother are of an over-weight woman who spent long afternoons lying on the couch watching TV while munching on potato chips and embarrassing you with her indolence when you had friends over, it may be hard to tolerate your daughter's curling up in the evening and doing the same thing, even if the length of her downtime, more like a half-hour each night, is substantially less than your mother's was.

One father, Dmitri, consulted with me because he was worried about his son's "effeminate" appearance and had several times lost his temper—inappropriate, he knew—and blasted him for acting "like a faggot." During our first two sessions, I was puzzled, for while the boy was not macho, he certainly didn't match up with his father's description of him. In our third session, however, when he came alone, Dmitri disclosed to me that when he was 10, he had been sexually molested by a man in his neighborhood who had invited him over for cookies and cider one afternoon. As we spoke, it became clear to me that Dmitri was terrified that if his son were anything less than hypermasculine in his attitude and appearance, he too might fall victim to abuse. Once his fears sur-faced, he realized that he'd be more likely to inoculate his son against abuse by educating him on how to prevent sexual harass-ment or abuse than by name-calling, and his entire attitude toward his son changed.

Whenever pejorative labels and gloomy predictions can be disinterred and brought out into the light of day, the specter of negative judgments can always be more easily exorcised, and their tendency to become self-fulfilling diminishes.

WHOSE LIFE IS IT ANYWAY?

Children deserve to celebrate their own triumphs and grieve for their own defeats. It is, as far as I can tell, the only true way to grow. Disentangling their accomplishments and failures from our accomplishments and failures is one of the hardest but most necessary of parental endeavors.

Our efforts to praise our children with the intent of bolstering their self-esteem will backfire if it is not clear who is being praised and if, in fact, the praise is even warranted. Is your son's ability to read second-grade-level books while still in preschool his success or yours? Did he really want to learn to read by the time he was 3, or did you push him to do so, hoping that you would stand out by raising a son who could read at such a young age?

Is your daughter really a "math genius," or does she simply take to it easily and perform at a high level because she has a talented teacher who can take the most mundane mathematical exercise and transform it into a fascinating project? She knows, from observing her classmates, that there are several other students who truly are mathematical virtuosos and operate at a higher conceptual level than she does. So constantly being showered with your verbal accolades may make her feel unseen and uncomfortable, fearful that you, and others, will eventually discover her true abilities and be disappointed.

Exuberant cheerleading of our children in response to behaviors and activities that they do not see as representative of who they really are can actually undercut their self-esteem, making them feel as if their true self is not worthy of expression. You may be thrilled that your daughter has made the volleyball team, but if her heart really isn't in playing volleyball—she felt pressured into trying out by you or by the coach—then your crowing about it to all of your friends and relatives is going to make her feel worse, not better, about herself.

Many times parents so completely engulf their child's victories that the only act of ownership left for the child is disowning the victory. In other words, you may force the child into rebellion because the decision to not read, or let the math grade slide, or not play volleyball, or play it poorly, may be the only decision left to a child, the only evidence that he is the author of his own life rather than a character in someone else's, namely, yours. As child psychologist Haim Ginott wrote, "If homework and high grades become diamonds in the parents' crown, the child may unconsciously prefer to bring home a crown of weeds that is at least his own."

We have already seen, in the case of Valerie and her son Tony, or Elliott and his son Brandon, how easy it is to overfocus on our child's achievements. This can happen when we feel that we have not lived up to our parents' expectations, as Valerie feared, or come too close to suffering the consequences of our own lack of ambition, as Elliott did. But I have also observed in my practice that even individuals who see themselves as tremendously successful may put too much pressure on a child to achieve.

Ask yourself the following questions to see if there's some likelihood that this process may be occurring:

1. Has your success occurred in a field or endeavor that is personally meaningful to you, or instead, one that you entered for other, less satisfying reasons?
2. Is your definition of success dependent on external criteria, such as financial reward, promotions, and recognition, and, thus, unstable or ephemeral?
3. Is the intensity with which you pursue success in one part of your life an attempt to obscure failure in another?
4. Do your efforts to be a success require such intensity that they severely compromise other parts of your life?
5. Are your efforts to succeed motivated mostly by a fear of failure?
6. Do self-defeating or self-destructive behaviors (addictions, affairs, workaholism, etc.) seem to accompany your success?

If you responded with a resounding yes to more than one of these questions, there's a great likelihood that you are, or will be, asking your child to provide you with the self-worth that you're not experiencing on your own. Give some thought to what you might want to change in your life so that your child feels freer to live his.

BE MORE OF WHO YOU WANT YOUR CHILD TO BE

Parents spend so much time trying to figure out why their children won't listen to them that they forget that their children are watching them intensely all the time. Asking your child to make changes while you steadfastly refuse to do so will diminish the possibilities for change.

You can't very well expect your daughter to defend herself against her more assertive playground counterparts if you devote yourself to being overly nice and keeping everyone happy at your own expense. She'll learn to speak out with a forceful, well-timed No! if she hears you saying it (especially if, when necessary, it is directed at her!). You can't very well expect your son to broaden his definition of recreation beyond watching television if you glue yourself to the tube for nine consecutive hours of professional football every Sunday. He'll be more likely to get outside for a bike ride if you haul yours out of the garage, knock the rust off, and join him.

I always insist that parents who are demanding changes from their children make some changes themselves—it tends to heighten our sensitivity to how difficult it really is to do something new or different and results in family leadership characterized by inspiration and motivation, rather than by criticism and sermons.

For example, I have coached soccer for a number of years now, at many different age levels, but recently decided to join an over-25 men's league, the first time I had played competitively since I was in high school. I was (painfully) amazed at how difficult it is to put into practice the supposedly simple skills and concepts that I had been teaching my young players, and the way in which I coached and spoke to my teams changed significantly as a result of this humbling experience.

One father I worked with, Felipe, was constantly exasperated by his 9-year-old son Hector's slow progress on the drums. "He gets the beat wrong over and over again, no matter how much he practices it. He's just not concentrating!" he complained to me. "The other day I felt like screaming at him to just play it *right* for once." I asked Felipe if he had ever played an instrument himself, and he said that he had taken some tuba lessons as a child, but that was about it.

Since he had a half-hour to kill at the music store where he took Hector for his lessons, I suggested that he use that time to consider picking up a few lessons himself. He thought that was a great idea. He'd never been crazy about the tuba and had fallen in love with rock-and-roll as a teenager, so he found a guitar teacher with an opening at the same time as his son's drum instruction.

Felipe's musical progress mimicked his son's, and it was only a few weeks later that he reported back to me, "You know, I'm so busy trying to figure out the same four chords my teacher has been working on with me for the past month that I haven't had time to listen to Hector's mistakes. My teacher's not rushing me or anything, but he's a young guy, and I've caught him rolling his eyes a few times as I fumble around. In fact, Hector even said one day, 'Dad, aren't you ever going to learn any other chords?' "

Confronting his own learning challenges was all it took for Felipe to become more tolerant of his son's seemingly glacial rate of growth.

DISTINGUISH BETWEEN CORRECTION AND CRITICISM

When children feel that their parents' expectations are excessive, they usually feel so discouraged that they abandon hope and become reluctant to try. Many of the children I work with wind up concluding that their parents' expectations are excessive not because of the actual expectations themselves, but because of how things are handled when those expectations are not fulfilled.

Children do need to be corrected and criticized at times: it's the only way they're going to learn what's right and what's best. But if it's consistently done in a disparaging, insulting, or humiliating way—"Your work habits stink!" "Your nails look disgusting.

Aren't you ever going to stop biting them?" "How could you not know the answer to this question yet? We've been over this a hundred times already!"—you will either incur your child's defiance and increase his resistance to your instruction or weaken his resolve and increase his helplessness, making him more dependent on you and on others.

A combination of empathic support and good-natured persuasion usually works best. Your child needs to know that you understand that he is having difficulties, and that he is not loved any less because of this. Comments like "I know this is hard, but you've done hard things before. Remember how hard it was for you to learn how to ride a bike, and now you ride without even thinking!" go a long way toward helping a child summon the resourcefulness to tackle a challenge.

Letting him know that you do have standards, but that he doesn't have to be perfect, will also help: "I don't expect you to not make mistakes—everyone does, and that's how we all learn—but I do expect you to do your best and to correct your mistakes when you make them."

Gently probing into the origin of an impasse is necessary at times, as well. "I've seen you use a dictionary before without much difficulty, and tonight you're really struggling. Is there something about this particular assignment that's different? Is something else on your mind?"

Sometimes, when you hear your words going beyond a legitimate registering of concerns and moving into the territory of an angry sermon or a blistering diatribe, it's better for you and your child to take a break. "You're looking pretty frustrated with this science project, and I'm never at my best once we get past nine P.M.," you might concede. "So what say we break for tonight and make a fresh start on it tomorrow?"

And while this may be stating the obvious, be sure *never* to correct your child's faults in front of his peers. It's guaranteed to make him feel less than good enough and also to make him furious at you for compromising his social standing.

The more sympathy, civility, and clarity children experience, the more cooperative and engaged they are likely to be.

HAVE COMPASSION FOR THEIR PASSION

In the last chapter I recounted the story of Tony, whose fascination with flying was initially ignored by his mother because of her inability to forgive him for not becoming accomplished in the ways that her family of origin would have valued.

In my experience, all children are willing to go to great lengths to promote their parents' acknowledgment of and admiration for their interests and ambitions. When a child's interests and ambitions resonate with her parents', it can be a joyously effortless experience to reinforce and stimulate this passion. Your daughter's burgeoning commitment to political activism is a moving reminder of your own, and the two of you sit at the computer every Sunday night, writing letters to local legislators about the ecological dangers of overdevelopment in your community. Your memories of collecting baseball cards are reinvoked by your son's shared interest, and the two of you spend hours at the kitchen table happily sorting out players by team, position, and ability.

But storm clouds may begin to gather when it's difficult for you to identify with what stirs your child, or, worse, when what stirs your child is directly counter to what stirs you. Jonah, a former peace activist who had become a university professor specializing in international conflict resolution, came to me with the goal of purging his 8-year-old son, Micah, of his interest in professional wrestling. "It's all he watches on TV, and all he wants to know about. I've tried to tell him the whole thing is a stunt, a sham, but he's buying every minute of it. When I asked him what he wanted for his birthday, it was wrestling action figures. I spend my days trying to help nations use diplomacy to avoid wars, and he's busy practicing head-butts on his 3-year-old sister!"

By distancing himself from any interest in pro wrestling, however, Jonah was not only cutting off a possible avenue of contact with his son but also running the risk of making Micah feel undervalued and criticized by a condescending father. In addition to pointing out that embracing some form of good-versus-evil melodrama tends to be a typical stage in children's moral development, I suggested that Jonah watch some wrestling shows with

Micah so that, if nothing else, he could learn more about it and possibly have a basis for establishing a dialogue with his son.

"After all," I said, "the United States doesn't completely cut off trade and diplomatic relations with other countries just because we don't wholly approve of their political system. Doing so would dissipate any leverage we have to facilitate progressive change in those countries."

Jonah got the point, and committed himself to watching a half-hour wrestling show with Micah each weekend. And while he didn't ever grow to look forward to this program, it did give him a better understanding of why it appealed to his son. "Some of these characters really are quite inventive!" he confessed. And his father's presence was something Micah really seemed to enjoy.

Coincidentally, I ran into Jonah at the supermarket a couple of years later, and he told me that Micah's interest in wrestling had passed (not surprisingly), but that he still joked with his father about how they used to watch it together.

Passion, by its very nature, is a healthy thing for a child (and an adult!). Quelling or repudiating that passion because of our own discomfort with what they are passionate about will only diminish the possibility that sparks from this fire will light other intellectual or emotional flames as well. One of the most concrete expressions of love is taking an interest in something that our beloved is interested in. When children feel this kind of love from their parents, it will ignite their love for and success in the world.

ASSIGN AGE-APPROPRIATE RESPONSIBILITIES

When parents are overburdened by their own responsibilities, there is a trickle-down effect and they overburden their offspring with too many responsibilities as well. Kelly, a single mother who worked full-time, expected her 14-year-old daughter, Casey, to come home from school each day, empty the dishwasher and set the table for dinner, meet her 7- and 9-year-old brothers when they got off the bus and give them a snack and keep an eye on them, and do a load of wash, all before Kelly got home at 5:30.

"It's the only way we can get by," Kelly told me during our first session. "If she does her part, the rest of the evening can go pretty smoothly. I can help them with their homework, fold the laundry, get the table cleared, and make lunches for the next day. Without Casey's help, I'd be up until midnight. I'm not asking her to do more than I'm doing—just to do her share."

This routine, however, was preventing Casey from completing her homework in the afternoons and participating in the cheer-leading intramural that a couple of her friends went to on Mondays and Wednesdays after school. She was not only whining a lot about being "stuck at home with my brothers," she was also subtly sabotaging the plan, by increasingly "forgetting" to do the wash or turn on the oven or be on time to meet the boys at the bus.

We arranged a compromise by which Casey would be allowed to go to the cheerleading class if she promised to help her mother out with the dishes and the laundry and do her homework after dinner on those days. Kelly agreed to have simple microwave meals and to have her sons stay in school for an aftercare program on the days that Casey took her class, picking them up on her way home.

Casey was pleased to be liberated from what had felt like an imprisoning regime and pitched in enthusiastically in the evenings out of gratitude for her mother's flexibility. Her brothers, as it turned out, benefited from the aftercare program because their homework was supervised there, so there was less need for Kelly's involvement in the evenings.

By unburdening Casey of what felt to her like an oppressive set of expectations, Kelly was rewarded with a more cooperative daughter.

Sometimes a child has too many responsibilities outside, rather than inside, the home. Kendra was only in third grade, but she was taking gymnastics, dance, and track, each of which required twice-a-week involvement. It was no wonder that she was suffer-ing from chronic headaches. She appeared to have not a moment in her life when she was free to read or think or play without some form of adult-imposed structure or supervision. Eliminating one of her activities, which turned out to be gymnastics, quickly led to a reduction in her headaches, and she continued to enjoy her dance classes and track meets.

Sometimes a child is not given a balanced-enough menu of

responsibilities. Ross, a fifth grader, excelled at both swimming and baseball, and his weeks were filled to the brim with practices, games, meets, tournaments, and clinics. In fact, he was kept so busy meeting all of his athletic commitments and staying on top of his schoolwork that his parents almost never asked him to do anything around the house.

He was not expected to make his bed or clear the table or feed the dog or rake the leaves. As long as he performed well in school and on the ball field, he was absolved of any other accountability. The problem was that he was living a very self-centered existence and failing to shoulder any of the normal responsibilities for his age level. Coddled and catered to, all he had to do was put on his various uniforms and "show up," and everything else would be taken care of.

His distorted perception of how the world worked revealed itself in school; his teacher reported to Ross's parents that he consistently had difficulty with group learning projects because he refused to do his fair share. "It's getting to the point that none of the other kids want to have him in their group, because he doesn't pull his weight and starts acting like a prima donna," they were told.

I suggested to his mother and father that he be given a basic set of responsibilities around the house, despite their concerns about overloading him. "If it turns out he has to miss a swimming practice or a batting clinic because he hasn't followed through, that really wouldn't be so terrible. To become a well-rounded person, he needs to be able to handle things when he's not the center of attention."

Rebalancing Ross's life so that there were other things on his plate besides receiving recognition for displaying his ample talents was difficult. He fought it at first, and had to sit out a couple of practices, but ultimately his parents' expectations led to improvements in his ability to work and play well with others.

BELIEVE IN DEVELOPMENT

It is remarkable to me that our life expectancy is years longer than any generation before us, yet we attempt to hustle our children briskly through childhood as if there was some hurry. One cartoon conveyed the essence of this by portraying a mother, arms akimbo, looming over her toddler, who was playing with toys on the floor. Her sneering comment: "All right, time to grow up."

Most children, despite our fears and their foibles, do grow successfully through childhood into adulthood. What comes with age, however unpleasant and worrisome, eventually tends to go with age as well. From the moment of our conception, our central nervous system is designed to drive us forward toward a mastery of ourselves and of the world, and to self-correct, compensate, and adapt when unanticipated obstacles and inevitable shifts present themselves.

Patiently allowing for and accommodating the naturally propelled maturation that all children experience can be difficult, but it is as much a parent's responsibility as is promoting that maturation. Of course, patience, while admittedly a virtue, is not a common commodity in a culture that places a premium on speed and instant response.

My clinical work with infants and toddlers often consists of no more than a strong request that their parents declare a moratorium on any comparisons between their baby and any other. Children grow in such unique and idiosyncratic ways that it is absolutely *useless* to fret about your young child's leisurely forays into language acquisition or physical mobility or pattern recognition. In five years, no one is going to care, or possibly even remember, that your daughter was the last one in her play group to sit up, or crawl, or put two words together to make a Zen-like sentence.

Likewise, in twenty years no one is going to care, or remember, that your son was the last one in his age group to remove his training wheels, or recall his locker combination, or ask a girl out, but chances are excellent that he'll have figured out how to do all three of these by then, and plenty more. Our children's lives unfold according to a secret blueprint that we (and they) will never have the privilege of seeing.

That's why a flexible response to our children's intellectual, social, sexual, physical, and psychological development across the life span is necessary to promote their entry into self-confident adulthood. And again, we have to be careful not to inflict our own emotional baggage on their lives.

Orrin, for example, contacted me because he was frustrated with his 5-year-old son, Larry. Two years before, Orrin had divorced his wife, Sharon, because he was gay and had finally decided, after years of private torment, that he could no longer tolerate what felt to him like a "fraudulent" marriage that required him to keep his homosexuality under wraps. Sharon, although initially hurt and confused by Orrin's decision, eventually came to accept it, and they had agreed to a fairly amicable joint-custody arrangement.

Orrin's concern was that Larry was not showing a healthy "gender balance" in his play. "All he wants to do is play with trucks. If we lived in a truck, he would think that he'd died and gone to heaven. I have lots of dolls available for him to play with, and other things, too, because I don't want him to grow up to be sexually stereotyped, to feel ashamed of his feminine side, like I did. But he's just not interested—everything is trucks and backhoes and steam shovels. One day I even tried to hide some of his trucks to see if he'd figure out something else to do with himself, but he threw this huge tantrum, and I finally just went and got them."

I asked Orrin what he recalled playing with when he was a child, and he said that he had never been interested in "typical boy stuff," like trucks or guns or soldiers. He had been more of an artist and remembers spending his time drawing and painting. I suggested that he take a morning to volunteer in Larry's kindergarten class to get a sense of what Larry's peers tended to play with.

When he returned, he acknowledged that most of Larry's male classmates were also very busy with "guy stuff, like the trucks and the building blocks—but I think they do that because they're probably already embarrassed to head over to the girls' section and play dress-up with Barbie dolls."

Orrin's live-in partner, Saul, had taken an active interest in Larry's development as well, so I invited him to a session with Orrin. Saul's experience as a child was different from Orrin's: "Actually, I was usually the dirtiest kid around, because I was always messing around outside. Even now, I love taking Larry outside with his trucks and making little roads and highways. Orrin is worried that if Larry plays with boy stuff, when he grows up he won't respect his father because he's gay, but I don't think there's anything to that. Plus, even though I loved that stuff, I eventually got interested in other things anyway, and I bet Larry does, too."

Hearing that his own partner had been a more stereotypical "boy" who had still been able to grow up with a healthy identity as a gay man helped Orrin to understand this stage in his son's development and, like Jonah, the pacifist professor who was so troubled by his son's interest in pro wrestling, tolerate it better. Larry's interest in trucks didn't exactly wane throughout the year, but Orrin was heartened to notice that his son had become somewhat less single-minded: "He still doesn't even go near the dolls I bought for him at home, but he's really taken to reading and loves to sit on the floor with a stack of books from the library, leafing through them and trying to figure out words."

SET LIMITS

No discussion of parenting would be complete without addressing the notion of how to set limits with our children. Even if it's true that children are innately good, all children need structure so they can develop trust in themselves and the world.

Discipline, the basis for that structure, is what teaches children the inner controls necessary to make them responsible for themselves and others, to be able to be autonomous and yet also accept the authority of others when necessary, to display initiative and channel their creativity, and to develop a working, flexible conscience.

Unfortunately, I have noticed how difficult it seems to be for today's parents to feel comfortable setting limits with their children. For one thing, we live in a culture that provides confusing messages about the importance of discipline, suggesting at times that it is injurious and inhumane, synonymous with oppression, rigidity, or imprisonment. In many ways, in fact, our society eschews discipline and promotes the belief that a *lack* of discipline is the hallmark of true freedom and maturity.

Parents wind up concluding that their efforts to impose discipline are not only unhealthy but actually "traumatic," interfering with their children's optimal growth and development, when the reality is that they'll never be prepared for life's inescapable challenges and responsibilities without having internalized a good amount of self-discipline.

Many of my patients also have difficulty setting limits because they believe that their children must "like" them, and most children will temporarily dislike anyone who interferes with their wishes being fulfilled. But children who sense their parents' eagerness for their approval will exploit it unmercifully, constantly blackmailing them with the threat of withdrawn love, leading to further overpermissiveness, which engenders further exploitation. What I have seen is that parents are best loved and appreciated over the long haul when they are willing to both gratify and frustrate their child in a fair, consistent, and developmentally appropriate way. Like surgery, setting limits may look traumatic from the outside but can ultimately have powerfully curative properties.

Another common obstacle to effective limit-setting is the notion that when a child's misbehavior has its origins in feelings of need or vulnerability, you cannot punish him for it. But just because you realize that your child is intimidating his younger brother because he feels displaced by him, for example, doesn't mean that there shouldn't be sanctions for his bullying. You can tenderly empathize and firmly establish guidelines for good conduct and consequences for bad. They're not mutually exclusive processes.

Finally, many parents feel that setting limits with a child will limit the child himself, rather than the child's undesirable behavior. It's as if they don't want to do anything that might in any way obscure what they find luminescent about their child. In truth, however, effective limit-setting liberates the child, teaching him that frustration is a temporary state that can be tolerated, that disappointment can be survived rather than avoided at all costs, that the resilience and resourcefulness that emerge when things don't go his way will eventually become his most valuable assets, and that his feeling whole does not depend entirely on the fulfillment of personal wishes, no matter how precious they may be.

To be effective and to accomplish these end results, limits must be implemented with a respect for the child's essential humanity and dignity. Limits that are accompanied by malice, excessive anger, capriciousness, physical punishment, or endless sermonizing tend to backfire, either fortifying a child's resistance to authority or humiliating or enslaving her, making her feel worse, and thus act worse.

Carmen, the single mother of 15-year-old Lucien, admitted to feeling powerless in the face of his complete defiance of her rules. "He comes and goes when he wants to. Sometimes he's gone for days at a time without telling me where he is. He goes to school or doesn't go to school, he has friends over at all hours of the night when he is home. What can I do? I can't keep him in the house or throw his friends out—he's six inches taller than me and fifty pounds heavier. I'm completely helpless."

I learned that Carmen's childhood had been dominated by the drug-related acting out of her older brother, who was eventually removed from the home by the police and then spent the next two decades in and out of jail. "I've tried to be very patient and understanding with Lucien because I don't want to lose him the way my parents lost my brother. I talk to him whenever I can about how dangerous a life he's leading, I try to help him see the mistakes that he's making, I tell him I know that it's hard being raised without a father. I've tried to be so supportive."

By emphasizing "patience and understanding" at the expense of limits and discipline, however, Carmen was abdicating her authority, making it very easy for Lucien to follow in his uncle's self-destructive footsteps. I offered her some strategies that she could use without having to get involved in a physical altercation with her son. She was to lock the door to her house if he wasn't home by curfew and report him to the appropriate authorities at school to address his truancy.

She was also to remove the door to his bedroom (adolescents value privacy more than almost anything else) and take all of his clothes from his bedroom and lock them in a suitcase in her closet, allowing him an outfit only when he had turned in the ones he was wearing (adolescents rarely leave for more than a day at a time without decent-looking clothing). His bedroom door and free access to his clothing were to be reinstated when he began attending school and obeying curfews on a regular basis.

The next several weeks were difficult and sometimes explosive ones, but Carmen, with the support of myself and her friends, hung in there. And once Lucien saw that his mother meant business and was taking a firm stand in response to his maladaptive behavior, he began to improve.

Carmen was able to realize that her son needed more discipline, rather than less, in order to regain control of his life, and that in offering it she could more effectively offset the terrifying destiny that she had envisioned for him.

LOOK AT THE BIG PICTURE

Carla, a 46-year-old mother of three, came to me for therapy shortly after being diagnosed with breast cancer. The subsequent months, filled with two surgeries, each followed by chemotherapy and radiation, were dark and scary ones for her and her family. After a year's time, however, she was delighted to receive a clean bill of health from her oncologist and felt as if she had been given a new lease on life.

Her response to this unexpected second chance was to radically alter her existence. "I endured so many sleepless nights wondering if I was going to die and vowing that if I didn't I was going to live differently, that I feel I have no choice but to make some real changes."

These changes included cutting back to half-time at her job and drastically trimming the number of activities her children engaged in. "I told the kids, 'Look, I don't know how long I'm going to live—it could be another fifty years, it could be just five—but I'll be damned if I'm going to spend it driving like a madwoman from place to place, never having a free weekend or a quiet evening at home because there's always some game or concert or recital or project going on.'

"I told them that they could each do one extracurricular activity at a time, and it couldn't be anything that took up more than two days a week. They can play soccer, but not travel to soccer.

They can be in a band, but not in the concert band and the jazz band at the same time. They can continue with Scouts, but none of this trying to do Scout stuff and youth group stuff at the church in one weekend. They all had some complaints, but, overall, I think we have a much better quality of life now, and it's really much more sane. I feel like I can breathe again."

As Carla spoke, I was ashamed to admit that I envied her. In response to the terror of dealing with a life-threatening illness, she had reclaimed and redefined her life, reestablishing as a priority the values that truly mattered to her: family connectedness.

How many of us would require a trauma of this sort to slow down, to question the frenetic pace we try valiantly to keep up with? How many of us would quickly forget about such a trauma once it had passed, and eventually resume the frenetic pace without so much as a single change, as if nothing had ever happened?

Most of the families I know and work with, my own included, need to be regularly reminded that there's something bigger than good grades or athletic exploits, something more than achieving and accomplishing and acquiring. We are eager to nourish our children's bodies and minds, but we often forget that it's just as important to nourish their souls.

That's why it's necessary to build into your family life habits and rituals that serve the purpose of awakening us to the wonder of the world at large. Do you take the time to greet your child when she comes through the door, listen to her laughter and marvel at her enthusiasm for life before you ask her how much home- work she's got? Are you able to see past your son's mediocre grades to really appreciate how diligently and lovingly he cares for the fish in his fish tank, and how wonderful his love of nature really is?

Does your family do something together that acknowledges that there is something going on in the world besides child- centered activities and entertainment? Can you volunteer together at a soup kitchen? Can you clean the debris out of the stream in the woods near your home? Can you volunteer to rehabilitate homes for senior citizens? Can you draw pictures that will liven up the children's unit of your local hospital?

Endeavors such as these help educate our children about the needs of the world at large and allow us to cultivate more of an "attitude of gratitude" and humbly appreciate the miracle of all that we do have, rather than sinking into a quicksand of disappointment and despair because of our preoccupation with all that we don't have.

Thirteen-year-old Melanie's parents scheduled an appointment because "we're at the end of our rope with our daughter. She's never satisfied with what she has. We give and give, but she's always got to have more. We've never seen a child so needy." Whether it was the latest computer toy or the most lavish wardrobe, guitar lessons, gymnastics, or ballet, whatever Melanie asked for she got—but it never seemed to make her happy.

I wondered if Melanie had experienced more than enough getting but not enough giving. As we learned in the chapter on forgiveness, it's hard to feel good about yourself if there's an imbalance between getting and giving. That is why many children who come across as *needy* start to behave differently when they're *needed*. It restores balance and diminishes guilt, along with the constant need to be punished for what you're feeling guilty about.

I recommended that Melanie's parents find an activity that required her to give of herself, rather than get, to see what impact this had. They returned a few weeks later saying that they had signed her up to volunteer at an after-school recreational program for children with Down Syndrome. While she had "done plenty of complaining" at first, they stuck to their guns and insisted that she follow through. And what they noticed was that she displayed a great gift for working with children with developmental disabilities, and in fact seemed very moved by them.

Over time, Melanie took her volunteer job more and more seriously and became ever less demanding at home. As her mother remarked, "The other day the head teacher pulled me aside on my way in to pick her up and told me what a fine job she was doing. It's like there's another Melanie in there that we never had the chance to see, and she never had the chance to show us."

One day, Melanie surprised her parents by announcing that she wanted to apply for work as a counselor at the summer camp the school system ran for children with Down Syndrome, which meant that she wouldn't be able to attend the camp she had been going to herself for the past several years. "When I heard that," her father said, "I realized that she was really growing up, and that maybe we've been missing who she really is because we haven't challenged her to express those aspects of herself."

By inviting Melanie to offer more of herself to the world, her parents changed both how they saw her and how she saw herself—for the better.

JUST LISTEN

If there's one piece of advice I find myself offering more than any other to parents, it is to say less and listen more. Children do need to be spoken to, of course—the ability to use words helps all of us to more effectively understand, bear, and express complex feelings like rage, sorrow, and fear. We cannot parent effectively if we don't talk to our children, telling them what they need to complete or how fine a job they've done, sharing with them our sympathetic depiction of what they may be feeling but can't yet articulate.

But talking is not a substitute for listening, because all children (and adults) need to have a "witness" for their experience, and good listening is the only thing that can provide that sense of having a witness. Good listening doesn't necessarily involve saying anything profound in response. Many of life's events and emotions are so profound that they simply cannot be fully contained by language. Trying desperately to attach words to experiences ultimately becomes alienating, leaving us feeling like we are not being held, not being tended to, that our greatest, most unspeakable essence is not being honored.

We have all, at times, felt something so deeply that even the most sensitively framed, eloquent response falls way short of the mark. "Just *listen* to me, for god's sake," we wish we could say, as we watch someone struggling to come up with an answer to the problem we have just described. "I just want you to *hear* me!" Children feel the same way. The notion that silence is a waste of time, that talking is the only way of relating to each other, is one that is peculiar to our culture. Sometimes it is when we say nothing that we speak most eloquently of our love for the person we are listening to.

One man I worked with told me that he recalled, as a boy, sitting and studying his grandfather as he silently whittled sticks and twigs into intricate sculptures and designs. "I'd sit there on the porch for hours, and I'm sure I learned more from him on all of those wordless afternoons than I've ever learned from anybody else."

Your child knows if you're really listening or not. He can tell if you're truly present, attending carefully to what he is struggling to put forth, or if you are simply biding your time as you mentally formulate a response to his comments, a solution to his problems. He can tell if you're going to embark on a dia*logue*, or a dia*tribe*. He can tell if you are rushing to comfort him before he is ready to receive comfort because of your own discomfort with what he has to say. He can tell if you're listening to his whole being with your whole being, or if you're trying to distill what you believe are the most essential parts of his narrative while you simultaneously compose lists in your head of phone calls you have to make and chores that need to be done.

Practice listening to your child as much as possible, and listening with an open mind and an open heart. Yes, the dream that she is relating makes no sense and seems to go on interminably. Yes, the tawdry dramas that take place on the playground seem repetitive and tiresome at times. Yes, the logic behind his defending why he didn't come right home after school seems shaky at best. Yes, the words she's using are harsh and angry, hurtful to let in. But in listening, you are allowing your child access to her deepest self, and it is only by having access to that deepest self that she can feel competent, complete, and worthwhile.

There are some parents I have worked with who have gone overboard in the opposite direction, who have to learn to keep in mind that good listening is not the same thing as tolerating an oral temper tantrum from a child. The child's need and right to

express her feelings does not mean that she has the right to bad-
ger or insult you, and it's appropriate to remove yourself, or the
child, when her airing of her feelings starts to verge on verbal
aggression or abuse.

But in my experience, such verbal aggression tends to occur
most often in families in which the child simply does not trust
that her parents will make the effort to listen to her if she speaks
at normal emotional volume. Bickering, screaming, demanding,
and insulting are the inevitable ploys of a child who feels she must
amplify her signal to an ear-shattering level to be recognized and
heard.

The more you listen to your child, and the more listened to
your child feels, the more you will know about who he is, and the
more supportive a caregiver you can be.

Seven-year-old Dante was referred to me because the Ritalin
that he had begun taking for the last two months to help him fid-
get less and focus more in school had not led to any noticeable
improvements. Unfortunately, I discovered, he had been medicated for an attentional deficit without fully taking into account
the possibility of alternative explanations for his behavior, such as
high-spiritedness, anxiety, depression, or learning disabilities.

"He's always been pretty hyper," his mother, Yolanda, explained, "and the teacher said that now that he's in first grade, he's
probably having a hard time staying focused because more seat-
work is required than when he was in kindergarten, which is why
he hasn't been concentrating."

In the course of one of my meetings with Dante, I asked him,
when his parents weren't present, if there was anything worrying
him. He told me that he had been having dreams "almost every
night" that his parents had died and left him alone. He said that
he was scared to tell anyone about these dreams because "they
might come true if I say them out loud."

When I related this to Yolanda, she told me that the father of
one of Dante's friends had been killed in a car accident at the
beginning of the school year. Because they felt that this was too
frightening for a child to have to think about, Dante's parents
hadn't discussed it with him, and he in turn had never mentioned

it to them, though they knew that Dante's teacher had told the boy's classmates about it so they would pay special attention to him.

It seemed to me, based on the dreams Dante reported having some months later, that this event had truly upset him and was substantially interfering with his capacity to focus in school.

I encouraged Yolanda and her husband to invite Dante to talk about his dreams when he had them, rather than keeping them to himself. I also had them all make a "dream catcher" together that would "catch" the dreams before they entered Dante's head at night. Finally, I suggested to Dante that, with his parents' help, he write a card to his friend conveying his sympathies.

Since his mother had said Dante had always been hyper, I did recommend that they pursue a psychological evaluation as well. The evaluation strongly suggested that Dante did, indeed, have a neurologically based attention deficit disorder.

With this in mind, it was agreed that he would remain on a low dose of Ritalin. But because we had helped Dante to release himself from his viselike anxiety by simply listening to him, the medication was suddenly able to do its job, leaving him better able to concentrate in class and follow his teacher's instructions.

_____ EXERCISE SEVEN _____

Most parents who want to make changes tend to bite off more than they can chew, rather than being more realistic about how much change they can all handle at one time.

For this exercise, you are to go back through the chapter and pick out *one* area that you'd like to use as a starting point for better parenting. It might be inviting your child to be your problem-solving partner, or being less vulnerable to others' advice, or being a better listener.

Then, come up with *one* behavior that would signify a step in the direction of change, but don't announce to your child that you're going to be doing anything differently. You might decide to practice listening to your daughter without interrupting or interjecting. You might decide to ask more about an interest that your son has and join him in pursuing it. You might ask your children to clear the table and load the dish-washer after dinner.

As you engage in this behavior, observe carefully how you feel, and how your child responds. What feels different? What feels new? What feels better? What feels worse? What was hard about making this change? Is this change that you have made something you could continue to do? If not, would another one be worth a try?

SEVEN

The Good Enough Parent

And Elijah fled into the wilderness, sat under a broom tree, and said, 'I am no better than my fathers.'

Rabbi Miezlish of Cracow was a successful merchant as well as a scholar. When his students learned that the rabbi's fortune had been lost as the result of a shipwreck, they wanted to break the news to him gently. One of his favorite students came to him with a question about a passage in the Talmud: "It says that we are to thank God for the evil that befalls us as well as for the good. How can this be done?" The rabbi explained the matter in terms of its hidden meaning, clarifying how every crisis is an opportunity for learning, how we do not always understand the ultimate result of what seems to be a tragedy in the moment. The student then replied: "And if my rabbi were to learn that all his ships had been wrecked, would he dance for joy?" The rabbi said, "Yes, of course!" "Well, then," responded the student, "you can dance—all your ships are lost!" The rabbi fainted. When he came to, he admitted, "Now I confess I no longer understand this passage in the Talmud."

No matter how carefully you have read the previous chapters, and how dutifully you have completed the exercises, I can guarantee you that there will still be times when you do not feel like you are a good enough parent, raising a good enough child. You will still experience moments when you feel hopeless and overwhelmed, lacking empathy, reacting with regrettable impulsivity to your child's flaws and foibles, despite all of your knowledge, understanding, and good intentions.

But just as you have been learning that there is no such thing as the perfect child, you must also learn that there is no such thing as a perfect parent. In fact, forgiving yourself for your imperfections as a parent is part of the process of forgiving your children for theirs. Compassion and respect, channeled toward ourselves as well as others, are always more healing and motivating than criticism and condemnation.

When we talk about being a good enough parent, what do we mean? Because we are in the midst of such extraordinary societal change, contemporary culture no longer supplies us with a clear, strong message about how effective parents are to behave. In previous generations, being a good enough parent seemed simpler and more clearly defined than it is in present times. If a mom kept a clean house, volunteered for the PTA, and baked cupcakes on her kids' birthdays, she was doing great. If a dad offered up firm discipline, provided sufficient financial support, and was around from time to time to play a game of catch or join in on a Scout camping trip, he was A-OK.

Now, as with many other endeavors, the definition of good parenting is far more complex, and the demands on people's time are so excessive that sometimes the response is simply to opt out. For those with demanding careers, it can be very difficult to fulfill both work and parenting obligations, and often it is the child who gets short shrift, not the job.

Peter, for example, was a partner in a hard-charging law firm for which he worked such long days that by the time he got home, all he wanted to do was be alone in front of the television or his computer, available only for a quick good-night kiss from his two children. If behavior or homework problems arose during his few waking hours at home, he viewed them as interruptions in his routine and passed them over to his wife. If she was not available, he would deal with whatever had to be taken care of in the most perfunctory way possible and then head back to his study or the den. The weekends he didn't go to the office were usually spent working around the house and yard or playing golf, activities in which he could have chosen to include his kids, but did not.

He and his wife came to me because their pediatrician was concerned about their 13-year-old daughter's disordered eating and weight. Shelly had already begun bingeing and using laxatives, and there was some evidence that she was purging after binges as well. She was five feet four inches tall and had gone from 118 pounds to 104 pounds in the last year, despite having grown more than an inch.

When I suggested to Peter that there were some ways in which he might contribute to her developing a more positive body image, which would in turn help to resolve her eating disorder, he acted only mildly interested but agreed without much resistance to give it a try. I proposed that he take a walk with her every weekday evening so they could both get some exercise and have some time together. I also recommended that they go out for an ice-cream cone together every weekend so she could learn to develop more pleasureable associations with food without having to punish or torment herself. "I like this idea!" Shelly said happily to Peter as we closed the session.

When they returned a couple of weeks later, I asked Peter how the walks and the ice-cream outings had gone. "Pretty good, I guess," he answered evasively, and right on his heels Shelly blurted out, "We took a walk *one* evening, the night after we met here, and that was all." She looked like she wanted to both yell and cry at the same time.

"Is Shelly telling the truth?" I asked Peter, looking at him squarely.

His eyes met mine briefly, then shifted to the side. "I guess so. Actually, I thought we did it a couple of nights. . . ."

"No, we didn't!" Shelly jumped in, before he could defend himself. "It was *one* time. That's all."

"It was a busy week for me," Peter said quietly, and then his voice began to rise: "I've got work to do in the evenings! I can't be counted on to take a walk every evening, there are things that have to get done."

"I believe you've got a lot of work to do, and perhaps taking a walk every weekday evening was biting off a bit more than you could chew. We can talk about coming up with a more realistic plan in a moment. But it's important to realize that helping

Shelly through a difficult time is something that has to get done, too."

We agreed that Peter would invite Shelly to walk with him *three* nights a week—Monday, Wednesday, and Friday—but upon their return session, I learned that this, too, had seemed too excessive a demand to Peter, and the ice-cream outing had also been postponed once again.

"I just don't think I should be expected to be involved with this," Peter asserted. "I work my butt off all day. I think I deserve my evenings and my weekends for myself. Someone's got to pay for these sessions, you know. If I wasn't doing my job, we wouldn't even be able to be here in your office."

I asked Shelly to leave the room for a few minutes, and then asked Peter, "What is the minimum amount of time you could commit to building a better connection with your daughter?"

"What do you mean?" Peter asked suspiciously.

"You felt that taking a walk five nights a week and going out for ice-cream once a weekend was too much. We adjusted it to three nights a week, and that felt like too much, too. But I still think Shelly should be able to count on *some* time with you, whatever amount it might be. So what feels to you, at this point in your life, like the minimum amount of time you could follow through on?"

"I don't know."

"It doesn't have to be a walk or an ice-cream cone. It could be a conversation at bedtime. It could be inviting her to help you water your garden. It could be teaching her a few golf strokes in the backyard."

Peter looked like a caged animal. "I just don't know," he said coldly. "Look, I'm hiring you to fix my daughter, I'm not hiring you to give me a hard time. If she's got some problems, you're the one who's supposed to come up with the answers."

"I'm trying to do that. But it appears that you don't agree with my prescription, which would involve Shelly having more time with her father."

"This is pointless," Peter snapped. "If you can't help her without my help, we'll find someone who can."

"You're free to do that. There might be other clinicians who have different ideas and would take a different tack. But if you're going to work with me, then I'd like for us to collaborate, so that we'll be more effective in guiding her through this."

"I've got to think about it, then," Peter said. "For now, I don't think we should schedule any more sessions."

"Then that's where we'll leave it. I'll be happy to give you the name of a couple of colleagues of mine whose work I can endorse, and I'll remain available should you want to check back in with me," I replied.

Not surprisingly, a few months later I got a call from another psychologist whom Peter had consulted, asking for my perspective on the case. She was running into the same roadblocks I had, except that Shelly's eating disorder had worsened. We compared notes and tried to develop some effective treatment strategies, including ones that might help engage Peter in parenthood.

Only a month later, I received a call from a psychiatric social worker at a hospital-based eating disorders unit, also asking for information about Shelly, who had recently been hospitalized there, her weight having plunged below ninety pounds. When I asked about her parents' involvement in her treatment there, she said that she had met with Shelly's mother, but that her father had not come in for the required family meetings, despite his promises to do so.

I was sure there were other factors contributing to Shelly's symptoms and decline besides her father's behavior, but his steadfast refusal to jump in and help rescue his daughter from a dangerous situation must have made her feel very unwanted and uncared for. Peter really *had* failed to be a good enough parent.

Much more typical of what I see, however, are the families in which parents exhaust and depress themselves trying to be good enough but never feeling that they are. Frantically attempting to meet every need, fulfill every wish, and be wonderfully, eternally present for their children, they suffer under the tremendous duress of trying to be what the essayist Nancy Mairs refers to as "G-d with skin on."

Darcy contacted me because she was "sick of feeling like a lousy mother." Thirty-six years old, with a son in the third grade and a daughter in the first, she was a highly accomplished scientist with a Ph.D. in microbiology who had chosen to work part-time so she could give more of herself to her family. Her current job involved working twenty hours a week in a biomedical research facility.

"What does 'lousy' mean to you?" I asked.

"It means that I'm not the mom I thought I was going to be."

"Who did you think you were going to be?"

"Someone who the kids could turn to, someone who tucked them in at night and told them stories, someone who volunteered at their school and got to know their friends and teachers, someone who made them good, healthy meals every night rather than doing takeout half the time, someone whose house didn't always look like a bomb had just gone off, someone who could really listen to them and what's on their mind without getting so distracted by everything." She paused, but only to catch her breath. "Need I go on?"

"That's a beautiful image of motherhood you've got there," I admitted, "but it also sounds like a pretty tall order to fill, particularly for someone who's working outside the home three days a week."

"But that's the thing, it's not like I'm working full-time, there are women who do that, there are women who have more than two kids, there are women whose husbands have worse schedules than mine does. He's home every night by six P.M., doesn't travel or work weekends, and I have friends who would cut off their right arm to have a husband who's home for dinner every night."

"Other parents notwithstanding, I'm left wondering how realistic it is for you to be working twenty hours a week and still expect yourself to prepare home-cooked dinners, volunteer in the kids' classrooms, keep an immaculate home, and always be emotionally available to them when they need you."

"But isn't that what a mother's supposed to do?"

"Within reason, yes. But I think you're going to have to choose where your energies go."

"Like how?"

"Well, if you're going to work outside the home three days a week, for example, then you might have to back off on volunteering in their classrooms, doing it every *other* week instead of every week. If you want to feel a little more patient and tender at bedtime, then you might have to turn the bathtime and reading over to your husband while you take a breather after dinner and try to get a second wind. Perhaps it's time to surrender your hopes for a consistently clean, well-organized home until the kids are old enough to really assist with that themselves."

"But those are all things that I want to be able to do," Darcy insisted.

"It's wonderful that you want to, and you can and should do some of them, but you can't do all of them, at least not all at the same time. And the children deserve a chance to develop some enjoyable interactions with their father as well as their mother."

Darcy grew teary-eyed. "I just don't know how much is enough. If I'm at work, I feel guilty that I'm not home. When I'm home, it's not like I'm so terrific to be with anyway. I don't get down on the floor and play with the kids, and I grow so weary of their fights with each other. My husband can really focus on them, he plays games and roughhouses and builds models—I'm usually off in my head, figuring out who's going to baby-sit when they have a day off from school, or how I'm going to pick up their soccer uniforms, or whether we've got any extra shoeboxes for their dioramas. Basically, I'm unhappy wherever I am."

No matter what Darcy did, and no matter how hard she tried, she had set the parenting bar so high that she would never be able to see herself as a good enough mother.

It was clear to me by the end of our first session that any straightforward efforts to convince her to ease up on herself were destined to be in vain. When reason and logic don't hold sway, there's usually more to the story than is being told, and it was those parts of the story that I knew we would have to address in subsequent sessions.

The process of recasting yourself as a good enough parent is similar to the process of recasting your son or daughter as a good enough child, in that you must journey beneath the surface and into the past to understand more about the origins of your expectations. I began the next session by asking Darcy to tell me something about her feeling of never knowing "how much is enough."

"No matter how much I do, I'm plagued by the sense that there's more I should be doing," she told me.

"Is this at home or at work?"

"More at home than at work. Like the other night, I decided I was going to start reading a book to my kids every night. They're both pretty imaginative, so we agreed on *Stuart Little*. They were very excited about this idea, and so was I, and it was really a lot of fun the first couple of nights. But a few nights into it we hit a chapter that was a little longer than the others, and they had a lot of questions to ask, and I was just so tired. I'd had a very difficult day at work. After about fifteen minutes, I told them we wouldn't be finishing the chapter that night, that we'd have to wait until the next night to get to the rest of it.

"But they were both upset about this so they kind of talked me into continuing, and I went ahead and finished the chapter, but by then it was way past their bedtime, and I still had to do the lunches for the next day and get the laundry done, and my mother's been sick all week and I hadn't talked to her all day so I knew she needed a call, and I just started getting this trapped, irritable feeling."

"Wasn't your husband available to give you a hand?"

"Well, he'd already supervised their homework that evening while I was out at a PTA meeting, and he had a bunch of telephone calls to make that had to get done by ten o'clock because he has all these clients who are in different time zones than we are, so he was tied up."

"So what happened?"

"So I finished reading, but I wasn't really enjoying it. I was reading it very fast because I wanted to get through the chapter, probably too fast for them, because I knew I had all these other things to do after they went to sleep. And they kept asking questions, which they should have a right to do—it's no fun listening to your mom read a book that you can't understand.

"But I got very short with them. I would answer in an annoyed tone of voice, and one time I scolded them, telling them they should stop asking questions and start listening more carefully. I just started to feel worse and worse, like I was ruining the whole experience for them, and for me, too. Instead of this pleasant, leisurely time together at the end of the day that I had planned, it became like a race, the opposite of what I wanted it to be.

"And when I tucked them in I was very abrupt with them, and I just felt so awful that their last encounter of the day with me was this very quick, distracted kiss, with my mind already on the other things I needed to do. I'm so tired of not enjoying my time with them and always thinking about the next thing that has to be done."

"In retrospect, how do you wish that you had handled that evening?"

"I don't know, that's my problem. It might have been better to just stop reading when it was their bedtime, even though we weren't done with the chapter, so that I could take my time tucking them in and then get to whatever else needed to be done. Or it might have been better to just continue reading until I finished the chapter, take as long as it took, not worry about their bedtime, and then give up on trying to do everything I had planned."

"Either of those would probably have been an improvement," I commented. "It sounds like the choice you made was the one that led to your feeling the worst—finishing the chapter, but doing so resentfully, and then feeling bad that you felt resentful."

"Exactly," Darcy agreed. "It's like whichever way I turn, I'm doomed. I never feel like I've done enough."

"I'd like you to take a moment to close your eyes right now, and to think about some of the first times you recall that feeling you've been talking about, the feeling that you haven't done enough."

Darcy winced at first, but then shrugged, slid down in her chair, leaned her head back, and closed her eyes.

"I remember that my parents used to have these nasty fights with each other, resulting in their not talking to each other for days," she began after a few moments. "But I would try to cheer them up, try to get them involved with each other.

"One time at dinner, they weren't talking to each other at all. There was this very stony silence. I started frantically telling jokes to try to lighten things up. And another time, I got my younger sister to help me put on a play in the evening, and we invited them into the living room to watch it, and I remember watching them so carefully, trying to get them to crack a smile or loosen up a bit."

"Did they?"

Darcy sat up and opened her eyes. They were teary. "I don't even remember, to be honest. All I remember is that I just hated that tension so much, and I did everything I could to try to make them happy."

"How do you think you did?"

"Not very well, I guess. They split up the year after I left home to go to college, and it was not a very mature breakup. Even now, I really have to be careful when we're having a family event, like one of the kids' birthdays, because the tension is so thick whenever they're in the same room. My father remarried pretty soon after the divorce, and that seems to be a pretty good relationship, but he still can't even be civil with my mom when they're in proximity with each other. And my mom has just become this recluse. Going out to dinner at the same restaurant with the same two friends every Saturday night is the extent of her social life. She wants nothing to do with my father's wife, won't even say hello to her or refer to her by name."

"How do you handle the friction between the two of them now?" I wondered.

Darcy sighed. "Oh, I try to tell my dad to be nicer to Mom when I know they'll both be over at my house. I've tried to establish a good connection with his wife, who I basically like, and I've sort of apologized to her for my mom's behavior, immature as it is, hoping she'll just tolerate it, which she does reasonably well.

"And I try to just ease my mom into things. When I know that she and my dad and his wife are going to be together for something, I sort of prepare her, remind her not to get too hurt, and try to really focus my attention on her, because my dad's got a partner who can focus on him.

"But they each put me in the middle still. My mom is wedded to this belief that my dad's wife broke up their marriage, since they had known each other before my parents divorced, and she'll still complain to me about having to deal with 'that homewrecker.' And my dad still complains to me about my mom, telling me how upset he is that she won't acknowledge his wife, even though they've been married almost twelve years now. It just doesn't end."

"Boy, it sounds to me like you're still doing as an adult what you used to do as a child to keep conflict between the two of them to a minimum."

Darcy chuckled sarcastically. "I guess you're right. It's still my job."

"And it's a job that you will never, *ever* be good enough at," I responded.

"Why?"

"Because it's not your job. You may have been invited to take on the role of making their relationship go more smoothly when you were a child, and you may still feel compelled to do so as an adult. But the fact is, it's a job that you will never succeed at, because it's their job, and it always was."

"So why do I keep trying to do it?" Darcy asked.

"Maybe because you still haven't forgiven yourself for not having succeeded, so you continue to persevere, hoping that someday, somehow, they'll figure out how to do it themselves."

"That'll be the day," Darcy said. "I don't imagine they'll ever change. There's certainly no evidence that they will."

"Perhaps that's why you still feel plagued by not feeling good enough as a mother," I proposed.

"What do you mean?"

"Maybe you're still so busy feeling like a failure as a daughter that you've transferred that belief to your role as a mother."

Darcy was silent for a few moments. "Do you really think that's so?" she asked.

"I don't know. But we could play around with it a little bit just to see, if you'd like," I suggested.

"What did you have in mind?" she asked.

"I want you to begin by keeping track of those moments when you feel like you're not doing enough as a mother. Make a note when they occur, in a pad or on a three-by-five card, or remember them the best you can in your head and write them down at the end of the day, so we have kind of a baseline sense of how often you struggle with this belief and what circumstances exacerbate it.

"And I'd like you do something else, as well. I would like you to write yourself a letter of resignation."

"What am I resigning from?"

"From being your parents' peacemaker. I want you to write a short note in which you resign from this position, explaining what duties you've chosen to relinquish and why you've decided to move on at this time. Please bring both assignments with you next time."

Darcy agreed to follow through, and in our next session she began by reading the resignation letter that she had written. It went as follows:

> To: My parents
> Re: Darcy's resignation
> I hereby resign my position as mediator between my mother and father. I have decided that they are entitled to have whatever kind of relationship they want to with each other, and that it is not in my best interests or their best interests for me to continue to try to arrange it for them.
> I will no longer perform the following duties:
> 1. Listening to one of them complain about the other over the phone
> 2. Making sure they're both comfortable with each other at family events
> 3. Feeling sorry for either of them
> I have decided that my energies would be best devoted to endeavors in which I have a reasonable chance of success, such as child-rearing, my marriage, and my research at work.
> Calls will not be forwarded.
> Thank you for your understanding.
> Sincerely,
> Darcy

I congratulated Darcy on her resignation, which she had obviously thought about with great care, and her plans to move forward with her life in ways that were bound to be more productive. She asked me if she should show the letter to her parents. My thoughts were that it was up to her, but that this was a situation in which actions would probably speak much louder than words. If she could follow through on what she'd written about, there'd be no reason for them to see the letter. On the other hand, if she didn't follow through, there would still be no point in showing it to them because it would upset them without serving any actual purpose. She decided for now to keep it for herself, but to use it as a reminder to stay clear of protecting her parents from each other.

I also asked to see the other part of her "homework," the log she had kept of those moments when she felt like an inadequate mother. As we looked it over together it was interesting to note that her feelings of not being good enough had more to do with her being unable to really be there for her children when they were together than with any actual failure to spend enough time with them.

"Now that you've given up one of your jobs, and one that was quite time-consuming as well as futile, you'll probably be able to do the job of mothering much more effectively," I suggested, "since that's a job, as you yourself put it in your resignation letter, at which you have a 'reasonable chance of success.'" I thought it was time to adopt a wait-and-see attitude, rather than urging any particular changes on Darcy.

In her next session Darcy reported that she was feeling much better about herself as a mother. "I think I was burdened by my role with my parents more than I realized. I was on the phone with my mom a couple of nights ago and she started to ramble on about how she had seen my dad and his wife at the restaurant she goes out to with her friends, and how uncomfortable it made her feel, and usually this would've gone on for a good fifteen minutes, but I didn't let it. I told her I was sorry she was uncomfortable, but it was in her power to create something more positive with them, and she was really stunned. I thought she had hung up the phone, she was so quiet! But I felt a lot better saying that than listening to her drone on. That's fifteen extra minutes I had with the kids right there, and there's probably plenty more where that came from."

"How about with your kids? Has that been any different?"

"A lot. When I start to doubt myself, or wonder if I've done enough, I just try to remember that I can't keep them happy or satisfied all the time any more than I can with my parents. One evening my son invited me out to watch him shoot some baskets, and I said I'd watch for a few minutes but then I had to get back inside. Of course, when I say it's time for me to go in, he says he wants to make just one more shot before I do, but he keeps missing that last shot, and keeps getting more frustrated, which of course makes him miss even more. Usually I would've just stayed out there waiting and waiting and waiting until he made that last shot, but feeling more and more annoyed with him, and with myself, for feeling so impatient.

"This time I was able to say, 'Honey, I know you'll make that shot, but I've got to get back to my chores. Come in and tell me when you've made it.' And I turned and went inside, clenching my fists the whole time because it was so hard. Sure enough, he came in a few minutes later and told me he'd finally made the shot, but he was angry with me and asked me why I couldn't have waited to see it."

"What did you say?"

"I said I would've loved to, but I had some other things to get to, and there'll be plenty of other evenings to watch him shoot baskets, and I was looking forward to seeing him play tomorrow. And he grumbled a bit, but he survived. And so," she added proudly, "did I."

Like Darcy, many parents need to free themselves of an inappropriate burden of guilt if they are ever going to be able to enjoy being with their children, to interact with them in a more relaxed and spontaneous way. This can be particularly true for divorced parents, who often seem to relieve their guilt in ways that make things worse, not better, for their children.

Bert had been divorced from his wife, Denise, for about a year, and had joint custody of their two sons. Dominick, 11, and Anthony, 9, spent every other week at Bert's home, but he was very unhappy with his inability to control them. "They seem to just do as they please," he said during our initial session. "If they don't want to do their homework, they blow it off. If they don't feel like shutting off the TV and doing their chores when I ask them to, then they don't. It's like I've got no authority anymore. I don't know why I have lost the capacity to be an effective father to my boys."

"What are some of the consequences for their behaviors when they don't follow your rules?" I asked.

"I talk to them and try to get them to understand the importance of getting homework or chores completed, but they just don't listen."

"So the consequence is that they are lectured?"

"I guess. . . ."

"Anything else?"

"Well, I've tried things like telling them I'll take away their allowance or restrict their TV time, but that doesn't seem to be working."

"What do you mean by not 'working'?"

"I mean that the boys still don't do what they're supposed to do."

"But do you deliver on the threats?"

"I try, but they always find a way around it. If I say no TV, I find out that one of them has sneaked downstairs and is watching in the basement. And the allowance doesn't seem to matter all that much to them, I guess because Denise gives them money too."

As Bert spoke, he sounded like someone who had basically given up, relegating himself to the role of impotent sermonizer.

"What does it feel like for you to have so little authority in their lives?"

"Terrible—I just feel like a total failure as a father."

I tried to point out to Bert that he had not made it clear to his children that there would be consequences to their actions. We developed a simple plan in which TV privileges would be granted only when chores and homework had been completed, and then agreed to follow up on the results in two weeks.

At the end of that time, Bert came in looking defeated. "It's just like the last time. I said there was to be no TV until I had checked their homework and their chores, and the first couple of nights things went fine. But then one night they said there was a show they really wanted to watch, and I agreed to let them watch it, and for some reason I hadn't checked beforehand to see if they'd done their chores, and they hadn't. So I went in and told them to turn off the TV and do their chores, but they didn't move, because they wanted to see the end of the show.

"So I let them do it, since there were only about ten minutes left. But by then it was getting late, and Anthony realized he had forgotten to study for his spelling test, so we sat down and did that, and by bedtime, neither of them had done his chores. And this kind of thing just kept happening after that night."

"Sounds like it happens because you *let* it happen," I remarked.

"How am I letting it happen?"

"By not following through on the plan, as we had talked about."

"I tried to. . . ."

"I know that. I can hear that. But something seems to get in the way of your being more clear and more effective. Your boys are not smarter or more experienced than you, yet they seem to be able to finagle things to their advantage pretty easily."

"I know. Why *is* that?" Bert asked, perplexed.

I thought it might be a good time to learn more about what had gone wrong with Bert's marriage to the boys' mother to see if that could help us to find some answers.

"We actually had a pretty good marriage, Denise and I," he began. "At least the first few years, when we were getting started, and the boys were little. But then she got this big promotion at work—she became a regional sales manager—and it seemed like she was working all the time, and we found ourselves growing apart. I finally discovered that she had been having an affair as well, with another manager at work, but to be honest it wasn't a big surprise. There wasn't much left between us by then."

"What are things like between you now?"

"Not very good, really. I mean, I think she cares for the boys, but I think she's still too focused on her work. Even when she's home she's on the phone or at the computer—that's what the boys tell me. The guy she was having an affair with, Lance, was also married at the time they met. He left his wife and wound up moving in with Denise, and they're still together. He and his ex share custody of *their* two boys, who are both teenagers, so they're over there every other week. And my boys say that Lance's boys bully them a lot, boss them around and tease them.

"I've talked to Denise about this, and she says the boys are just trying to get my sympathy, that when the four kids are together they get along fine, and that Lance is good with Dominick and Anthony. But I find it hard to believe. I just don't think my sons would be making up these stories about Lance's sons."

"How guilty do you feel about your sons having to manage such a difficult situation?"

Bert didn't hesitate. "I feel awful. I don't blame myself alone for the end of my marriage to Denise. I know that both of us were at fault, but whenever I think of Dominick and Anthony being so neglected by their mom, or having to fend off Lance's sons, I get this terrible feeling in my stomach. I wish I could be there for them all the time. I wish they didn't have to put up with so much."

"How might that contribute to your reluctance to say no and stand firm when they're at your place?"

"I've thought about that, and I suspect it's a big factor. I'm very conscious of wanting to enjoy them and wanting them to enjoy me. I bought a nice little townhouse only ten minutes from their mom's place, and I set it up with them in mind, so they've each got their own bedroom and the basement is a playroom. I'm not dating anyone right now, so I really focus on them when they're with me."

"But do you feel as if you need to abandon your authority as a way of making up for what you believe they're not getting at Denise's home?"

"I guess so. I feel like they've got it so hard over there, I want my home to be a haven for them."

"There's nothing wrong with creating a pleasant, satisfying environment for them, but how will they learn to be more responsible and cooperative without expectations and consequences?"

"You're right, I know. It's just that sometimes I can't bear to disappoint them when they're with me because they're so used to being disappointed at their mom's house."

Bert seemed to be trying to expiate the guilt he was feeling for not having been able to make his marriage to Denise work, and for putting his boys in the position of having to deal with two very different households, by becoming a softie and coddling the boys, protecting them from any distress or frustration. But the expiation had a price to it: he was incapable of setting realistic limits for his children. Consumed with Denise's not-good-enough mothering, he was feeling and acting like a not-good-enough father.

Knowing that there are as many stories as storytellers in any family, I told him I thought it would be a good idea if I met with Denise and Lance to learn more about what life for the boys was like in their home. Bert was agreeable to this plan, and so were Denise and Lance, who came to my office the following week.

Naturally, Denise's version of her marriage to Bert was somewhat different. "If Bert told you that I started investing more in my work life when I got promoted to regional sales manager, he's right, but I doubt that he told you that he was never around himself. He works with his dad. It's a retail furniture business, and his hours were always horrendous. I had been involved in sales before the boys were born. I stopped working for a few years and then got back into it once they started school.

"But if Bert had been more involved with me, I probably wouldn't have even taken the promotion, and I probably wouldn't have gotten involved with Lance. I was feeling neglected for a pretty long time. You can't imagine how lonely I was, with those two little boys, no job, and a husband with a seventy-hour workweek."

"How do the two of you manage your work and home life at this point?" I inquired of Lance.

He replied, "I do a lot of work from home, so I'm usually there when my boys, and Dominick and Anthony, are coming home from school. And I can cover for Denise when she travels because I have some flexibility in my schedule."

"I'm rarely home later than six-thirty, in time for dinner, and I don't really have to travel more than two or three days a month now," Denise said. "Bert makes it seem like I'm *always* away, but that's not the case, and I'm usually able to schedule my trips during the weeks that he has the boys anyway, so it doesn't really affect them."

"How do the four boys get along with each other?" I asked.

"Up and down," Denise said. "I think it's been an adjustment for all of them, and for Lance and me as well."

"There have been times recently when the four of them are all outside doing something together," Lance added. "Like over the weekend they all got involved with putting up our tent so they can do some sleeping out now that the weather's warmer. I'm hoping that maybe they're starting to get used to each other. My boys do gang up on Denise's boys, and I've had to stay on top of that. It's certainly more peaceful when my boys are with their mom, or when Denise's boys are off with Bert," he admitted.

The scene that Denise and Lance were describing was not quite as dreadful as Bert had envisioned. While there was certainly a big difference between the boys' life with their father, in which there were no other adults or children to contend with, and their life with their mother, in which time and attention were more divided, it seemed clear that their needs were being attended to in both households.

I then scheduled a session with Bert and the boys together, and I made sure I had some time with Dominick and Anthony without their father in the room. During that time alone, they shared with me their struggles to adjust to their parents' divorce and to make the transition back and forth between two different households. They certainly had plenty of complaints, as most kids do, but their complaints weren't limited to one parent and seemed to spread fairly evenly across the board.

They felt, for example, that Lance favored his boys over them, and that Denise was more interested in what Lance had to say when there was a conflict than in what they had to say. But they also griped that their time at Bert's was boring because they hadn't yet made any friends in that neighborhood (both parents had agreed that the boys would continue going to their original school, which was in their mother's neighborhood), and all they did when they were over there was watch TV or ride their bikes around the cul-de-sac.

In other words, life for them was imperfect, as it is for every child whether their parents have split up or not, but the imperfections were not confined to either household. Nor did it seem that the boys were being neglected or traumatized in any serious way.

When I shared that view with Bert, he seemed greatly relieved, although a little disappointed as well. It was as if he was glad to hear that the boys were not being treated as poorly as he had imagined, but was having trouble coming to terms with the fact that it wasn't a simple matter of his home being heaven and Denise's home being hell. She wasn't quite the neglectful mother that he had created in his mind.

"We had talked about the possibility that you were having difficulty setting limits with the boys because you felt so guilty about what you had 'put them through,' but it appears that they're not as bad off as you had imagined," I summarized.

"You're right—although I still believe Denise and Lance probably put on the best face possible when they spoke with you."

"I'm sure they did," I agreed, "but I also spoke with Dominick and Anthony, and they didn't sound all that outraged by their life with their mother and stepfather."

"Then why would they complain about it so much to me?" Bert wondered.

"It sounds to me like they're astute enough to realize that it softens you up a bit and enables them to scoot around some of the rules you keep not enforcing."

"You mean they're trying to manipulate me?"

"I wouldn't rule that out," I concurred.

"So how do I handle it when they complain about how their stepbrothers treat them, or how their mom is never home and they're stuck with Lance? Just ignore them?"

"I think you could suggest that they take up their complaints with their mom and their stepfather."

"But I don't think anyone over there listens."

"Perhaps they don't. But I think it's worth a try to see if they would. And you can offer to help the boys word their complaints in a way that would make it more likely that they'll be listened to, which would be a skill they could use in many other life situations as well. Whatever the outcome, it would be better than letting them manipulate you into allowing them to behave so irresponsibly. If you let them get away with that, you're being just as unavailable, in your own way, as you accuse Denise of being."

That last comment seemed to jolt Bert. He agreed to stick with the original plan that we had made, linking TV rights with completed chores and homework for at least another two weeks, and to begin discouraging the boys from complaining to him about their life at their mother's while encouraging them to raise these issues directly with those involved.

When he returned a couple of weeks later, he seemed more pleased and confident. "They pushed it, and tried the same business that I talked about last time, but I didn't yield and that TV wasn't turned on one time until everything had gotten done, and I mean *everything*."

"How did they push it?"

"One night, just a couple of nights after we last met, we were finishing up dinner and I was going over what needed to be done before they watched their favorite TV show. Well, almost like it was on cue, Dominick began to talk about how they never get to watch this show at their mom's because Lance's sons hog the TV and watch something else, and there's no way he can do his chores and his homework in time to watch it.

"And I could feel that bad feeling starting up, like they should at least get to watch it at my house no matter what, even if they're not done with what they need to finish. But instead, I suggested that he talk to his mom and Lance if he thinks he's being treated unfairly at their house, and that at my house he could videotape the show to watch another time but the chores and homework were not negotiable.

"What did he say?"

"Oh, he grumbled and said there was no point in talking to his mom, that it wouldn't make any difference, anyway."

"And what did you say?"

"Well, I was kind of torn. Part of me believed him, but I remembered what you said about the importance of teaching them to speak their mind, and I just said that I still thought it was worth bringing up with their mom. And then he accused me of taking Denise's side, and I realized how ridiculous this debate was, all over a TV show, and how we were getting off the subject of his needing to do his homework and load the dishwasher, so I just ended it right there. I told him he could watch the show that night if he did what needed to be done, or he could forget about it and waste the evening debating with me. And I also reminded him he could have the chance to watch it at his mom's, too, but he'd have to take care of that himself. And that was that."

"How did it feel to shift your interaction with him in that way?"

"Great. It was a big relief for me to be that clear with him. And what was funny was that once Dominick went upstairs to do his homework, Anthony kind of whispered to me that they usually do get to watch that show at their mom's, it was just during the basketball playoffs that Lance's sons would commandeer the TV in the evenings. So that made me feel a little better about standing firm, too."

By realizing that he had not consigned his sons to a miserable life simply because he and their mother had created separate households, Bert was better able to overcome his guilt and regret and offer his boys more of what they needed. A father who had convinced himself of his own unworthiness had redefined himself as good enough.

As I said at the beginning of this chapter, today's parents are besieged by unclear, and often conflicting, messages about how to successfully fulfill their role as caregivers. With every media-worthy crisis or tragedy, be it a high school shooting, a drug overdose, a suicide, or a car crash, experts appear, attempting to retrospectively make sense of what are, in essence, incomprehensible events, usually by pointing the finger at ineffective parents.

Unfortunately, what parents are told they are to do is not always consistent. For example, shortly after the 1999 murders at

Columbine High School in Colorado, there was a strongly worded editorial in our local paper about the importance of parents' remaining involved enough with their teenagers to know what they're up to: get acquainted with their friends, volunteer at their school, and sit on their bed and talk with them at night was the advice, and it was surely good advice at that.

On the same day, in the same section but on a different page, there was an article focusing on parents' *overinvolvement* in their teenagers' lives. High school guidance counselors and academic advisors in college were noting that even the parents of graduating seniors still wanted to "be involved," often, they believed, to an unhealthy extent. "I have parents calling me to find out how their son is getting along with his roommate, or how their daughter is doing in chemistry," one university dean commented. "That's the kind of thing I would never have encountered ten years ago. They're not really letting their children become adults."

What parent wouldn't feel somewhat confused by the opposing directives embedded in these two articles? I work with parents every day who struggle mightily with these dilemmas, and of course I wrestle with the same uncertainties myself. How much is enough? How much is too much? What is the difference between empathizing and enabling? What is the difference between constructive and destructive criticism? When are we pushing too hard and when are we backing off too quickly?

There is no final answer to these questions, however. The ultimate bible of child-rearing has not been written, nor will it ever be. Parenting is more art than science, and being a good enough parent depends less on what you do and more on the spirit in which you do it. That is why acknowledging that you are far from perfect, that you have made mistakes as a parent, and will do so again, is so essential. And remember, children do not enter the world with a preset notion of what ideal parenting is. If allowed to, they will forgive any lapses in reliability, attention, or patience that turn out not to be chronic.

So while I can't provide you with a comprehensive syllabus on how to know with certainty if you're acting like a good enough parent, I can offer you some guidance when it comes to dealing with the doubts that many thoughtful, contemporary parents are contending with.

ALLOW FOR RESILIENCE

Many modern parents adhere almost religiously to the tenet that the hurts and sorrows from long ago have crippled them forever and there is no way for recovery, regeneration, and regrowth to occur. We are then trapped into believing that the same holds true for our children, that the hurts and sorrows we can never prevent them from experiencing will cripple them as well. This belief can tighten like a tourniquet around an entire family, leaving everyone gasping for relief.

Since we may feel as if our hurt and sorrow were the result of our being raised in a dysfunctional family, we may conclude that we are unworthy and incomplete, unable to effectively minister to our children because of what was "taken" from us as children. To feel ready for and deserving of parenthood we stubbornly devote ourselves to psychologically cleansing and repairing ourselves, as if we were a house that needed to be spotless before going on the market. The reality is that our childhood pain has usually sensitized and ennobled us, and remembering this can emancipate us to raise our children with less anxiety.

It's also important to emphasize that people, including children, have evolved to thrive, not perish, under real-life conditions. Human beings are not delicate and brittle, but supple and hardy, motivated by challenges and responsibilities and able to psychologically metabolize dissatisfaction, frustration, and even trauma. Treating ourselves, or our children, as excessively fragile deprives us all of the chance to have faith in ourselves and diminishes our capacity to learn from disappointments, recover from hurts, compensate for our handicaps and disabilities, and capitalize on our potential.

As parents, we must bear in mind that hardship does not automatically translate into psychological damage, and that we can choose to wallow in victimhood or celebrate the human capacity to triumph over victimization.

Medical science has demonstrated the many ways in which the human body can be surprisingly resilient and survive physical injuries and infections of the worst kind. But the human *spirit* is resilient, too, and can also survive the emotional injuries and infections that we must all at some point endure.

KNOW YOUR LIMITS

Well-meaning mothers and fathers are sometimes convinced that being a good parent means being constantly attuned to their child's every thought and feeling. Yet such attunement is neither possible nor desirable, and pursuing this too conscientiously actually robs a child of the experience of sorting out his or her own interior struggles and uncertainties, an experience that is crucial to the development of self-respect.

We might hope that trying to discuss and put into words each nuance of what our children are living with will immunize them against feeling any loneliness, fear, or ache, but these feelings are part of the human condition, and to some extent need to be accepted as such rather than avoided.

Communication between parent and child is, as we all know, of supreme importance, but of equal importance is learning how to think, feel, and act on one's own. This means making the effort to engage with a child, but also remaining aware of the need sometimes to disengage and let a child work out a problem on his or her own. The two intertwined processes create a person who feels confident that he is connected *with* others, but comfortable about being different *from* others.

ALLOW FOR A RANGE OF FEELINGS

We are all indoctrinated in the belief that parental love is a natural reflex, a spontaneous swelling of warm, pleasurable feelings that have no choice but to crescendo at the first whiff, glimpse, stroke, nibble, or sound of our child.

But being a loving parent doesn't mean that we will always feel loving. Sometimes we are more likely to feel like a dry ravine where the river of affection has, for mysterious reasons, ceased to flow. This can be very disturbing to those of us—that is, most of us—who had expected those warm waters to flow perpetually.

Unfortunately, parenthood has been sanitized and valorized to the extent that the natural ambivalence every parent feels has become proscribed. We are expected somehow to be *unfailingly* understanding and supportive, which deprives us of the opportunity to experience any spontaneity in our emotions and makes it equally difficult for our children to be open to the full range of human feelings. Parents who feel that they constantly have to be on "good behavior"—never distracted, never impatient, never disappointed—place great pressure on their children to be the same way, which can be quite constricting.

Acting as if you feel equally loving no matter what your child is doing and what you are actually feeling perpetuates a fraud and confuses your child, who intuits that there is *something* lurking behind that façade of pleasant beneficence, even though she can't quite put her finger on it. Often, she will create or provoke some conflict to bring to the surface the tension that she senses—quite accurately—to be there.

The reality is that breaks and ruptures in your empathy for your child are both normal and expected, and they have a hidden pay-off, which is that they help normalize your child's own breaks and ruptures, so she knows there is nothing permanent about them, or anything to make her feel that she is a bad person.

Sometimes when I'm working with parents who feel they must put aside every negative, critical thought they're having, I ask them to take five minutes a day to write out all the thoughts that make them uncomfortable. Knowing that there is a time and a place for that negativity, and releasing it into the collective parental ether, is often a great relief and allows them to discharge the tension that has been inexorably building up.

All of us suffer the slings and arrows of outrageous offspring, but the anger, hate, and resentment we feel are not the opposite of love: *indifference* is. That is why we have to create an atmosphere of tolerance for the complex mixture of feelings that is an unavoidable part of family life, indeed of any richly hued, passionate relationship.

ALLOW FOR DOUBT

One rabbi I studied with suggested that the surest way to ascertain the depth of people's faith was to gauge the quality of their questions: the more intense and troubling the questions, the more profound the faith.

I have similar feelings about parenthood. Child-rearing is too elaborate an endeavor to insist on clear-cut certainty and consistency. The sheer variety of situations we are confronted with in workaday family life makes it highly unlikely that we will always follow through on our tightly held convictions. Often, we will be hard-pressed to even remember what those convictions are.

The fact is, some introspection and flexibility have real virtue. By not being rigid we teach children the value of their persistence, demonstrate open-mindedness, foster their ability to think and express themselves on their feet, and help to conserve our energy for larger, more productive battles. Giving in from time to time or providing children with the opportunity to persuade you to do things their way will not harm them. On the contrary, you are more likely to ultimately build their capacity to work in partnership with others.

Naturally, there's always someone in the vicinity who appears to have all the answers, who knows exactly what to do and follows through with crispness and clarity. But to my mind, the parent who doesn't experience any uncertainty may be very closed off to precisely those complexities that make children the unique, remarkable people they are and may refuse to allow new and essential information about them to be processed and incorporated. Besides, parents who don't seem to recall having any uncertainty, like your know-it-all aunt or your judgmental father, may be suffering from the benign amnesia conferred by the passage of time.

As one exasperated mother remarked to me after summarizing all of the "surefire" advice she had been given about her daughter, "I know I'm not always sure of what I'm doing, but all these people who think they know everything, to my mind have a lot to learn."

DON'T BECOME OVERRESPONSIBLE

The optimistic belief that all children want to do well, perform successfully, and emulate and gratify their parents fosters the unavoidable conclusion that if there are any departures from this sunny prognosis, it must be their parents' fault. This was aptly captured in a cartoon which depicted a ragged-looking, multiply pierced young adult complaining to his buddy: "My life has been totally screwed up for years, but thus far neither of my parents has stepped forward to claim responsibility."

Children do indeed want to grow and develop in healthy ways; however, the road to maturity and self-sufficiency is not only paved with an eagerness to please but simultaneously littered with thick dollops of impulsivity, self-centeredness, arrogance, and impatience.

While some of the parents who come into treatment resemble Peter, the father who refused to accept any responsibility for his children's difficulties, much more typical are those parents who enter my office as if they were entering the woodshed, their beleaguered heads bent in anticipation of the verbal whipping they are certain I will administer to them for having been the sole source of whatever problem their child is experiencing.

One of the reasons we are vulnerable to such self-criticism is that when we have a child, we are reminded of the grandiosity of our own childhood, when we were convinced, temporarily at least, that we were the center of the universe and everything happened because of what we did or didn't think or do.

This narcissism is of course irrational, but it provides great comfort to a child, giving him a sense that he has control over his world, that he engineers the family's experience. The alternative, which is to assume that the universe operates without any input from him, is terrifying to a child.

So the little boy who concluded that his parents divorced because he wasn't always nice to them becomes the father who assumes that his daughter's lack of friends is the direct result of his not having been nice enough to her. The little girl whose father blamed his inability to accumulate much money on having "too many kids" becomes the mother who convinces herself that her son's poor grades are also her responsibility because she wasn't always available to help him.

Parents who remain wedded to the belief that they have failed as parents convey that belief to their children, who then become convinced that they must ultimately fail as well. You can take active responsibility for being part of the solution to your child's problem without having to assume that you were somehow the sole cause of it.

LET THEM GO AND LET THEM GROW

I've lost track of the number of parents who come to my office saying, "I've been to every one of my son's basketball games," or "I have never missed one of her plays," or "We have never left our daughter with a sitter or in day care." Often these statements are made when their child is having difficulties and are meant to defend the positive, substantial role the parents have played in their child's life.

Most of us were taught to believe that by being very vigilant and attentive, we could avoid, or help others avoid, harm. But being overly vigilant and attentive with our children can actually increase their vulnerability to harm, in the sense that they won't develop the self-confidence and savvy necessary to handle the many surprises and setbacks, challenges and choices, that life will inevitably present.

Leaving them with a difficult teacher for a semester rather than rescuing them by hastily insisting on a transfer, giving them the chance to be coached by someone other than yourself, going away with your spouse for a long weekend and leaving them with the capable, but not necessarily entertaining housekeeper who's worked for you for years, are legitimate decisions to make, and help instill in your children a sense of faith in their capacities.

There will always be disappointments, even dangers, that we cannot keep our families safe from. Recognizing this can help us to realize that our physical and emotional presence is not always possible, or even desirable.

SELF-CHANGE VERSUS SELF-BLAME

There is a Hasidic story about the son of a rabbi who went to worship in a nearby town. On his return, his family asked, "Well, did they do anything different from what we do here?"

"Yes, of course," said the son.

"Then what was the lesson?"

"Love thy enemy as thyself."

"So it's the same as we say. And how is it that you learned something else?"

"They taught me to love the enemy *within* myself."

Constantly blaming yourself for your parenting mistakes is like taking the wrong medicine: we keep ingesting it in larger and larger doses, hoping it will produce results, but of course it never does. A guilt-drenched parent always raises a guilt-drenched child.

I believe there is nothing wrong, and much that is right, with recognizing that you have blown it in an interaction with your child, but this recognition is most useful when it is seen as information that can be used for self-growth rather than self-indictment, a way to prevent subsequent blowups rather than as a reason to engage in extended mourning over what has gone wrong.

Likewise, it is appropriate to apologize to your son or daughter for having overreacted, but this is best done in tandem with pointing out the behavior that contributed to your overreaction: "I should not have screamed at you like that, but when I repeatedly ask you to shut off the TV and get moving on your homework, and you ignore me, I find it very difficult to control my temper." Nobody feels good when they have unloosed their fury on a child, but this fury can carry with it an important message: "If you are consistently going to behave inappropriately or uncooperatively, you will generally not like the consequences." When children can find some meaning in a startling or upsetting exposure to parental rage, their sense of security will be only temporarily shaken, rather than significantly impaired, and feelings of closeness and trust can be restored, often at a higher level.

Parents who can remind themselves to understand and accept their weaknesses teach their children that the essence of being a human is to continuously fall short of our goals, and yet to keep striving just the same. As the Japanese proverb states, "Success means falling down seven times, and getting up seven."

EVERYONE SUFFERS BY COMPARISON

Comparing our children to other children is destined to wash away their self-esteem, but comparing ourselves to other parents will have a similar effect. We may be determining how we stack up against a friend, a neighbor, a colleague, a sibling, a grandparent, maybe even against a fictional character in a movie or novel, but no matter who it is, we're destined to lose out in the process.

No other parent had the same childhood, or has the same child, as we do, and because of this, it is pointless to try to assess our standing as parents by looking through the lens of someone else's life. Besides, it's impossible to know what really goes on in someone else's family. While it's easy to imagine that parenting comes to others as easily as breathing, what I have seen is that raising a child brings even the most self-confident individuals to their knees at some point, whether they admit it or not.

There's nothing wrong with a little healthy competition with other parents, real or imaginary, old or young, if the result is that it motivates you to excel, and to be the best mother or father you can possibly be. But beyond that, it's always best to trust that despite your fantasies about your counterparts, you are likely to be the best parent your child has got, and to go ahead and act in ways that make good on that trust.

MAKING THINGS EASY CREATES GREAT DIFFICULTIES

Finally, it is important to bring to parenting a humble respect for its enormous complexity. Expecting it to go smoothly can only result in even more suffering than every parent is likely to experience. Not every child-rearing question has a concrete answer, and not every family conflict has a workable solution. Children need us the most when they are least pleasant to be with, and, as we have seen, even loving parents don't always feel in love with their children. As soon as you get through one crisis, another one is guaranteed to appear on the horizon.

These unsettling but unavoidable realities need to be gently embraced, rather than ferociously battled. The wisdom of this approach will result in a family life that is enjoyed, rather than endured, and will allow for your hard-won feelings of good-enoughness to take root and spread their healing, compassionate energies among every family member.

EXERCISE EIGHT

Often, when the standards we hold ourselves to as parents are most unattainable, there is an associated history. Early in the chapter we saw how Darcy's time-honored belief that she needed to be her parents' peacemaker—an impossible task—carried over into her parenting and led her to constantly feel like a failure both as mother and daughter. Her decision to eventually resign that position was liberating, and enabled her to be more realistic about what she could do, and to feel better about what she did do.

Ask yourself the following questions to see if you can determine the origins of your impractical beliefs about what you should be able to do as a mother or father.

1. How well did you meet the expectations that were imposed on you as a child?
2. How realistic were those expectations?
3. What happened if you could not meet those expectations?
4. How many of those expectations have you internalized, and to what extent is your self-respect contingent on your performance in these areas?
5. What would it be like to begin releasing the least realistic of those expectations? What would begin to live and breathe? What would begin to wither and die?

EXERCISE NINE

The quote from Elijah with which I opened this chapter speaks poignantly to the desire we all have to compare well with our parents when it comes to parenting. This can sometimes be hard to do, however, because our image of our caregivers is always rooted in the past and seen through the lens of our childhood.

Many mothers and fathers don't feel good enough because they are struggling with the internalized representation of their own mothers and fathers. You may have grown up thinking your father was the most wonderful man in the world, and thus constantly feel as if you fall short. Or you may have concluded that your mother was awful and believe that you must do *everything* differently from her to compensate for the damage that her maladaptive parenting incurred.

Give some thought to how realistic your portrait of your parents' parenting is, and think about how your perspective on the way you parent is affected by this portrait.

To create a more realistic portrait, it's often a good idea to do a little psycho-archaeology—to dig around and create a more full-bodied depiction of your mother or father, the way Alex did in Chapter 3.

For example, Tanya constantly criticized herself as a mother. When I asked about her own mother, she went into a state of rapture. "My mother was a saint," she said glowingly. "She was the most wonderful mother a girl could have. She was like a best friend to all of my friends, and to this day many still stay in touch with her, sometimes even more than they stay in touch with me! I'll never be able to fill her shoes."

It was my belief that one of the reasons Tanya was so disappointed in herself as a mother was that she compared herself to an idealized image of her own mother, one that she would never successfully match up to.

Tanya had a sister, Vera, older by eight years, whom she didn't see very frequently, but who was coming into town for a business trip. I suggested that she take advantage of this to talk with her about Vera's recollections of their childhood.

When she returned, she had a great deal to fill me in on. "We shared a lot about growing up, and it was surprising for me to learn that Vera had some real complaints about Mom. For example, she always felt resentful that Mom got so involved with her and her friends, as if Mom was competing with her to see who could be better liked. And she also said that she didn't think that Mom and Dad had a good marriage, and that Dad had had an affair at one point, which was something that I didn't have a clue about! I'll tell you, it was a real eye-opener talking with Vera and seeing things from a different angle."

As Tanya began developing a more down-to-earth profile of her mother, she found that her hitherto relentless self-criticism began to ease.

EIGHT

The Good Enough Marriage

There is no problem for which children are the solution.
Annie Lamott

We have seen how your ability to see your child as good enough is always filtered through the prism of your individual experience. But there is another prism through which your view of your child is also refracted—your relationship with your spouse.

With each child that arrives, your marriage becomes another set of interlocking triangles, and triangles are always accompanied by the eternal ebb and flow of loyalty and betrayal, rivalry and alliance, love and hate, remorse and guilt. While child-rearing is a tremendous opportunity for a couple to deepen their commitment to each other and become stronger and more unified, it is also one of the most fertile of breeding grounds for marital conflict. This reality was captured in a cartoon I came across in which a mother said to a father as their son was casually entering their room: "Do you want to tell him he's taking all the fun out of our marriage, or should I?"

Nora and Frank, for example, were the parents of 2-year-old Jackson, who had been regularly hitting and kicking his mother when he did not get his way. It quickly became apparent that Jackson's obstinacy coincided with a severe decline in his parents' approval rating of each other. "He's not much of a dad," Nora complained about her husband almost right away. "Most of the time, he gets home from work too late to spend any time with Jackson, and even when he's home earlier than usual, he just says hi, grabs something to eat, and then heads upstairs to work on the computer. I have to beg him to give Jackson a bath or read him a story. I shouldn't have to encourage a father to be with his son."

Frank was just as dissatisfied as his wife. "Since the day we brought Jackson home from the hospital, Nora hasn't paid any attention to me at all. Everything is Jackson, Jackson, Jackson. 'Do you want to hear what Jackson did today?' 'Come on, Jackson, show Daddy how you can draw!' 'We can't go out this weekend with our friends because I don't want to leave Jackson with a sitter.' I mean, who's she married to, him or me?"

An insidious cycle had been set into motion: The more Frank felt that Nora preferred Jackson over him, the angrier he felt, anger that was conveyed through neglecting his son, the tiny rival for his wife's affection. And the more Nora felt that Frank neglected Jackson, the more she invested in her relationship with her son, trying to make up for her husband's absence by being two parents instead of one. This of course left Frank feeling more neglected by his wife, leading him to be more neglectful of his son, which in turn engendered an intensification of Nora's involvement with Jackson.

By the time they came to see me, an active state of hostility existed in their household, sex had vanished, and they had drifted dangerously apart. No wonder little Jackson was so frustrated and angry, I thought. Between feeling neglected by his father, engulfed by his mother, and overwhelmed by their growing animosity toward each other, it's a wonder he's not hitting and kicking everyone in sight, rather than just his mother.

Over the weeks that followed, as I got to know Nora and Frank better, it became clear to all of us how they were both unwittingly engaged in writing new editions of old family histories. Frank's apparent indifference to Jackson upset Nora because she recalled her own father as distant, seeming not to care much about her. "I remember one time we were at church, and a friend of the family who hadn't seen us for a while asked my father, 'So what grade's Nora in now?' I was so embarrassed. Not only did my father have to stop and think, he actually came up with the wrong answer!"

Nora's consuming love for Jackson upset Frank because it

reminded him, without his being aware of it, of all the love and attention his mother had lavished on his younger sister, leaving him feeling ignored and excluded. "It was so obvious that she wanted a daughter more than a son. I felt so *disposable* once she was born, like I was some sort of stand-in until the real child came along. I was looking through my mother's purse one time when I was a kid, and I remember seeing one or two pictures of me but about a dozen of my sister. She was always the star in my mother's eyes."

Sorting out the origins of their reactions to each other helped to gradually shift this destructive cycle in a more constructive direction. Frank learned to express himself more directly when he was feeling neglected by Nora, rather than retaliating by ignoring his son. He also discovered that the more interest he displayed in Jackson, the more fun Jackson was to be with and the more interest his wife displayed in him, both of which naturally increased his motivation to be an involved father.

Nora learned that a more satisfied husband makes for a more proactive, vigorous father. She tried not to be so completely absorbed by her son, but to make her marriage more of a priority. She began asking Frank how his day had gone before moving the focus onto Jackson, for example, and she agreed to hire her 15-year-old niece as a baby-sitter once a month so that she and Frank could get out as a couple on Saturday nights. She also took me up on my suggestion that she act more swiftly and firmly when Jackson displayed aggressive behavior, rather than trying to "talk him into stopping," as she had previously been doing.

Meanwhile, as Jackson sensed the warming shift in the marital climate and experienced more time with his dad and more space with his mom, his aggressive behavior diminished. Parenthood had led this mother and father to reexamine, and heal, their old wounds, and as their past was rewritten in the present, their future became much brighter.

The past that we replay in our interactions with our children is not always the family-of-origin history. Sometimes we are replaying painful episodes from our marital past. Kevin and Chantee were at loggerheads when it came to how to handle their 14-year-old daughter. Cassandra was a bright, high-achieving ninth-grader who was repeatedly sneaking out of the house late at night for secret rendezvous with a boyfriend neither of her parents was crazy about. Douglas was 18 years old. He had left high school without graduating, was working at the nearby supermarket bagging groceries, and living in an apartment with friends—hardly the partner these parents envisioned for their dazzling daughter.

"I think this guy's bad news," Kevin announced. "We've got to do everything in our power to prevent them from getting closer, but my wife has this attitude like, 'Let them be, let them be.' Well, how can I 'let them be'? Am I supposed to sit back and let her hang around with a good-for-nothing eighteen-year-old who didn't even have the sense to finish high school? Am I supposed to just *let* her go out and see him whenever she wants, *let* him get her pregnant, *let* him ruin her life before she's even gotten started? What kind of a father would allow that to happen?"

Chantee spoke with equal intensity. "You can't make our house into a prison, Kevin. She's going to go out, she's going to see guys, she's going to have boyfriends. If you don't let her see Douglas, then we're basically forcing her to sneak out at night. I hope to god she's not having sex, I hope to god she's protected if she does, and I hope to god she's not going to get pregnant—but you can't keep a 14-year-old girl in jail when she hasn't committed a crime."

"But she has committed a crime—the crime is sneaking out in the middle of the night to do god-knows-what with this yo-yo," Kevin interrupted angrily. "We should do everything in our power to prevent them from seeing each other. And we've got to have her adhere to a curfew, which you never do. The other night she came in at one-thirty in the morning and her curfew is eleven-thirty at night, and what did you do? Nothing! You just let her go up to bed. If we don't take a stand here, this goofball's going to screw up her life, and ours, too. Are you ready to raise her baby, Chantee? Are you ready to become a grandmother?"

"Of course not," Chantee retorted. "But you're making it so that she never wants to be home anymore, because you're always fighting about this, telling her she can't go out, telling her when she has to be home, telling her she has to check in, telling her Douglas is bad for her and that he's not to come near the house. I sent her up to her room that night so you wouldn't scream at her. And if you don't stop screaming at her, she won't even be home at one-thirty—she'll stop coming home altogether. I mean, you have so many rules for her, like she's a bad kid or something, and she's not—she's just in love. He may not be the greatest catch, but he's a sweet guy—she could do a lot worse. Our daughter is in love, *head over heels* in love. Don't you even remember what that's like, Kevin?"

"I guess not," he replied venomously, and Chantee glared back at him.

The dynamic of the cycle was easy to see: The harder Kevin tried to squelch Cassandra's relationship with her boyfriend, the harder Chantee worked to try to free Cassandra from her oppressive father. The more Kevin condemned Douglas, the more Chantee supported this underachieving young man. But what was not clear to me was what had set these two parents—both of whom were very concerned about a relationship they thought might threaten their daughter's future happiness—on such a collision course.

As is usually the case when things have reached an impasse this unbridgeable, these parents turned out to be hostages to their respective pasts, unable to respond to their daughter's needs in a rational way.

I used the time I spent alone with each of them to try to shed some light on what had led them to this apparent dead end.

Chantee told me that Kevin's behavior brought her father to mind. "My dad was in the military, and he demanded total obedience. He used to literally sit on me if I dared to defy him, if I opened my mouth to speak my mind. I hated him, and I couldn't wait to leave home, and I probably did so too early, before I was ready. That's why I married Kevin when I was only nineteen—I just couldn't take it any longer. Even now it's difficult for me to be with my father. He hasn't changed all that much. He's *still* got to have things his way all the time."

"I hear the ways in which Kevin is like your father. Are there ways in which he is unlike him as well?"

"Well, he was never like this until Cassandra started seeing Douglas. That was one of the things I liked about him at first. He seemed so different from my father, much kinder and more open-minded. But since Cassandra hit adolescence, it's like he's changed into someone else, someone identical to my father."

"But he's not identical," I tried to point out. "He's simply responding, during a *particular* phase in your daughter's life, in ways that are reminiscent of how your father used to respond to you all the time."

"Say it any way you want—my father was impossible, and Kevin's acting the exact same way."

During my time with Kevin, I detected that Kevin was haunted as well, but by a different ghost. He told me that in the early years of their marriage, Chantee had had a short-lived affair, which he learned about by accident after it was already over and which had left him with feelings of rancor and mistrust toward his wife that persisted to this day. "I can't believe I was made a fool of all those months when she was involved with someone else. If I hadn't come upon some letters she had hidden in a drawer, I probably still wouldn't know about it."

"Do you think she'd be unfaithful again?"

"That's the thing—I just don't know, and I can never be sure. But I will always remember the feeling of discovering those letters. It was like a knife in my chest. I literally sunk to my knees, I was so hurt and shocked."

"How long ago was this?"

"Oh, it was early in our marriage, when Cassandra was still little—I'd say almost ten years ago, now."

"How much longer before you'll be able to put it to rest?"

"I don't think I'll be able to," Kevin said, his eyes smoldering. "You can't turn back the clock. What's been done is done. I can't ever forgive her for betraying me in that way."

"Forgiving her wouldn't mean condoning what she did, though," I attempted to explain. "It might mean that you can release yourself from your feelings of having been betrayed so the two of you can remove an old roadblock that gets in the way of your marriage."

"Would *you* forgive your wife if she had an affair?"

"I would be very hurt and very angry, just like you are. But I would hope that we could learn what we each contributed to the conditions in which the affair occurred, and find a way to heal the pain and move forward."

"Well, you're a better man than me." Kevin scowled, unconvincingly.

It wasn't hard for me to see how Chantee was symbolically trying to liberate herself from her father by subtly supporting Cassandra's risky efforts to liberate herself from Kevin. And it was just as easy to see how Kevin's unsuccessful efforts to control and limit Cassandra's relationship with Douglas was a belated response to Chantee's having "snuck out" and cheated on him years before. The work that lay before us involved getting the two of them to recognize the phantoms from their past and putting those phantoms to rest so that they would cease to sabotage the present.

Until Kevin could differentiate his daughter from his wife, and until Chantee could differentiate her husband from her father, Cassandra would remain without the steady, lovingly imposed limits she needed in order to manage her first love relationship without getting in too deep.

The marital disrepair that usually accompanies family life can commence as soon as the baby is born. In a previous book, *Things Just Haven't Been the Same: Making the Transition from Marriage to Parenthood,* I explained how the early stages of child-rearing, which usually involve a deleterious combination of hormonal changes, sleep deprivation, unrelieved tedium, financial stress, social isolation, increased involvement with in-laws, and a decline in sexual satisfaction, are often so demanding that even the best of marriages suffer and are slow to regain their prior resiliency.

But the demands of child-rearing do not end as children grow up. The strains of working outside the home, running a household, staying on top of homework, maintaining a schedule of appointments and activities that appears to rival D-day in its complexity, setting limits, being attentive, and fulfilling the thousands of other endless endeavors that make up the life of a modern parent can create a breach in the most solid relationship.

Our marriage, which ideally offers a sanctuary in which to sort out or gain respite from the intense, unrelenting effort and emotionality of parenthood, often becomes nothing more than the sinkhole into which we dump our worst, most disconsolate emotions. Spouses find themselves divided, rather than unified, by their children and prone to taking out their anger not just on each other but on the children as well, through neglect, aversion, aloofness, or hostility.

Naturally, this wreaks havoc on the potential for our child to be, and be seen as, good enough. As we saw in the two short cases presented above, the complaints that parents present about their children quite frequently reflect underlying fractures in the spousal subsystem. And this process can take a variety of forms. In one family, for example, a woman feels too intimidated by her husband to criticize him openly, so her outspoken criticism of her daughter becomes a substitute for her unspoken criticism of her husband. In another, a father may express his anger at his wife by ceding too much power to his son, quietly fanning the flames of rebellion while undermining Mom's efforts to be in charge while he's away at work.

But family processes are always bidirectional. Children, far from being passive observers or victims of a flawed marriage, will tirelessly attempt to take care of an ailing relationship in a variety of inventive ways. Sometimes their tactic is to be as "good" as possible, hoping that if they get enough A's, score enough goals, win enough medals, earn enough accolades, and are dutiful, kind, and submissive enough, they will somehow heal their parents' relationship and woo them into a state of shared pride and pleasure.

Sometimes their tactic seems counterintuitive, but it still has the same goal. By being so difficult to raise that their parents couldn't possibly consider separating, by deflecting ill-will directed from one parent to the other, by relentlessly forcing to the surface subterranean issues so that they can finally be dealt with and grown through, these children are investing great effort in the restoration of their parents' marital bond.

Let's take a look at a family in which a child's problem behavior had, as its source, a fissure within his parents' marriage, and how the process of repairing that break enabled all of them to deepen their emotional as well as their spiritual bonds.

The Feldman family entered my office for their first session one afternoon and briskly took their seats. "We're in crisis, and we don't have a lot of time to sort this out," Steve began, cutting right to the chase without even saying hello. "Jeff's bar mitzvah is less than three months away, and he's not even close to being ready to lead the service or chant his Haftarah. He's not practicing regularly, he's not taking it very seriously, and I don't know what he thinks is going to happen when he's called up to read, but at this rate it's going to be an embarrassment for him, and for all of us."

Already aware that this was going to be a treatment that did not proceed at a leisurely pace, I turned right to Jeff, a smallish, bespectacled seventh-grader, and solicited his opinion: "Does your dad have reason to be concerned about your preparation for your bar mitzvah?"

"No," he snapped. "I'm getting it done, I'm just not getting it done perfectly, like he thinks I should. Plus, he's making me do more than I have to do. I've already got to do the whole Haftarah, rather than half, like my friends who are sharing their bar mitzvahs with another kid. Now he's saying I've got to lead part of the service, too, and I don't think that's fair. Almost none of the other kids have to do that."

"Is that true, Steve?" I asked.

"He's right, there's no one else in his class with the same bar mitzvah date, so he can't split his portion in half. But I know there are other kids who lead part of the service as well. Just a few weeks ago we went to the bat mitzvah of a classmate of his and she led the service from start to finish. Don't you remember, Jeff?"

"So I'm supposed to be just like Cheryl, is that it?" Jeff shot back. "Cheryl's a dork! She had all that time to practice because she doesn't have any friends. She spends her whole life inside, studying. I don't care what Cheryl did. I just don't want to have to do more than my fair share."

"What about the basic portion that you are expected to know," I asked him. "Do you feel as if you'll be ready to chant it by your bar mitzvah date?"

For the first time, I sensed some hesitation from Jeff, but then he quickly recovered. "I'll be fine," he responded, looking at the floor.

"I don't know how you think you'll be fine when you don't practice, and when you do practice, I've got to be standing over you
the whole time, making sure you don't wander off to get a snack
or check to see if you've gotten any e-mails. Jeff, this is Hebrew
we're talking about—it's another *language,* and I've heard you—
you haven't really learned it yet."

"Who is helping him to learn it?" I inquired.

"We hired a tutor, a real nice guy, who Jeff meets with once a
week—that is, when Angela gets him there," Steve said, tossing an
angry look at his wife. I had been so absorbed in trying to sort out
what was going on between Steve and Jeff that I had almost forgotten she was there.

"Steve, he's missed a total of two tutoring sessions since we
started a few months ago," she said, her eyes blazing. Then she
turned to me. "Steve thinks I should have made Jeff meet with his
tutor last week, even though he wasn't feeling well. Poor Jeff was
completely wiped out, he was fighting a cold and had barely made
it through the school day, and I just couldn't see pushing him to go.
I thought he needed the evening to rest and recuperate."

Steve jumped in. "I don't know, Angela, when I came home
that evening he looked pretty comfortable to me, the two of you
in the family room, drinking hot chocolate and watching TV
together."

"Oh, this is ridiculous," Angela said, glaring at Steve. "For god's
sake, can't he have an evening off when he's not feeling well, when
he doesn't have to practice for his bar mitzvah? Just one evening?
He's twelve years old, Steve, what is the big deal?"

"The big deal is that he's not prepared, that he basically manip-
ulated you into feeling sorry for him so he didn't have to meet
with the tutor, simply because he didn't feel like it, not because he
was sick, and we've got a bar mitzvah coming up that he's not
going to be ready for. Would I mind if he missed a tutoring or practice session if he was more diligent and making more progress? Of
course not. But we're coming down to the wire here, and I honestly don't know what's going to happen on April tenth when the
rabbi calls him up and he's got to read in front of a hundred and
fifty people."

Not feeling that it was necessary for Jeff to witness any more conflict between his parents than he had already seen, I excused him from the room and spent the remainder of the session with Steve and Angela.

"Angela, your husband is very anxious about the possibility that Jeff will not be adequately prepared for his bar mitzvah. I can't tell if you share his concerns."

Angela's tone of voice shifted from angry to confused. "I'm not sure I know enough about all of this to be concerned. Steve is Jewish and I'm not, and while I agreed to raise Jeff as a Jew and have him go to religious school, I haven't had any experience with bar mitzvahs before. To be honest," she said a little guiltily, "I've never even been to one."

"I've invited you to join Jeff and me at synagogue, so that you can see a few bar or bat mitzvahs and learn what they're all about, but you always have a reason not to," Steve said.

"Is that true?" I asked her.

"I guess it is," Angela agreed, looking cautiously at Steve. "Look, Steve, I'm really out of my element here. I know this bar mitzvah is important for you, but I can't tell how important it is for Jeff. What I do see is that you're making him miserable by constantly being all over him to practice and learn his part, and he feels like you're asking too much of him."

"I wouldn't have to be all over him if you would simply do your part," Steve said, looking exasperated.

"But what *is* my part?" Angela pleaded. "What, exactly, am I supposed to do? I've worked with you on the guest list for the party, I was the one who found a good photographer, I'm the one trying to organize the food we'll be having."

"But a bar mitzvah is more than a party, honey," Steve said. "It's an important ritual in Judaism, a coming of age ceremony, not just a giant birthday bash for a thirteen-year-old."

"So what is it that you expect me to do?" Angela repeated.

"Show some interest in his learning what he needs to know. You take over sitting with him while he practices. Make sure he goes to the tutor, even if he's not feeling a hundred percent. Why am I always the one playing the heavy?"

"Honey, I can sit with him when he does his part, but I wouldn't know if he was doing it right or doing it wrong. I can't read a word of Hebrew. What good would it do?"

"How important is Jeff's bar mitzvah to you?" I asked Angela, noticing, out of the corner of my eye, Steve leaning forward with interest to hear her reply.

"Right now," she said softly, "I really don't know. [I could see Steve fling himself back in his chair in exasperation.] It seems like nothing more than a big hassle, a source of tension for everybody. One of the reasons I stopped going to church thirty years ago was because I thought so many religious rituals were hollow and meaningless, more trouble than they're worth."

Steve jumped right back in. "See, this is why he's not making progress. You don't care about this bar mitzvah. You're sabotaging it."

"Steve, I'm not sabotaging it," Angela replied, her voice rising again. "If you want Jeff to have a bar mitzvah, then by all means have a bar mitzvah. I've been as supportive and as helpful as I could be. And I'm not stopping him from practicing. But you can't expect it to matter as much to me as it does to you."

Turning to Steve, I asked, "What have you done to help Angela understand more about why this event is so meaningful to you?"

"Well, like I said, I've invited her to go to services with Jeff and me, and she hasn't gone."

"What else?" I pushed.

"What else could I do?"

"You could share with her stories from your own bar mitzvah. You could show her the translation of the selection that Jeff will be reading so she knows what it's about. You could invite her to contribute to the service by finding or creating a special reading or piece of music. You could ask her what role she wants her family members to play in the ceremony. There's a lot of places to begin."

Steve was silent, but Angela wasn't. "He's right, Steve, now that I'm thinking about it, you haven't really brought me into this very much. You accuse me of only caring about the party, but that's the only part you've asked for help with. You're correct, I don't have much interest in going to services, but I've never really liked going to services, church or synagogue. How can you expect that Jeff's bar mitzvah will matter to me when you haven't taken the time to let me know why it matters so much to you? And you've completely excluded my family. You're busy trying to enlist your relatives to participate in the service, but what are mine supposed to be doing the whole time?"

"But this goes way back," Steve responded. "I remember whenever I had to be away on a business trip during the week, somehow those were always the days that Jeff was 'sick' and you didn't send him to religious school. You were always eager to help him with his homework in elementary school, but when it came to his homework from Hebrew school, you acted like it didn't exist."

"How much can one person do?" Angela almost shrieked. "Why do you get so nuts about all of this? He's being raised Jewish. He's going to have a bar mitzvah. I don't know what else I can say!"

Tension being as high as it was, I decided that I needed some time alone with each parent to see what they had to say without their partner in the room. I began with Steve, who, I learned, was the son of two Holocaust survivors, one of whom, his father, had died almost two years earlier.

"How did being raised by survivors influence your definition of yourself as a Jew?" I wondered.

"It's very complicated, because my parents hadn't been raised to be very religious themselves, and they certainly didn't raise me to be religious. We only went to synagogue on Rosh Hashanah and Yom Kippur. We didn't light candles on Friday night. Being identifiably Jewish was something they understandably had grave reservations about.

"But there was always a very strong belief in the importance of being Jewish, so my decision to marry someone who wasn't Jewish was gut-wrenching for me—my parents were incredibly upset at first. But once it became clear that I was not going to convert and that we were going to raise our children Jewish, and of course, once they saw what a good person Angela was, they grew to accept her and really love her."

"What impact did being raised by survivors have on your thoughts about Jeff's bar mitzvah?"

Steve took a long, slow breath, sighing it out. "It's been a very powerful experience, preparing for this bar mitzvah. I wasn't a very observant Jew growing up, or even as an adult, but when I think about what we went through as a people and how much we survived, I gradually came to see his bar mitzvah as a statement about who I am and my heritage. It's a way to say, 'Look at how amazing it is that I'm here, that my son is here, that we're alive!' "

"What would your father be thinking about all of this if he were still alive?"

"I've thought a lot about that, too, particularly because the date of Jeff's bar mitzvah is right around the anniversary of my dad's death. I guess it would be really wonderful for him to see that he had survived for a reason. He was a very depressed man. He lost just about his whole family in the Holocaust, and I know sometimes he didn't believe there was any point to living after such tragedy. But he always came alive for his grandchildren, and I think that if he were here, he'd rejoice. And it would prove to him that I hadn't given up on Judaism just because I had married outside the religion."

While Steve's words were very moving and very meaningful, it was also easy to see how much pressure was being placed on Jeff's slender shoulders as his bar mitzvah neared. He wasn't simply being asked to learn some ancient prayers and receive the blessings of his family and congregation as he prepared for an adolescent rite of passage. He was being asked both to redeem his father in his deceased grandfather's eyes and to be a public testament to the enduring resilience of an entire religion. Quite a load for a seventh-grader to carry, I reflected privately.

My time with Angela was also instructive. In asking about her religious identity, I discovered that she had become disenchanted with Catholicism early on and had devotedly steered clear of any formal religious identification since her Confirmation as a teenager.

She also told me, however, that she had recently reconnected with a childhood friend who was part of a progressive church, and who had been encouraging her to read some books by modern theologians, books that had helped her to see more clearly how to forge a Christian identity that was actually quite compatible with her personal and political beliefs.

"A new world has started to open up to me. Suddenly being a Catholic doesn't seem so archaic, so rigid. I've even gone with her to a couple of services at her church and have been thinking about joining a discussion group on 'Feminism and the Bible' that the pastor there is going to lead."

"What does Steve think about your growing interest in creating and reclaiming your own religious identity?"

"To be honest, I haven't really talked about it. There's been so much going on with Jeff that I haven't wanted to get into it with him."

"Are you concerned, though, that he might have mixed feelings about your quietly beginning to pursue this path?"

"I'm afraid so," Angela said, looking worried. "I mean, let's face it, it's lousy timing. Here he is trying to prepare all of us for this public declaration of his family's Jewishness, and after almost thirty years I'm starting to want to go to church and read the New Testament." She rolled her eyes sadly at the irony of the situation.

"How much does Jeff know about your religious identity?"

"If you had asked me that at any time up until last year, I would've answered, 'Nothing.' I've basically shunned religion since childhood and was perfectly content to follow my husband's lead—join a synagogue, enroll Jeff in Hebrew school, and educate him as a Jew.

"But one afternoon this friend I was telling you about, Abby, was over, and we were just chatting about church, and Jeff was there, and he seemed very interested. He started asking her all kinds of questions that I couldn't answer, about Jesus, about the difference between the Old Testament and the New Testament—it was really neat for me to see his mind opening up. Later that night, when I was tucking him in, it was the first time he asked me about what religion was like for me when I was growing up. It was something we had never talked about before."

"Have these discussions been pursued by either of you?"

"Not really—although the other day I was reading this book that had been written by a female minister, and Jeff wandered over and read a little over my shoulder, and asked what it was about."

It seemed to me that Angela's spiritual journey, as moving and meaningful as her husband's, must have posed something of a conflict for Jeff. Being a good son to his father meant taking on the mantle of young Jewish adulthood through becoming a serious, thoughtful, well-prepared bar mitzvah. But being a good son to his mother would mean being free to explore and identify with her spiritual yearnings, too. No matter which way he moved, he would inevitably feel that he was letting one of his parents down.

No wonder he was approaching his bar mitzvah with such half-baked efforts. This was the only way for him to walk the tightrope he was on, an unsatisfying solution to what appeared to be an unsolvable problem.

I brought Steve and Angela back together without Jeff for our next session and shared with them my thoughts about the quandary their son was in. To their credit, both immediately understood and were open to my suggestions for how to release him from his loyalty bind.

"It is up to both of you to convey to Jeff that you will be working together to help him study for his bar mitzvah. Steve, you can do your part by making this ritual a family ritual rather than a personal one. You need to invite Angela into the process of the bar mitzvah by sharing with her its significance for you and by treating her as your partner in raising Jeff rather than as some auxiliary relative who's there simply to help coordinate the reception.

"You also need to see Jeff as Jeff, not as the symbolic representation of all of Jewish survival or as a vehicle for vindicating your intermarriage in your parents' eyes. Maybe it's really enough for him to just learn his Torah and Haftarah portions without having to lead the service as well."

"Angela, you need to join forces with Steve to help Jeff through this rite of passage while still feeling as if you are entitled to pursue whatever spiritual quest is meaningful to you. You don't have to give up on your own heritage to successfully co-parent your son. And he needs to know that he's not betraying you and what you believe in by more assiduously completing his preparation for this ceremony."

Steve followed through by scheduling a meeting for the two of them with the rabbi, who offered numerous suggestions as to how Angela and her family could contribute to the bar mitzvah service. And Angela set up a separate meeting with the pastor that she had been so impressed with at her friend's church, finding that she was finally able to talk about her long history of ambivalence about Catholicism. This, she told me, enabled her to feel more positive about not only her own religion, but her husband's as well.

With a more cohesive parenting unit in place, things quickly improved. Steve told his son that it was up to him if he wanted to learn any of the "extra" components of the ceremony, which was a great source of relief for Jeff. Steve and Angela also established a regular half-hour practice session every evening after dinner. Even if Steve was unable to be home at that time, Angela agreed to insist that Jeff use this time well or he'd lose his rights to television or computer time.

Angela also agreed to go to services with Steve and Jeff for the next few Saturdays so she'd have some familiarity with what was going to take place at Jeff's bar mitzvah. In return, however, she asked Steve if he would join her for services at church some Sunday after the bar mitzvah.

Steve surprised her by agreeing, and then shared with both Angela and me a very beautiful story, one that neither Jeff nor Angela had ever heard before. His mother had actually been rescued from the Nazis by a group of Catholic nuns who had hid her for many months and arranged for her safe passage to the United States. This story became the basis for Jeff's speech from the pulpit as part of his bar mitzvah. Angela reported back to me in their concluding session how moving his words had been, and how they helped to assuage the feelings of both sides of his family by reminding everyone that courage and compassion are not confined to any one race or religion, and can show up in even the darkest of times. By rescuing their son from his competing loyalties to them, Steve and Angela had finally allowed Jeff not just to succeed, but to use his success as an instrument of healing for the wounds in their relationship.

We have seen how a child is more likely to be good enough if he is being raised by two people in a good enough marriage. Here are some strategies for creating such a marriage.

1) Decide Where Your Loyalties Lie

Family therapists try to help couples distinguish between vertical loyalties and horizontal loyalties. Vertical loyalties extend either up, to our family of origin—our parents, grandparents, siblings, cousins, aunts and uncles—or down, to our children. Horizontal loyalties extend across, to our spouse.

It is not always possible to strike a satisfying balance between vertical and horizontal loyalties. When you override your husband's objections and invite your parents to join the two of you for dinner on his birthday because you don't want them to feel left out, you are choosing to be a good daughter over being a good wife. When you work twelve hours a day in the business your father started and ignore your wife's wishes that you be home for dinner at least a few nights a week, you have opted for vertical loyalties at the expense of horizontal ones. When you "look the other way" and allow your daughter to watch TV after your husband disallowed it because of her back talk the night before, you are pledging allegiance to her over him.

In general, I believe that *families function best when a couple's horizontal loyalties take precedence over their vertical loyalties.* This means that children, grandparents, and any other contenders for love, power, and loyalty have to be constantly reminded that your marital relationship comes first.

Naturally, such prioritizing cannot occur all the time. When there is a newborn in the house, for example, and the baby wakes up crying, the parents must attend to the child no matter how much it interferes with whatever time they were hoping to enjoy together. However, as we saw in the case of Frank and Nora, children need to see that their parents' relationship with each other is sound and intact. This helps them to internalize a healthy model for intimacy, something they can carry with them throughout childhood and use as a basis for establishing their own intimate relationships as they grow.

Likewise, grandparents also need to be shown that you and your partner are the ones in charge and running the show now. They had their chance to raise children, and no matter how they did, at this point it's your turn. Thus, you will tell your mother that you appreciate her advice regarding the "dangers" of the family bed, but that you and your partner have made your own decision about that matter. And you will tell your father that you understand how upsetting this may be to him, but you have decided not to interfere with your daughter's relationship with a boy of a different race. Remaining vulnerable to your parents' opinions and somehow believing that they still "know best" is natural, but child-rearing decisions need to originate with your children's parents, not their grandparents.

The process of maintaining horizontal loyalties can be done in many ways. When you and your spouse either agree about how to set limits for your child, or make your disagreements known in private so that no one else is brought into the negotiations, you are maintaining good horizontal loyalty. When you ask your children to move over so their parents can snuggle on the couch together or leave them with a sitter so the two of you can go out to a movie together, you are maintaining good horizontal loyalty.

Remaining faithful to your marriage, in the fullest sense of the word, can be a challenge, but the more you do it, the better off you and your children will be.

2) View Differences as Assets, not Liabilities

Marriage is the union of two individuals, and no two individuals are ever alike. But the experience of starting a family together will highlight the bedrock differences between them as no other life event can ever do. The contrast between how a mother and father were raised by their parents, for instance, will become most glaringly exposed when they take on the task of raising children. The wife who felt that her authoritarian parents did a great job raising her and her brothers may clash with her husband, whose very liberal parents seemed, in his eyes, to be right on target.

However, you do not have to be identical to your partner or give up your uniqueness to join together as effective parents. Just as Steve and Angela discovered in the course of helping their son prepare for his bar mitzvah, there are always respectful compromises that make it possible to honor our differences, and even to use them to enrich ourselves and our relationship.

3) Accept Gender Differences—and Feel Free to Escape Them

The different ways in which men and women seem to *instinctively* handle parenthood are another source of potential tension. Even in the very first days of parenthood, fathers will hold, talk to, play with, and smile at their child in a way that is distinct from mothers. Subsequent approaches to communication, limit-setting, instruction, managing anger, conveying affection, and a host of other parental endeavors also appear to be strongly influenced by a parent's gender.

Despite the lasting influence of the women's movement, the men's movement, and the participative childbirth movement, parenthood still continues to beckon many individuals into performing traditional, sex-stereotyped roles. Men often respond to family life by feeling more responsible for being good providers, while women often shift their focus from the office to the home and take on more of the child-rearing responsibilities. If such transitions do not seem to be occurring quickly or tangibly enough, anxiety begins to surface, often expressed through complaints and criticism of each other.

Conversely, from the woman's point of view, the transition may be happening all too rapidly, as she finds herself alone in the role she thought she and her partner had agreed to share equally. Couples need to be sensitive to each other's expectations about the parental roles each expects to play—and they need to be prepared to be flexible when those expectations turn out to be unrealistic.

4) Communicate Your Needs

My experience observing hundreds of marriages over the years (including, most closely, my own!) has yielded what is for me the irrefutable doctrine that it is our determined efforts to *avoid* conflict that actually precipitate the worst conflicts. When we bury what we believe, censor what we think, or edit what we say so as to avert a dispute in the present, we are ultimately laying the groundwork for a battle royal in the near future.

Communicating clearly and effectively is always the key to addressing and resolving differences of opinion and defusing the possibility of escalating conflict. It also models for your children the verbal strategies and techniques they will need for their own lives.

Perhaps the most important aspect of good communication is being precise about what it is that you want. One of the most abused words in co-parenting dialogue is "help." For example, many times a woman will say that she wants "help" from her spouse in a child-rearing matter, but when that help is forthcoming, she still doesn't seem satisfied. "My husband will look over my son's math homework if I ask him to, but if I don't ask, he doesn't bother," she complains, prompting him to respond, "But all you have to do is ask, and I'll do it. What more do you want me to do?"

In this case, what she wants isn't so much "help"—which implies that she is the principal caregiver, her husband merely an auxiliary—but a *shared sense of responsibility and commitment* in enhancing their son's abilities in math. What she really wants is for this to matter as much to her husband as it does to her, to take an interest without her having to prod him to do so. Until this is made clear, and until she creates the opportunity for this to happen, she will always feel like he's letting her down, and he will always feel that whatever he does is never enough.

I often encourage parents to ask themselves three questions before they communicate a need to their spouse:

1. What is it that I really want my partner to do more or less of?
2. Is what I am asking of my partner something he or she is actually going to be able to do, knowing who he or she is and what other demands he or she is contending with? If not, who else might be available to provide it?

3. What am I doing to increase the chances that he or she is going to respond to my request in a positive way?

Such questions help us to state our requests more clearly, and to make them more realistic as well.

5) Forgive Your Partner and Yourself

As we saw in the case of Kevin and Chantee, unresolved marital issues can contaminate not just the marital relationship, but the parent-child relationship, too. In Chapter 6, we learned that children need to be forgiven for not fulfilling the conscious and unconscious dreams their parents have for them. Forgiving them doesn't mean we don't hold them accountable for their behavior, but that we release them from the unwritten contract that insists that they devote their lives to satisfying and completing ours.

The same holds true for marital forgiveness, because our mate, like our child, will inevitably disillusion us as well. A marriage partner is always at least partially selected to replicate, validate, mirror, or repudiate some unexpressed aspect of ourselves or our parents. While we might like to believe that we come together as individuals in our own right, it's more accurate to acknowledge that, to some extent, we join up to inhabit each other's fantasy worlds. And whenever we look to another person to redeem some aspect of the past, we are bound to be disappointed, for that is a job no one can do.

The process of forgiveness emancipates our partner from the prison of our fantasies, and allows us to see and appreciate our partner for who he or she is, allows our partner to be, in essence, good enough. In a working marriage, this usually stimulates mutual feelings of forgiveness on our partner's part, so that we too are liberated and feel good enough as well.

Because our spouses are usually the ones closest to us, they are often the afflicted beneficiaries of our blame when family difficulties arise. "How did you expect her to turn out when you've spoiled her all these years?" "He didn't make the hockey team because you were always late getting him to tryouts." "The learning disabilities come from your side of the family, not mine." "He's developmentally delayed because you used to get high when you were pregnant with him." But holding your spouse hostage by constantly wielding these tightly held grudges does nothing more than keep you and your entire family under siege.

The steps that move us toward a state of marital forgiveness are really no different from those that move us toward a state of parental forgiveness. Acknowledging the realistic and unrealistic expectations we have been carrying for our spouse; finding ways to seek constructive, rather than destructive, entitlement in an effort to create a better relational balance; speaking the right words and performing the meaningful rituals that will help us each to heal the painful past—all of these can be applied to our marriage as well as to our children.

A patient of mine once told me that the key to her happy marriage of more than fifty years was "eventually running out of the energy it took to stay angry with him." Once her anger no longer absorbed all of her energy, she mused, her feelings of fondness and gratitude for her husband had more room to flourish. Forgiveness helps us to release the energy bound up in our hurt and resentment and channel it in more loving ways.

_____ EXERCISE TEN _____

MARITAL FORGIVENESS MEDITATION

Forgiveness in a marital context requires acknowledging the wounds you have inflicted on each other. Such wounds can include:

1. Abuse (physical and emotional)
2. Abandonment (physical and emotional)
3. Infidelity
4. Loss of money, job, or reputation
5. Loss of health
6. Loss of freedom

7. Parenting difficulties and disagreements
8. In-law difficulties and disagreements
9. Division-of-labor difficulties and disagreements
10. Sexual difficulties and disagreements

Take a look at this list, and put a check next to those you think you are responsible for and an X next to those you think your spouse is responsible for.

Pick one that has a check next to it, and think about how you might earn forgiveness from your partner for having inflicted this wound. Tell your partner you are sorry for what you have done, and ask your partner what you could do that would help to heal the wound. It might be through doing some kind of penance, expressing some kind of remorse, "making up for" what was done or not done in some way. Continue this process with all subsequent checked behaviors.

Now pick one that has an X next to it. Think about what your partner could do or say that would help you forgive him or her for having inflicted this wound. If you would like, let him or her know, so he or she can think about whether he or she wants to follow through or not. Continue this process with all subsequent X-marked behaviors.

When you have gone through both the checks and the X's, take about five minutes to reflect upon the ways in which your partner has been a positive, loving presence in your life, rather than a disappointment. If competing, negative thoughts begin to intrude on your meditation, allow them to simply bubble up and disappear and gently bring yourself back to a positive frame of mind. Try this exercise daily, and notice how your feelings of resentment and anger eventually begin to dissolve, to be replaced by more kind and compassionate feelings.

As you forgive, and find yourself experiencing more kindness and compassion, remind yourself that your child will very likely be involved in an enduring, intimate relationship as he or she matures, and that the more positive your feelings are for your child's other parent, the more positive your child's feelings for his or her life partner will one day be.

Allow this reality to motivate you to further melt your anger and bitterness, and to release the love that is locked in all of us.

NINE

The Good Enough Divorce

*Nor will failures interfere with holiness, for genuine holiness
is precisely a matter of enduring imperfections patiently.*

Thérèse of Lisieux

If finding effective ways to parent as partners and see our children and each other as good enough is daunting when a mother and father are married, it's even more of a challenge when they are separated or divorced. At this juncture, enormous strength and self-restraint may be required to collaborate sensibly as co-parents, let alone simply to make sure you don't murder your ex.

Not only must divorced parents contend with the sometimes overwhelming personal distress that accompanies the dissolution of any marriage, but they must reassure their children that they will always be there for them, though they have chosen not to be there for their former spouse. And they must also encourage their children to feel free to continue to love and care for that person, no matter how much anger and hurt there is between them.

Like their parents, the children of divorce are also experiencing a myriad of strong emotions, and the guilt, remorse, fear, grief, and ire that are inseparable aspects of a dissolving family unit will express themselves in numerous, sometimes problematic, ways. Trying to fathom the depth of whatever problems could propel their two beloved parents to stop living with each other, dealing with their anger at both Mom and Dad, adjusting to the prospect of new households, schools, neighborhoods, stepparents and stepsiblings, witnessing expressions of antagonism and malice between their caregivers, and feeling alone and unprotected, longing for the family that can no longer be, will leave even psychologically robust children feeling temporarily unnerved and unhinged.

However, while divorce is always painful, if the divorcing parents don't divorce the child, but remain available as parents in spite of their own pain, the suffering of all concerned will fade over time. In fact, while few children are eager for their parents to divorce, once they are relieved of the unspoken tension or vitriolic anger that are part of most failing marriages, they may be better off.

Children develop in healthy ways in postdivorce homes when their parents remain unified as mother and father even though they are no longer husband and wife—when they can come to agreements and make child-rearing decisions with a minimum of friction and bitterness, when they provide their child with guilt-free access to their other parent, when they don't let their guilt transform them into becoming excessively permissive, when they don't inappropriately turn to their child for support and nurturance, and when they give their child room to experience and talk about their often conflicting emotions.

But this is a tall order, and the normal feelings of resentment and victimization on the part of divorcing parents, coupled with their unavoidable desire for revenge, can sometimes trigger a torrent of emotions that bring out the worst in everyone.

Let's take a look at how one divorced mother struggled with these feelings successfully enough that she was able to help ameliorate a difficult situation involving her daughter, and in the process foster her own growth and healing as well.

Greg and Pauline scheduled a session with me because of their concerns about 7-year-old Jeanne's interactions with Pauline. Greg and Vicky, Jeanne's mother, had separated when Jeanne was 3 and were now divorced. Greg and Pauline had been married for about a year now, after having dated for more than two, "more than enough time for Jeanne to get used to things," according to Greg.

But despite Jeanne's having known Pauline for almost three

years, she could still be quite hostile and standoffish. "It's really absurd. She acts like Pauline is not even there most of the time," Greg continued. "She'll start to talk about something that happened at school, and Pauline will ask a question or make a comment, and without even looking at her, Jeanne will say something like, 'I was talking to my father.'

"She comes down and says good night to me, but not to Pauline, which I think is very rude. She'll find ways to avoid being alone with Pauline, even if it means coming along with me for something I know she doesn't want to do. And Pauline's never been anything but kind and friendly with her from the very day I introduced Jeanne to her."

"What has this been like for you, Pauline?" I asked.

"It's very painful," she said sadly, tears swelling in her eyes. "I've tried to be patient all along, and it's not like I'm trying to replace Jeanne's mom, or anything like that. But for her not to even say good night, or acknowledge me in a conversation, or show me even the most basic kind of respect—well, it's really becoming unbearable. And I don't dare discipline her or anything, but if I even ask her to help me out with something, you know, get dinner on the table, or give me a hand bagging up the grass clippings after I've mowed, I can forget it.

"It even extends to my parents. They've gone out of their way to treat her just like their other grandchildren. They send her birthday presents and Christmas presents, and when they visit they usually bring her something special. They've really taken the time to get to know her and what she likes, like these American Girl dolls that she's into, but she won't even write them a thank-you note when she's gotten something from them. And that makes me a little angry. It's one thing if she's going to be disrespectful of me, but when she's like that with my parents, it feels even worse."

"How has it gone when you have broached this subject with Jeanne?" I asked Greg.

"I've basically gotten nowhere, which is why we're here," Greg responded. "I've told her that she doesn't have to love Pauline in the way she loves her mother, but that she's got to treat her with respect. Her two older brothers have been good about this, they get along with Pauline quite well, so it can't really be Pauline's fault. And even they have gotten a little tired of how nasty Jeanne can be with Pauline. The other day my older son, Daryl, said, 'Dad, you've got to do something about Jeanne—she's becoming such a spoiled brat.'"

"What are the custody and visitation arrangements these days?" I asked.

"I get the kids every other weekend and one evening a week. I usually take them all out to dinner, and then back to my house to finish their homework, maybe watch a video if there's time. So it's not like they don't see their mom much, or that Jeanne is with my wife all the time."

"And what's your relationship with Vicky like?"

Greg took a long breath before answering, and Pauline turned to look at him. "Chilly, I would say. The marriage was just one of those marriages that was never meant to be. We were in our early twenties, and not very grown up. We had our first child within a year of being married, and then had another two, hoping that things would improve, but they never did. By the time Jeanne was born I knew it was over, and we hung in there together a little longer—you know, 'for the kids'—but I really can't even remember a time that we were truly happy together."

"So where do things stand now?"

"Well, as I said, we're not on very good terms. We can't seem to agree on anything related to the kids. We worked with a mediator during the divorce process, but that didn't help, and by the end, we weren't communicating at all except through our attorneys. Nowadays she's on me if I pick up the kids five minutes late or drop them off five minutes early, she complains if they come home without having finished their homework, she makes plans on weekends when she's supposed to have the kids and then can't understand it when Pauline and I don't agree to cover for her. It's a mess."

"Has she remarried?" I inquired.

"No. She's been seeing a guy—his name is Willie—but it's a very up-and-down relationship because Willie is still married. Apparently, and I've learned this from a friend of mine who knows him, he's left his wife once or twice but then goes back to her.

Sometimes I think how Vicky treats me is dependent on what's going on between Willie and her. If they're getting along, then she's pretty reasonable with me. If she and Willie are on the outs, then I feel like I pay the price."

"What is your relationship with Vicky like?" I asked Pauline.

"Pretty much like my relationship with Jeanne," she replied with a sarcastic chuckle. "I'm just kind of there. If Vicky can avoid dealing with me, she will. If I pick up the phone when she calls, she'll say hi and then quickly ask to talk with Greg or one of the kids. If no one else is home, she'll ask me to have one of them give her a call back. She's civil, I guess, but barely. I have the sense that she'd prefer that I not exist."

It was hard to ignore how closely Jeanne's treatment of Pauline mimicked her mother's, although clearly Jeanne's brothers were not replicating the pattern in *their* interactions with their step-mother.

Before I brought Jeanne in to solicit her perspective, I decided it would be best to meet with Vicky and see what she had to say.

"Does Vicky know that you've contacted me about Jeanne?"

"Yes. Because we have joint custody, I had to check in with her about this. She wasn't enthusiastic about the idea, but she didn't stop me or anything like that, either. She just said something vaguely hostile, like, 'If you want to waste your money on coun- seling a girl who's got nothing wrong with her, be my guest.' That was her basic attitude."

Vicky was decidedly unenthusiastic when I invited her to join me for a session, but she reluctantly agreed. "I guess if you think it'll help, I'll come, although I don't know what this has to do with me. They're the ones who are having problems with her."

She did have plenty to say once she got to my office the next week, however. "I'm not surprised to hear that Jeanne's not crazy about Pauline, to be honest," she began, "because I think they've played this all wrong from the very start. As soon as Pauline was in the picture, Greg expected the kids to treat her like she was their mother. It's like he instantly discounted me and made her into the New and Improved Mom."

"Have you gotten to know Pauline at all?"

"Sort of. I mean, we've had numerous interactions over the years, although we've never sat down and talked or anything like that. Honestly, she seems a little fake to me, always cheerful and smiling, so eager to be your friend. I'd have a hard time spending much time with someone like that. It's like the pressure's always on to be in a good mood."

"What are things like between you and Greg?"

Vicky sighed. "I don't know why he's so difficult. I'm sure he's told you that our marriage was not a great one by any means. And our divorce was a disaster, one for the books. But he still makes things harder than they have to be, and since he got involved with Pauline he's shown no flexibility whatsoever. We used to trade off weekends if one of us had a commitment, but now that he's married, that's all changed. 'It wouldn't be fair to Pauline, she and I have made other plans' is what I always hear. Meanwhile, if he shows up twenty minutes late to pick up the kids, I'm supposed to delay whatever it is I'm doing until he gets there. It's a real double standard, as far as I'm concerned."

"Have you been involved with anyone since your marriage ended?"

"That's another saga," Vicky responded. "I've been seeing a guy, Willie, and we have this really great relationship, but the problem is that he's married. He's planning on leaving his wife, but until he does, it makes things very hard. You know, seeing a married man is no picnic. Everything has to be done on the sly. I'm alone on weekends and holidays—I'll be very happy when he moves out and we can bring things into the open."

"How long have you been seeing each other?"

"Almost three years now."

"And he still hasn't left his wife?" I asked.

Vicky fairly bristled. "Look, I've been through the end of a marriage. It's not easy to do, and it requires a lot of thought and planning. He's got a couple of kids as well, although they're pretty much grown up—only one of them lives at home now. I think he's just waiting for the right time."

"When does he say the right time will be?"

"I don't know for sure. I guess he's thinking when his youngest son moves out. Then he'll make his move."

For the time being, I filed away my skepticism about Willie's readiness to leave his wife for Vicky after three years of promising to do so, and instead brought the focus back to Jeanne.

"What has Jeanne had to say about life at her father's since Pauline's been in the picture?"

"She definitely doesn't like Pauline, I know that. She says that all Pauline cares about is keeping the house clean and buying new clothes. I know you haven't met Jeanne yet, but she's like me—no-nonsense—and she's got what I call 'built-in bullshit radar.' She can size someone up in seconds and sniff out any phony-baloney."

"What have your sons said about Pauline?"

"They seem okay with her, I guess," she replied, her tone shifting from biting to almost wistful. "They certainly don't go into tirades about her like Jeanne does. But they're also older and more independent and less involved with Pauline. They're both adolescents now. They've got their own lives, and I guess they just tolerate her."

"Do you think they would say that they see her as a fraud as well?" I inquired.

"If you asked them to be truthful, I think they'd say yes."

My next step was to meet with the three children together and listen to how they described the situation. Daryl and Winston, Jeanne's older brothers, did indeed seem to have adapted fairly well to their father's remarriage.

"Pauline's kind of cool, actually," said 15-year-old Daryl. "She's very nice to my friends, and they all like her a lot. She and Dad get along well, and she's younger than he or my mom, you know, so it's like she understands things a little better—you know, like when I want some privacy or when I want to go out with some friends. She's even stood up for me a couple of times with my dad. When I wanted to go to this big concert a couple of months ago, it was Pauline who helped convince my dad that it was okay for me to go, that it wasn't going to be some drug-fest, like he thought.

"Plus, she has her own advertising firm, and she's gotten us into some shoots, and we've met a bunch of famous people who are doing radio and television commercials for her agency, athletes and movie stars, which has really been neat."

Thirteen-year-old Winston was less exuberant and more detached, but he had no difficulty acknowledging the advantages of Pauline's presence in their life. "I guess it's been nicer visiting my dad since Pauline's been around. She's a pretty good cook, and now they've got a house, not that shabby apartment my dad was in when he and my mom first split up, and Pauline's made it look really nice. I don't love her like my mom or anything, but I guess she's all right."

Jeanne, however, had nothing positive to say at all. "Well, I can't stand her," was her opening salvo after her brothers finished their songs of praise. "She gets on my nerves."

"In what way?" I asked.

"I don't know. She's just so, so—so stupid!"

"C'mon, Jeanne," Daryl instantly interjected. "You've just never given her a chance. She's tried hard, and she's been really nice to all of us, and you know it."

"No I don't," Jeanne insisted. "It's like she's the boss of the house now, but she's not my mom, and I don't have to listen to her."

"Jeanne, you don't have to love her, but you could be a little nicer to her," Winston tried. "It's not like she's some witch or something."

"That's what you think," Jeanne replied tartly, folding her arms and scowling.

I asked Daryl and Winston to have a seat in the waiting room and spent some time with Jeanne alone to give her a chance to sort out her feelings without having to fend off her brothers.

"It sounds to me like you've got some real complaints about Pauline," I offered.

"You bet I do. I wish she wasn't there. I wish she'd just go away."

I noticed Jeanne's eyes glistening and her face reddening. "You look like you want to cry," I commented gently.

"I just can't stand her," was all she could muster, as the tears started to flow down her cheeks.

Jeanne's tears, and her inability to be more specific about her negativity toward her stepmother, suggested to me that she was in more conflict than she was letting on. Perhaps she didn't feel entitled to have good feelings about Pauline, despite wanting to do so.

"What would your mom think if you liked Pauline?" I asked carefully.

"What do you mean?" Jeanne asked, sounding perplexed.

"Well, sometimes children worry that their mother will be upset if they have a good relationship with a stepmother. Like it might make her feel like she's not as important to them anymore."

"My mom doesn't like Pauline. She's said so. I think my mom would be mad if I liked being with Pauline, because Pauline's not my mom."

"You're right—Pauline's *not* your mom. Nobody can ever replace your mom. But you can still have a good relationship with Pauline without her being your mom."

"I can?" she said in wonderment.

"Of course," I said. "She's not there to take over being your mom. But you can be comfortable with Pauline and still love your mom."

A sad look came over Jeanne's face again. "Pauline knows I like dolls. And she's bought me some stuff for my dolls, like clothes, but I never play with them. I hide them, because one time my mom saw what I was dressing my dolls in and asked where I got them, and when I said from Pauline, she was mad."

"That must have been very hard for you, to feel like you couldn't enjoy what you had gotten from Pauline because it made your mom so mad."

Jeanne nodded dolefully and quietly started to cry again.

"Maybe I can talk with your mom about this, and help her to see that just because you like what Pauline gives you, it doesn't mean that you love Pauline more than you love your mom."

Jeanne brightened suddenly and seemed almost giddy with relief. "Could you?"

"I'll give it my best shot."

Having been entrusted with this duty, I called Vicky and invited her back for a session.

"Well, have you solved the problem yet?" Vicky snapped as she took off her coat and settled into a chair.

"Not yet, but I think I can with your help," I answered.

"How can I help? She's fine when she's with me."

"You can help by giving her permission to have a better relationship with Pauline."

Vicky looked startled momentarily, then recovered. "What makes you think I haven't given Jeanne permission to like Pauline? If she likes Pauline or doesn't like Pauline, that's her decision, not mine."

"Except that your opinion matters a great deal to Jeanne, and because you're her only mother, she may feel as if she's betraying you if she develops a relationship with her stepmother. And nobody, no matter what age they are, wants to betray their mother."

"But why should I care if she has a good relationship with Pauline anyway?"

"Because it'll be hard for Jeanne to have a good relationship with her father if she can't figure out a way to get along with her father's wife. And it'll greatly increase her self-confidence and her ability to forge healthy, satisfying relationships with the opposite sex if she has a good relationship with her father."

Vicky took some time to mull this over. "I never thought about it that way," she eventually responded. "I guess, as I think about it, I didn't have much of a bond with my father—I always thought he disliked me—and I haven't had great success with men over the years, either. My marriage to Greg was actually my second. I'd been married for a short time a few years before, and it was a very abusive relationship. And now I'm seeing a great guy—he probably treats me better than any man ever has, but he's married to someone else."

Vicky's face reddened in the same way her daughter's had when she became sad. "But I've never tried to stop her from having a good relationship with Pauline—I've never told her not to like her."

"Maybe not in so many words," I offered, "but in the way you talk to Pauline or about Pauline when Jeanne is in earshot, or in the way you respond to her when she talks about Pauline, you may be giving her the unmistakable message that it's a threat to you if she dares to enjoy her stepmother."

"So how can I give her this permission you talked about, the permission to feel more positive about Pauline?"

"I think you need to monitor carefully how you sound when you refer or speak to Pauline, so Jeanne doesn't pick up on your hostility toward Pauline. And I also think you need to sit her down and tell her that while it has taken some time for you to adjust to the fact that your daughter is going to be partly raised by her father and a woman other than yourself, you now understand that you have to let go and allow her to develop whatever relationship she wants to with her father and stepmother."

"I can say that, but I don't know if I can do it," Pauline said, her voice quavering a bit.

"I think you'll be better able to do it if you say you're going to do it," I proposed.

I invited Vicky back for another session, and she told me she had embarked on a conversation with Jeanne about her relationship with her father and Pauline. She reported that not only had Jeanne been very glad to have been liberated from the fear of being disloyal to her mother, but that her daughter had also planted another seed for her.

"She told me she liked the fact that Daddy was married again, but that she'd like me to marry again too, so 'things would be equal.' This really floored me! And then, of course, she asked me when I was going to marry Willie. And that really got me thinking about whether I'm ever going to marry Willie, whether I've got any future with this guy. So I've decided to set a deadline with him and give him two more months to make up his mind. If he's ready to move out by then, even if he doesn't move in with me, that'll be a step in the right direction. If not, then I think it's time to walk. I've got better things to do than invest all my hopes in a relationship that's not going anywhere."

In a follow-up session with Greg and Pauline a couple of weeks later, I learned that Jeanne's treatment of Pauline had begun to shift noticeably. "One night she came down and said, 'G'night,

Dad, g'night, Pauline' and I almost fell off the sofa," Greg related, laughing. "And just last night, when I had to run the boys over to school for a band rehearsal, I assumed she would be coming, but she wasn't. She said she wanted to stay home and color. It was the first time since we've been married that she's voluntarily been alone with Pauline."

"And it's not like we did anything together," Pauline added. "She just sat at the kitchen table drawing while I made the lunches for the next day—but it felt nice just the same. The thing that amazed me was Sunday night, when I walked by her room and saw that she was playing with her dolls, and all these clothes and accessories I had given her were spread out on her bed. I didn't think she even had them anymore! And she saw me and gave me this great smile, and a little wave. She didn't have to do or say any more than that. It just made me feel like I had finally become a real person to her."

Jeanne's relationship with her father and stepmother continued to improve in the ensuing months, and in the meantime Vicky scheduled a couple of sessions for herself once she realized that Willie wasn't really planning on leaving his wife. "I've learned that I deserve to be something more than second fiddle in some married guy's life. No matter how much we enjoyed each other when we were together, and how great I felt when I was with him, the fact is, he went home each night to be in bed with his wife. And that's not good enough for me."

As she freed her daughter to be a good enough stepdaughter, to enjoy being with her father and his new wife, Vicky found that she too felt good enough, and that freed her to insist on having something better for herself as well.

Here are some additional thoughts on how to create a family life after divorce that contributes to the development of good enough children.

1) Give Your Child Room to Feel

Although children can successfully survive divorce without being traumatized, there is still no denying the impact divorce has on a child's emotional state. As painful as it may be to do, because it stirs up such guilt, divorced parents must provide their children with an opportunity to give voice to their complex emotions so that these are not buried and destined to express themselves later on in unhelpful or destructive ways.

When parents divorce, the child must come to terms, usually for the first time in her life, with very deep feelings of loss, with the bitter reality that the sacred family bonds thought to be inviolable do not always hold firm. She yearns for the parent who is no longer present every day and for the familiarity and comfort of whatever family routine has been forever disrupted.

She must fight off her fears that, if Mom left Dad or if Dad left Mom, then Mom or Dad could leave their children, that if her parents stopped loving each other they may stop loving her, that if their being angry resulted in their not wanting to live with each other anymore, then they may not want to live with her when she makes them angry. Children will be better able to cope with these potentially overwhelming psychological problems if they feel free to talk about them with an understanding parent.

Often, it is mistakenly assumed that divorce does not affect babies or toddlers because they are "too little" to know what's going on, but even small children are acutely aware of the significant changes occurring in a divorce and find ways to express their concerns. I saw one 4-year-old boy, Walter, whose parents had separated a couple of months before and who was chronically "losing" things—his toys, his books, his stuffed animals. When I asked Walter what the worst thing he ever lost was, he replied, with dead seriousness: "My father." Helping him to express his feelings of having lost a parent, and, later on, making sure that I spoke with Walter's somewhat neglectful father about being more timely about his visitations with his son, led to Walter's being better able to keep track of those belongings he had some control over.

Three-year-old Aisha was referred to me by her pediatrician because she was constantly picking at and reinfecting a gash on her thigh. I learned that she had hurt herself while running up to her room in tears upon learning from her father that her mother would not be returning home. As she was helped, through our playing together, to mourn this loss, she no longer needed to keep calling attention to the physical injury that symbolized the emotional injury incurred by her mother's departure.

Naturally, it may at times feel like a Herculean task to listen to your child talk about missing or longing for the very person, your ex-spouse, whom you may be either longing for yourself or wishing never to see again, but she needs room to express this just the same.

On the flip side, that doesn't mean you have to accept the brunt of your child's blame for the end of your marriage, no matter how much grief and anger is being expressed. "I know you're angry with me for divorcing your dad," you might say, "and you're entitled to be angry that things have changed, but you also have to remember that both of us were involved in this decision."

2) Avoid Loyalty Binds

As we saw in Jeanne's case, described above, children often find themselves paralyzed by their loyalty to their divorced parents, unable to pursue their own self-interests because of their constant dread of offending or betraying someone they love very deeply. Yet it can be difficult for an aggrieved parent to support his or her child's connection with an ex-spouse. There is an irresistible urge to "set the record straight" and give a child an earful or two about what Mom or Dad is really like, so that our offspring remains our ally, loves us best, and is protected from experiencing the same hurt and disappointment that we did.

However, it is always best to allow children to come to their own conclusions about their parents. Children may idealize their parents not because they really believe their parents are ideal but because it is through the process of idealizing that they begin cultivating *within themselves* the very attributes that they believe they see, or want to see, in their caregivers.

After having worked with hundreds of children of separation and divorce over the years, I have seen that the vast majority of them are eventually able to assess each of their parents accurately, and should be trusted to gradually discern their parents' specific strengths and weaknesses without having to be goaded into doing so by an injured party.

I have also noticed that many children are more likely to identify with and idealize the parent they see the *least*, because they never get the chance to more objectively evaluate the phantom parent's character. That is why one parent's effort to prevent a child from having a relationship with his or her other parent often succeeds brilliantly in encouraging that child to worship the other parent—precisely the outcome one was trying to avoid.

Of course, if you sincerely believe your child to be endangered in any way by your ex-spouse, there is certainly no reason to sanction their having a close association with each other. But short of actual danger, no matter how difficult it is for you to allow your child to have an unencumbered relationship with his other parent, you must work toward that goal.

One thing that may help is to do your best to remember what it was that attracted you to this former partner in the first place. After all, there must have been something there or you wouldn't have married him or her. Being able to recall and be reminded of those positive qualities may take the sting out of your child's motivation to be close with him or her, and make a complicated situation more bearable.

You certainly don't have to be friends or lovers with your ex-spouse, but if you can find ways to support each other as parents and remember that neither of you can replace the other, your child will be better able to integrate the positive aspects of each parent while feeling loved and protected by both.

3) Help Your Child Avoid Self-Blame
Children are very egocentric. They generally assume that whatever happens, happens because of something they did. When it comes to cause-and-effect perceptions, children, particularly young ones, will almost always conclude that they were the cause of the effect.

In a divorce, children are at a loss to comprehend what could possibly have created such an irreparable tear in their parents' marital union, so they are quick to assume that it must have something to do with them, that they weren't somehow *good enough* to keep their mother and father married. That is why it behooves divorced parents to try to head off their children's tendency to self-blame, and to be particularly sensitive to any signs of it in the immediate aftermath of a separation.

Donovan was an 8-year-old boy who was referred to me because of a sudden obsession with keeping the house clean. He wasn't getting his homework done, playing outside, practicing his trumpet, or getting to bed on time because he was so intent on vacuuming the living room, cleaning the toilets, keeping the sink clear of dirty dishes, picking up his and his two little brothers' toys, and sweeping the kitchen floor.

Donovan's parents had separated two months before, and I learned that shortly before they made the decision to separate, they had gotten into a terrible argument. When I talked to Donovan, he told me that he recalled the fight being started by his father, who came in yelling about the house always being a mess.

It became clear through our discussions that Donovan had come to believe that if he could somehow make the house spotless and uncluttered, his parents would reunite. Only when I had each of his parents explain to him that their reasons for separating had nothing to do with the neatness of the house was Donovan able to begin releasing himself from his housekeeping duties and go back to being a kid.

4) Give a Realistic but Tactful Explanation for the Divorce

Separated or divorcing parents often ask me for a formula to explain this transition to their children, but such an explanation depends on many factors, such as a child's age and maturity level, the nature of family relationships in the predivorce and postseparation home, the reasons for the divorce, and the role of stepparents.

I haven't found it helpful to submit the commonly offered reasoning that a divorce occurred because "we stopped loving one another," since the child is then likely to conclude that you might stop loving him as well. In general, I believe it's better to focus on the fact that there were real differences between you and your ex-spouse, differences that were significant enough that the two of you could no longer feel right together as a couple. As your child matures, you can then slowly add additional information about what those differences were.

On a related note, if your ex-spouse is absent or neglectful when it comes to time with your child, I don't suggest reassuring your child that this parent loves him anyway. He'll grow up with a very distorted notion of what love is, and be likely to conclude that the fault lies with him rather than with his parents.

You don't have to vilify your ex-spouse, but you can again point to the differences between the two of you when it comes to parenting. "I'm not exactly sure why your mother is not visiting you on the weekends as she had agreed to—you'll have to bring that up with her to find out—but I do know that this is one of the reasons we couldn't continue living together, because we had such different ideas about what being a good parent is all about. You don't have to agree with me or dislike your mother, but we couldn't keep the family together when we felt so differently about what family means."

5) Keep Conflict to a Minimum and Away from the Child

King Solomon was perhaps most famous for a "custody" decision, albeit one that involved two mothers, rather than a mother and a father. While this case was a difficult one, it clearly involved a real mother and a false mother, so it wasn't as difficult as some of the modern custody disputes I have been called to testify in. In most custody battles there is no false parent, and both parties tend to believe that they are, indeed, looking out for the needs of the child, rather than their own self-interest.

Yet despite this belief, I have seen many families in which real parents unwittingly act like "false" parents. While saying that their first priority is the child, their willingness to rip her apart with their competing claims on her makes it clear that preserving their personal sense of triumph over the other parent is actually much more important to them.

One set of divorced parents spent an entire session arguing

about where their 11-year-old son should go shopping for his school clothes one September. This conflict seemed to churn up all of their disagreements about how their child should appear and behave.

"In ten years, your son is not going to remember where he eventually wound up doing his shopping," I warned them, "but he will never forget the fact that the two of you couldn't put your differences aside and come to an agreement about this."

Another divorced couple I worked with constantly insulted each other's competence as caregivers and seemed unable to understand what this was doing to their children, so I asked them each to bring a picture of their children to the next session. When they arrived, I took the pictures and propped them up on an empty chair, then handed each of them a pair of scissors and directed them to put a slash across these photographs every time they said something critical of their former partner's character. They got the message and were much more civil with each other from then on.

Still another couple, warring for more than *two years* about a disputed custody and visitation schedule, finally called a truce when I commented to both of them: "The two of you seem to be more in love with your positions than with your child."

Children of divorce do best when they see their parents treating each other with respect and civility. Every time they are in attendance during a conflict, or privately drawn into the conflict as jurors, go-betweens, referees, or confidants, they suffer immeasurably. As one 12-year-old told me, "I don't care if my parents like each other, or even agree with each other. I just wish I didn't have to hear what they *think* about each other all the time."

One of the most dangerous outcomes of ongoing complaints and recriminations between former spouses is that they inevitably wind up attributing to their children the worst qualities of the other parent. Like the attributive processes we have examined in previous chapters, this can sometimes create a self-fulfilling prophecy in which the child then comes to embody the very qualities that are projected onto him, *whether they are accurate or not*.

Fourteen-year-old Adam was constantly reminded, "You get

angry just like your father does," by his mother, who had divorced his father years before. Because his parents rarely saw or spoke to each other, it seemed to me that Adam's mom was funneling her anger at his father toward their son. And since Adam saw his father infrequently and had no real familiarity with him, he learned, with his mother's "help," to identify "being angry" with "being like Dad," since he knew few of his dad's other qualities. Not surprisingly, Adam grew to cultivate his anger as a way of identifying himself with his absent dad, his only male role-model, and establishing himself as a man.

Other problems are also likely to surface if parents constantly disparage each other. It is my belief, for example, that children who begin having problems in school when their parents split up are often victims not so much of the separation itself but of the rancor surrounding it.

Drowning in the remaining riptides of marital contention, being forced to swallow too much uncensored input about their parents' defects and indiscretions, and constantly trying to monitor any tiny shifts in temperament that might allow them to prepare for another emotional tidal wave between their parents, they simply shut down. Having learned *more* than they need to know at home, they choose to learn *less* than they need to learn at school

Finally, as is the case when their parents are married, children will often create problems in an attempt to force their mother and father to put aside their differences and collaborate as a cohesive caregiving unit. No misdeed is beyond the pale if a child believes that it will even temporarily elicit cooperative support from parents who are usually at odds with each other.

Protecting your children from divorce-related turmoil is critical in helping them adapt to what is, after all, a momentous change. They need to be able to move forward with their lives, rather than become consumed by attending to yours.

6) Good Enough Custody Arrangements

All divorcing parents search for the perfect custody arrangement as a way to stave off their remorse and guilt, but such an arrangement will always remain elusive. What I have seen is that, as with most aspects of child-rearing, the specifics of the decision are less important than the spirit in which the decision is made and implemented. The process of determining custody and visitation can become a deadly invitation to act out the unresolved conflicts that linger from a terminated marriage. Alternatively, it can provide a welcome opportunity to complete unfinished marital business and emancipate both partners to move on.

There are numerous factors to consider when developing an appropriate custody arrangement, including the child's temperament, the parents' conjoint capacity to communicate and cooperate with each other, each individual parent's availability and competence as a caregiver, financial realities, whether the child has a strong preference for one parent or the other, and which schools and neighborhoods are going to be home base.

What most parents must come to grips with, however, is that they will no longer have unrestricted access to their child's life. At times there will be stories, victories, celebrations, encounters, tribulations, and adventures that they will not be directly, or even indirectly, privy to. This is a great loss, and parents may try to offset it by attempting to make themselves the sole sun around which their child must obediently orbit.

Being inflexible about custody and visitation, sabotaging agreements that have been made, chastising or reproving their ex-spouse for the ways in which they parent, and making transitions sticky and unpleasant—all are strategies divorced parents use in an attempt to wrest control of their child away from the other parent and claim, or reclaim, it for themselves. If you can allow your child to revolve unfettered around *two* suns, rather than just one, however, she'll be better able to prevail over the vagaries of divorce.

Remember, too, that no custody arrangement will be permanent, and that many children will at some point express an interest in living with their noncustodial parent, especially when their noncustodial parent is also their same-sex parent. Understanding this as a developmentally appropriate desire to broaden and deepen their identity, rather than as a rejection or lack of appreciation of you, will enable you to participate in the decision-making process in a more balanced way.

I have worked with many children who are told that a change in custody or visitation will never be considered, and who then inventively begin to create difficulties in an effort to facilitate such a change, hoping that if everyone sees how poorly things are going in one household, they'll be more easily transferred to another.

Unless safety issues are at stake, making it clear that additional time with a noncustodial parent, or even a change in custody, are possible will decrease the likelihood that your child needs to act out his desire and will encourage him to more objectively discuss and evaluate his motivations.

7) **Taking Steps Toward a Good Enough Stepfamily**

About 1 million American children watch a mother or father remarry each year and begin a stepfamily. The word "step" in stepfamily is actually derived from the middle English word for "bereaved," which is appropriate since a stepfamily does not come into existence without some kind of loss in the life of one or both partners. Because these losses have not always been fully acknowledged, grieved for, and put to rest, stepfamilies are often very fertile incubators for struggles that leave everyone, adults and children alike, feeling not good enough.

Stepchildren must find a way to honor their stepparent without dishonoring their birth parent, and often have the additional challenge of working through rivalrous feelings toward stepsiblings. Stepparents must take on the challenges of a new marriage and maintain an alliance with their own children while simultaneously helping to raise stepchildren who may resent their very presence in their lives.

No wonder psychological research suggests that it usually takes several *years*, not months, for a stepfamily to finally congeal and begin to experience some harmony. In fact, one of literature's greatest tragedies, *Hamlet*, can be interpreted as the story of an enraged stepson who is tormented by his feeling that his mother remarried so quickly after the death of his father that she never even mourned him. ("The funeral baked meats did coldly furnish forth the marriage tables.")

My general advice to stepparents who want to avoid a tragedy is to move slowly, to respect the loyalty children always have for their birth parent, and to not expect them to embrace with open arms someone whom they may see as an intruder. It is also important to remember that because the children may have already seen one marriage end in bad feelings—feelings that may still be simmering—their lack of affection for a stepparent may be rooted in their fears that this marriage, too, is doomed. In fact, the majority of second marriages don't survive, so when a child reasons, "Why bother getting close to my stepparent, when it's likely that he and my mother are just going to get divorced, too?" he's not thinking irrationally.

I have also concluded that many of the behavior problems I see in children who are trying to adjust to a stepfamily are calculated to test the solidity of this new marriage, to assess whether it has staying power. "If my father and his new wife can withstand the onslaught of my obnoxiousness and belligerence without coming apart at the seams," a child may be unconsciously thinking, "they'll be able to handle anything."

With this in mind, as with any successful family, the marital unit must stand firm. Working together as a team, modeling mutual respect, demonstrating affection, and making couples time a priority, are always the best ways to reassure children that the new marriage that is forming has a very good chance of becoming an enduring and fulfilling one.

After all, despite whatever grumbling and complaining they so freely offer up, children instinctively know they're better off if their parents are happy. Family life is more pleasant, conflicts are less frequent, and children feel free to attend to their own business and, ultimately, to leave home, if they don't have to worry about Mom or Dad still feeling consumed by loneliness, hurt, or anger.

Remember, also, that despite the inevitable struggles inherent in the formation of a stepfamily, the process also holds great promise. The children may finally have the opportunity to experience a contented, well-functioning marriage and may also eventually forge deep and enduring relationships with stepsiblings and half-siblings no matter how rocky the initial jostling for position.

Every family transition has embedded within it a loss and a potential gain. Actively cultivating the gains while realistically accepting the losses are the surest ways to help children and their parents navigate these transitions successfully.

8) Getting Better, not Bitter

Our discussion of divorce would not be complete without one more mention of forgiveness, for if there is ever a rupture in which creative healing is called for, it is when a marriage has come to an end. Whether there was a severe violation of marital trust (physical or sexual violence, substance abuse, or chronic infidelity) or whether marital bonds decomposed for subtler, less dramatic reasons (growing apart, no time together, different career trajectories, meddling in-laws), there are always ample grounds for feelings of vindictiveness and a tendency toward destructive entitlement.

Forgiving yourself and your partner for the hurts that you were each responsible for doesn't mean you condone what was done in the past. It simply means you are declaring that both of you are human—flawed, imperfect, but human—and by dint of this deserve to learn from your pain and then put that pain to rest so you can implement what you've learned in more successful ways than you have ever done before.

In doing so, you will free your children from unnecessary suffering, but you will also free yourself to become more like the good enough parent, partner, and individual you have always dreamed of becoming.

——————————— **EXERCISE ELEVEN** ———————————

When a marriage has ended, we will forever question why it was that we tied the knot in the first place. Yet there must have been something that originally drew us to our partner, ill-fated as that partnership may have turned out to be, something about him or her that we found, and maybe still find, to be charming, attractive, touching, or tender.

This meditation on forgiveness is similar to Exercise 5, described in Chapter 5, but focuses on your former spouse rather than your child. Feel free to change gender and pronouns as necessary.

Find a comfortable position, close your eyes, and take some deep breaths, in through your nose and out through your mouth. Keep breathing in this way until you find yourself in a slow, peaceful, effortless rhythm. (*Pause for a minute.*)

In your mind, place yourself in a setting that feels very safe and very pleasurable. It may be real or imaginary, from your past, from your present, or in your future. (*Pause for a minute.*)

Once you have located yourself there, I would like you to go back in time and remember when you first met your child's father. As his image forms in your mind, recall what it was about him that you found inviting, appealing, engaging. As you gaze at him, think about the love you felt for him, love that changed over time but that was still real when you were first feeling it. Put gently to the side any angry or negative thoughts or feelings about him that surface, and just for this moment allow yourself to feel in all of its fullness this original love. (*Pause for a minute.*)

Imagine that he is now able to talk to you about all the things that he never spoke to you of before, about his pain, fears, vulnerability, loneliness, sorrow, grief—about all the ways in which he aches. Imagine as he speaks that you are able without any effort at all to open your heart to him, to listen plainly, quietly, lovingly, attentively. (*Pause for a minute.*)

Imagine that in the process of listening you naturally begin to feel within you a melting away of all your hurt and anger, and that your heart starts to fill, instead, with mercy, with understanding, with kindness and grace. (*Pause for a minute.*)

Now tell him that you forgive him for all his flaws, defects, failures, and imperfections, for all the ways in which he has disappointed, enraged, injured, and disillusioned you.

And tell him that you would like him to forgive you for all of your flaws, defects, failures, and imperfections, for all the ways in which you have, knowingly and unknowingly, hurt and angered him. (*Pause for a minute.*)

And in your mind, imagine now that your child has been watching you this whole time, silently bearing witness to the great courage you have shown in releasing yourself and her father from the pain of the past. Remind yourself that this child could not have come into being without the partnership with her father. Listen as she tells you how much better she feels now that you are forgiving her father, how she no longer has to carry the burden of your hurt and anger, how she is finally able to freely love both of her parents without tension or fear.

Extend your arms to your child and bring her in toward you, and feel her give in to your warm embrace. And thank her father for joining you in the creation of your child, and accept his gratitude to you in return.

Continue breathing deeply and quietly for a few moments, cherishing the feelings of forgiveness and compassion that you have begun to discover and invite into your life. Promise to hold these feelings close to you as you awaken and move through the rest of your day.

TEN

Questions, Answers, and Reflections

I love what I cannot be
As well as what I am

Marge Piercy

Over the years, I've heard the innermost feelings of thousands of parents—not just through conversations with my patients, but by sharing experiences with my friends and family, and with the many people who have read my books and articles or attended my workshops and lectures. Some of them are expectant or brand-new parents, some are experienced parents with grade-school, adolescent, or young-adult children. But whether they are old hands at the job or just beginning, and whether they're birth parents, stepparents, or adoptive parents, all of them face problems and all of them seem to be seeking the same solution in one form or another: perfection.

What will ultimately give parents real satisfaction in their family lives, however, is not the Perfect Child, but the Good Enough Child. I hope that by now you understand that seeing your child as good enough does not mean feeling hopeless and defeated, "settling" for the child you've got while yearning for the imaginary child that forever eludes your grasp. Raising and loving a good enough child is something different, the process of adopting the radical, wondrous, and liberating belief that your child is already terrific, and sustaining that belief no matter what twists and turns your family journey follows.

The good enough child is a child who does not feel that he has to be a different child or a better child to be loved, cherished, and supported. The good enough child has his share of problems, frailties, and imperfections, but he is much more likely to mature and blossom anyway because he is secure in the knowledge of his parents' capacity to accept him for who he is, even if his problems, frailties, and imperfections never completely disappear.

When the good enough child's behaviors suggest that he has some learning or growing to do, these behaviors are not ignored or indulged but instead honestly acknowledged *at the same time* as his many talents and attributes are warmly celebrated. This enables him both to more effectively address his weaknesses as well as to capitalize on his strengths.

The good enough child experiences a deep sense of appreciation, not so much for what he does but for who he is, and is free to become the person he feels destined to become, even if this requires a courageous departure from the paths his parents have so eagerly prepared for him. The good enough child revels in his parents' deep and profound pleasure in the miracle of his mere presence and carries internally wherever he goes a sense of purpose, wonder, and joy that is not contingent on external criteria.

Most important, the good enough child, through seeing himself mirrored in his parents' loving and compassionate eyes, grows up to become an adult who can give and receive love with his own friends, his own partner, and, eventually, with his own good enough child.

In *The Good Enough Child*, I have shown you how it is possible to raise children without harsh judgment or unrealistic expectations, and with the capacity to handle your own and your children's flaws and virtues, failures and successes, in a spirit of acceptance and unwavering love.

You have learned to translate the bewildering, infuriating, disappointing, and disillusioning behaviors that children display, to understand that all such behaviors are a request for love, and to respond with sensitivity and generosity rather than with rage and irritability at these difficult times.

You know how to listen to your children rather than talk at

them, how to instruct them with kindness rather than criticize them with contempt, how you can even grow from, rather than suffer through, the vagaries of parenthood, and in the process become a more fulfilling, and fulfilled, individual, the architect of a richer personal and family life.

The elemental irony and mystery of child-rearing is that *children are most likely to grow and change for the better only when they can trust that they'll be loved even if they stay the same.* When you work wholeheartedly on accepting the imperfections of your children, you are cultivating the most crucial and fundamental component of parenting, the "art" from which all other parental arts body forth. It is this art that I hope I have taught—for it *is* learnable—in *The Good Enough Child.*

To make sure I've covered all the bases I can think of, I will use these final pages to address some of the most common questions parents have asked me over the years, questions that may not have been addressed specifically enough in previous chapters. I hope that my answers amplify and clarify the beliefs I have put forth in this book and speak to its themes in a helpful way.

You stress the importance of stepping back in order to allow children to become themselves, not the fulfillment of parental expectations. But how do you know when you've gone from disengaging to abandoning your responsibilities as a parent?

Knowing how and when to let go and release your child from your expectations is, for many of us, the most difficult task of parenthood. The process cannot wait until adolescence, but must begin to be practiced in your child's first years. We have such difficulty with this process because letting go runs counter to our innate desire to protect our children, to keep them safe from harm.

My general advice is to assess your child's developmental stage and establish those areas in which you, as a parent, need to remain firmly engaged in her life. If you are raising a toddler, for example, you obviously cannot allow her to wander around the neighborhood without supervision, but you might have to allow her to be pushed around a bit by a strong-minded age-mate at the tot lot without rushing to rescue her, so that she learns how to defend her turf.

If you are raising an adolescent, it's not appropriate to tell him which extracurricular activities to take or which colleges to apply to, but you can certainly make it clear that he must maintain a certain grade point average if he wants to use the family car on weekends, and if he uses drugs or alcohol, there will be serious consequences.

Clearly defining the issues in which you *need* to remain involved will help you to gradually relinquish those areas for which your child can assume responsibility.

You have spoken about the need to assign consequences to behavior, but I'm never sure what consequences are appropriate.

First of all, I tend to recommend positive consequences over negative consequences. It's generally much more effective and pleasant to award your son a sticker for every day that he does not call his little sister a provocative name and promise him a special dessert after he's earned five stickers than to constantly come up with punishments every time he belittles her. It's better to reward your daughter with an extra thirty minutes of nightly phone use after she's gone one month without blowing her curfew than to keep taking something away every time she comes home late.

Sometimes, however, a negative consequence must be invoked. My general rules are that these should have some logical relationship to the misdeed that earned them, that they should be harder on the child than on the parent, and that some kind of learning should occur as the result of the consequence. It is not always possible to accomplish this each time, but as the old song goes, two out of three ain't bad.

If you have discovered that your son lifted a coveted Pokémon card from his buddy's backpack, for example, you can have him return the card and write a letter of apology. If your daughter was caught smoking at school, she can be told that she just bought herself a ticket for the six-week smoking-education class at the local hospital.

Sometimes a helpful but tiresome task is all that's necessary.

Cleaning a bathroom, raking leaves for an elderly neighbor, stuffing five hundred envelopes for the PTA mailing—all go a long way toward teaching a child that his behavior had a negative impact on others and needs to be changed.

Parents who are trying to devise a suitable consequence will sometimes seek to deprive the child of whatever he finds most meaningful. If what he is deprived of is something that offers nothing more than entertainment value, like watching TV or playing video games, that's fine. However, if it's something like Scouts or wrestling, which are growth-promoting and ultimately build self-confidence and self-respect, it's best to choose some other form of deprivation.

What are your thoughts on the use of psychotropic medication to help children improve their behavior?

Currently, there is so much controversy on medicating children that it is difficult for parents to know what is best. I have seen numerous children who have been inappropriately diagnosed and medicated for a "disorder" and numerous parents and educators who look to medication as a substitute for the hard work necessary to help children grow and learn to the best of their abilities. However, I have also worked with children who, after suitable diagnostic work, were prescribed medication that provided significant symptomatic relief for them and a reduction of anger and frustration for their entire family. And I have met with parents who are so opposed to the use of medication that they rule out an intervention that might hold some genuine curative power.

While we are constantly learning more about the genetic and biological roots of our behavior, I believe it is simplistic to assume that how we think and what we do are purely the result of our synaptic chemistry. And even if there *is* a neurochemical component to problem behaviors, that doesn't automatically require a medical intervention. How we think and act has at least as much effect on our neurological circuitry as that circuitry has on our behavior. It's definitely a two-way street. For example, much research has shown that activities like exercise, prayer, writing, meditation, and positive thinking have significant and far-reaching impact on our neurochemistry.

It is clear that the psychotropic medications available these days are much safer and more neurologically precise than ever before, but I still tend to exercise great caution before recommending that a child use medication, for a variety of reasons. First, many of the newer remedies, effective as they might be, have not been studied over a period of years, or specifically on children, meaning that we don't really know the possible outcomes of long-term, or even short-term, use. Second, every prescription has *some* side effects, and the potential for psychological or physical addiction is always present no matter what is prescribed. Third, many children are resistant to taking medication because it makes them feel like they are abnormal or "sick." Finally, it is unwise to deny a child the opportunity to first develop the internal resources necessary to compensate for a weakness or master a challenge, because these opportunities, over time, build character and teach her about her own inner strengths and capacities.

If nonmedical interventions such as behavior management, psychotherapy, or tutoring have been given a good try but have not yielded good results, then I think that medication should be considered, but only *after* a medical and psychological evaluation has been completed.

My own belief is that most of the distractibility that teachers or parents observe in children, for example, is the result of anxiety, depression, misdirected or unexpressed anger, high-spiritedness, inappropriate educational placement, or learning disabilities, rather than of an actual, neurologically based attention-deficit disorder or attention-deficit hyperactivity disorder. The diagnosis of ADD or ADHD *cannot* be conclusively arrived at until these other possibilities are ruled out, and they can't be ruled out simply by filling out a few questionnaires in the guidance counselor's or pediatrician's office.

And even if a diagnosis of ADHD can be made, that doesn't automatically mean that psychostimulant medication must be prescribed. There are numerous strategies that help a child stay focused and organized without medication.

On the flip side, if medication is recommended and turns out to be effective, there's never any reason to feel that you or your child have failed in some way. Children (and their parents) have to learn that they can't do everything themselves, and that sometimes it's a sign of strength and maturity to acknowledge a problem and ask for help.

How can I tell whether my child's motivations in a particular area are more his than mine?

This is a question I wish more parents would ask, because it suggests an awareness that sometimes children consciously or unconsciously go after goals with an intensity born of their desire to please their parents rather than themselves.

There's nothing wrong with a child's *wanting* to please his parents, of course. In some ways that desire is the basis for many of his achievements. But when a child's devotion to fulfilling his parents' wishes gets in the way of fulfilling his own wishes, he will never feel truly gratified by his accomplishments, no matter how great they are.

I always suggest asking questions and listening as carefully and objectively as you can to your child's answers. The way your child answers the question "Do you really want to do the extra-credit science fair project, or are you saying you want to because you know I want you to?" will reveal a great deal about his motivation. He may say no, not really; he may say yes, and be able to explain why; or he may say yes, but not be able to come up with any sound reasons for doing so.

You can also learn a lot just by observing. Does your son go to hockey practice enthusiastically, or does he constantly complain about having to get ready and never know where his skates are? Does your daughter seem genuinely excited about the assignments in the gifted and talented classes she was recommended for, or does she approach them lethargically or resentfully?

Sometimes the intensity or perfectionism a child brings to his

activities is itself problematic, suggesting that he's more ambivalent about them than he's letting on. When children can't get
anything less than an A+ on every single assignment without
dissolving into tears, or can't sleep at night because they're going
to have to miss a soccer practice next week because of a friend's
birthday party, that's a sign that there's too much pressure,
whether internal or external.

Even if you feel that the pressure has not come from you, it's
important to consider the possibility. Many times parents tell me
they've made it clear to their child that it's okay for them not to
get straight A's, not to qualify for the all-county swim meet, not to
get the top scores at the violin recital, but the manner in which
they say it or the way they ultimately react depending on whether
or not these high standards are met may not be congruent with
the words they speak.

For children to really feel good enough, they must believe that
they are authoring their own lives, not participating in a drama
from yours.

*My husband and I have always worked extremely hard at school and at our
jobs, yet our sixteen-year-old son seems to have absolutely no work ethic at all.
He's always looking for the easy way out, always looking to cut corners. If
parents are supposed to be their children's main role models, why isn't he modeling himself after us?*

First of all, just because parents are significant role models does
not mean that children automatically become just like their parents. One of a child's most important developmental tasks is to
forge his own identity, not just mimic others'. If you and your husband are such workhorses, your child may feel that there's no
room for him to establish himself as a separate entity by working
hard as well. His niche may be found elsewhere.

Also, children are very astute observers of their parents' satisfaction with their lives. The two of you may be very conscientious,
but the life you have created through all of your conscientiousness may not seem all that appealing to your son. If he observes a
mother and father who are constantly tired and irritable, with no

time to relax and enjoy themselves, for example, "hard work" may seem, to your son, like a surefire recipe for unhappiness.

Finally, remember that not everyone discovers something worth working hard for during childhood. While many very successful and fulfilled adults knew what they wanted to do with their lives from as far back as they can remember, many others take years to discover where their interests and talents lie. Your son is 13, not 33. It's okay to give him some time to discover himself, at which point you may be pleasantly surprised to see him digging in and working just as hard as you do.

Is the process of seeing your child as good enough the same when you have a child by adoption as it is when you have a child by birth?

In some ways yes and in some ways no. It's the same because no matter how we begin our family, through birth or adoption, we have dreams and wishes we expect our children to fulfill. In that sense, all parents have to go through identical stages as they learn to relinquish unrealistic expectations and appreciate their children for who they are, rather than for what they do.

On the other hand, because adoptees have a lineage that is not genetically connected with their parents, the family's journey through these stages will have its own special twists and turns. All children must answer the question "Who am I?" but adoptees must answer an additional question: "Who might I have become had I not been adopted?" Their parents must struggle with a similar issue: "What would our family be like if we'd had a child by birth instead of by adoption, or if we had adopted a different child from a different place at a different time?"

I have worked with many adoptive parents who have an easier time than most birth parents accepting their child as good enough because the child is more easily seen as his own person, a "clean slate." As one father confessed to me during a workshop I led for adoptive families, "I feel a whole lot more comfortable when it comes to my adopted son having problems than my birth son having problems because I know that my adopted son's problems don't have their roots in *me*. I figure it's the result of his birth parents' genes or having been in an orphanage for the first eight months of his life, so I can deal with him without feeling guilty. But when my birth son is giving me fits I start blaming myself, wondering what it is that he picked up from my gene pool, or what it is that we didn't do right during his early years, that is making him so difficult."

On the other hand, I have worked with adoptive parents who have a *harder* time than most birth parents accepting their child as good enough because, without necessarily being aware of it, they, like Sam and Tovah in Chapter 5, constantly compare their child to the fantasy birth child that they haven't quite let go of.

What's most important is realizing that every child deserves the chance to blossom into the person he is meant to be. With an adoptee, this means remembering that while you may be his "real" parent, his filiation with his birth parents must also be honored so that this essential part of his being can be fully understood and incorporated.

What role does a child's temperament play in her being seen as good enough?

Mark Twain wrote that "temperament is the law of God written in the heart of every creature by God's own hand, and must be obeyed, and will be obeyed." While I don't believe temperament has to be defined quite so dramatically, most pediatric and psychological research supports the belief that children enter this world with a congenital "wiring" all their own, one that produces not a single, immutable personality, but a dynamic matrix of relatively stable personality characteristics that influence how they engage with the world.

I believe it is important for parents to understand this so they don't fall into the trap of finding fault with themselves or feeling personally indicted when their children display traits that they find irritating, embarrassing, or unappealing. But while a child's temperament is really nobody's fault, it would be a mistake to equate temperament with destiny and give up on having any influence on a child's sense of well-being.

For it is not just the child's temperament but the interaction between her temperament and the way in which you perceive and respond to it that will help to determine whether she sees herself as good enough. In particular, when a child's personality attributes take on pejorative psychological meanings in her parent's eyes, and when these attributes don't yield easily to contrary evidence—when we can *only* see tearfulness as manipulation, boundless determination as defiance, bookishness as withdrawal, or shyness as cold rejection—the stage is set for conflict and alienation.

Unconsciously trying to justify our negative feelings about our child by ascribing negative motives to her is not uncommon, but the more we are able to handle the difficult aspects of her temperament with humor and compassion—and not take them so personally—the more we will be able to find pleasure in each other.

Is there a "good enough" approach to helping my child do his homework so that we don't wind up in screaming matches every evening?

Homework is one of the first things children need to learn to be responsible for on their own. Because of this, it is not surprising that there are frequent family fights around homework—fights that may echo previous ones having to do with bedtime, toilet training, and feeding—as parent and child struggle to determine who's really in control.

My belief is that the *primary goal* of homework is not pleasing or impressing parents and teachers, getting good grades, or even, necessarily, mastering academic material, but *acquiring the skills that will enable children to autonomously manage their lives.* Making choices about how much and how hard to study, where and when to study, how to balance academic responsibilities with social life and extracurricular activities—this is where the real learning occurs.

Thus, parents play a very important role when it comes to their child's homework, but that role needs to be clearly delineated. Becoming overly embroiled or invested in your child's homework, such that you wind up caring and doing as much as he does, or more, will set up a pattern of dependency that makes it impossible for him to develop the self-reliance necessary to succeed.

On the other hand, not making the time to quiz or test him,

allowing him to rush through assignments in a careless manner so that he can get to football practice on time, giving him the answers to questions because you're too impatient to allow him to struggle, or tolerating procrastination so as to avoid a battle will all lead to the same result—a child who can never feel confident about his capacity to compete and achieve.

The objective is to gradually cultivate and stimulate your child's internal motivation and intellectual curiosity, and his capacity to persevere on his own without being able to count on instant success or gratification. And this cannot happen overnight; it takes years of modeling, appropriate supervision, and advice.

I know of few families in which there are never any blowups when it comes to homework. But if you're finding that screaming matches are occurring on a regular basis, it's time to reevaluate your understanding of the point of homework and your role in your child's completion of it.

How do I know when it's time to consult with a professional to assist me in the process of seeing my child as good enough, and what kind of treatment should I seek out?

Because of the often bewildering intensity and complexity of the parent-child bond, even the most conscientious, loving, and well-intentioned parents will go through phases in which they become preoccupied with their children's flaws and failures. If these phases begin to seem more like the norm than the exception, then it's time to consider meeting with a therapist to gain some new perspectives and insights.

Usually, the sooner you notice an unhealthy interaction between yourself and your child and strive to make changes, the more quickly anticipated changes will come about. The longer a problem is allowed to endure, the more entrenched it becomes. If a conflictual situation didn't get to where it is overnight, it certainly isn't going to resolve itself overnight either, even with the guidance of the most skillful therapist.

One of the things that seems to keep parents from consulting with a professional is the fear that psychotherapy is a vague, interminable ordeal that will proceed without any tangible recommendations or useful endpoint. As you have seen in many of the cases presented here, however, with commitment and an open mind it may only take a few sessions for constructive changes to begin taking root.

Regarding who to seek treatment from, it's helpful to remember Dr. Winnicott's observation "There is no such thing as a baby." This does not apply only to the first stage of life. Children's problems at *any* stage of development do not emerge or reside within them but instead need to be seen as symptoms of the family's emotional system, the wondrous tapestry woven by each member's individual threads.

With this in mind, my experience has been that it is generally most effective to work with someone who will treat the family as a whole rather than the child as an individual. The more the entire family participates and invests in changing maladaptive patterns, the more quickly they will all see the positive results they are looking for.

Successful treatment almost always begins when parents start doing things differently, even before their children do. I have noticed time and time again that mothers and fathers who become more aware of the attributions they make, alter the ways in which they inadvertently contribute to or reinforce problematic behaviors, acknowledge the individual or family dilemmas that their children are trying to resolve, and cultivate a climate of family forgiveness, inevitably notice improvements in their children, *even if their children are behaving no differently.*

So don't let anger or resentment build for very long. Even a check-in from time to time with an experienced clinician who has a systemic perspective can prevent serious difficulties from germinating and keep your family's emotional muscles in good shape over the long haul.

Throughout the months that I have been writing this book, my family, like yours, has been in a state of constant transformation. There have been periods of great joy and periods of great grief, weeks in which life flowed like the sweetest and calmest of rivers, and weeks in which life was fraught with turmoil and anguish, moments when I have been fully present to my wife and children with unyielding love and abundant care, and moments when I have responded with appalling carelessness and an inexcusable disregard for their basic needs and wants.

With every passing day—as son, brother, husband, father, therapist—I find myself more and more humbled by the complexity of family life, because family life is always filled with both tremendous promise and great peril. We are never as alive or as vulnerable as we are when we are with our family.

I have had the privilege of studying regularly with Phyllis Stern, a very wise and seasoned therapist, for over fifteen years now. One recent afternoon I flopped down in my regular chair in her office, put aside the stack of patient charts I always bring with me, and instead of talking about cases, lamented my disappointment with this book, a book whose growth she had been witness to from its inception.

I spilled forth all my concerns about whether what I was writing had any value, whether I had provided my readers with the insights and strategies necessary to envision their children as good enough, whether I had conveyed as clearly and as honestly as I could my adamantine respect for the courage and compassion it takes to raise a child well.

After patiently hearing me out, she responded, as she has done so many times before, with simple, good-natured understanding: "I guess it'll just have to be the good enough book."

I hope you have found it to be so, and that you will let me know any further thoughts you may have on the subject of *The Good Enough Child*.

Index

BOOKS BY BRAD E. SACHS, PH.D.

THE GOOD ENOUGH CHILD
How to Have an Imperfect Family and Be Perfectly Satisfied
ISBN 0-380-81303-3 (paperback)

Respected psychologist Dr. Brad Sachs helps recognize unrealistic expectations placed on children and helps parents to free themselves from the crippling belief that a healthy family should be absolutely perfect.

Appropriate for the parents of toddlers to teens.

"Sachs provides clear and realistic guidance for all parents." —*Washington Post*

THE GOOD ENOUGH TEEN
Raising Adolescents with Love and Acceptance (Despite How Impossible They Can Be)
ISBN 0-06-058740-7 (paperback)

Sachs presents a developmental overview of what parents can expect from their children during adolescence, then delineates the five stages in the journey toward accepting a child for who he or she is. With prescriptive tools and strategies for parents, including checklists, quizzes, and exercises, and numerous case studies from the author's own practice, *The Good Enough Teen* is vital help for any parent with a teenager.